What readers have said about *The Book of Leadership*:

'Full of seriously good leadership wisdom – a must-read for those who aspire to greatness' – **Richard Koch, bestselling author of *The 80/20 Principle***

'This wonderfully wise and insightful book is loaded with practical, thought-provoking ideas on leadership that can profoundly affect your life' – **Brian Tracy, bestselling author of *How the Best Leaders Lead* and *Eat That Frog!***

'One of the most stimulating books to read on leadership. Everyone can be a leader who has focus, passion and caring' – **Philip Kotler, Professor of International Marketing at the Kellogg School of Management**

'You simply must read this book – easily applied lessons, with guaranteed results' – **Philippa Snare, CMO, Microsoft**

'This book contains many valuable lessons in leadership and is an engaging and inspiring read' – **Olaf Swantee, CEO, EE**

'Full of inspiring insight to help guide you to the very essence of leadership – the ability to make a difference every step of the way' – **Ronan Dunne, CEO, O2 Telefónica UK**

'A very human approach to the topic of leadership and all the more readable for it' – **Robert Senior, CEO EMEA of Saatchi & Saatchi**

'The wisdom in this book will, if adopted, enable you and your team to get world class results' – **Sir Stuart Rose, Chairman, Ocado and former CEO, Marks & Spencer**

'A very practical guide to excellence in leadership. Read it all or dip in – either way it will be time well spent!' – **Jon Moulton, Chairman, Better Capital**

'A world class leadership book for people and avatars alike' – **Philip Rosedale, Founder, Second Life**

'Anthony has a natural knack for probing questions that get to the root of the matter, the numerous insights from these answers have been skilfully crafted into a thoroughly readable and enjoyable book' – **Michael Birch, Cofounder, Bebo**

'Loaded with wisdom and suitably peppered with a good dose of wit – a truly refreshing read' – **Sahar Hashemi, OBE, Cofounder, Coffee Republic**

Anthony Gell has interviewed hundreds of the world's most iconic CEOs and business leaders. He is the founder and CEO of LeadersIn, a community dedicated to sharing wisdom from world leaders in their field. Before launching LeadersIn in 2012, Anthony was the Regional CEO of a global publishing and conference company. In 2008, he launched both a consulting business and The Business Voice (bvo.com), which provides a free library of interviews under the brand 'Leaders In Business'. Anthony is an avid public speaker and has been asked to interview business leaders and present at many leading institutions, including London Business School and Imperial College, London.

For more information about Anthony, and to connect with him visit www.anthonygell.com.

The Book of

LEADERSHIP

HOW TO GET YOURSELF, YOUR TEAM AND YOUR ORGANISATION FURTHER THAN YOU EVER THOUGHT POSSIBLE

Anthony Gell

piatkus

PIATKUS

First published in Great Britain in 2014 by Piatkus

7 9 10 8 6

Copyright © 2014 by Anthony Gell

A CIP catalogue record for this book
is available from the British Library.

ISBN 978-0-349-40340-3

Typeset in Palatino by M Rules
Printed and bound in Great Britain by
Clays Ltd, St Ives plc

Papers used by Piatkus are from well-managed forests
and other responsible sources.

MIX
Paper from
responsible sources
FSC
www.fsc.org   FSC® C104740

Piatkus
An imprint of
Little, Brown Book Group
Carmelite House
50 Victoria Embankment
London EC4Y 0DZ

An Hachette UK Company
www.hachette.co.uk

www.littlebrown.co.uk

Contents

Part One: SELF Leadership – it all starts with *you*!

Part Two: TEAM Leadership – building and leading world-class *teams*

Part Three: ORGANISATIONAL Leadership – building and leading world-class *organisations*

Dedications

To my father Peter –
for being the most inspiring person that I know and for
teaching me more than anybody I know

To my wife Shaheena –
for being great in every way and the best partner in life
I could have ever wished for

To our daughter Saniya –
for the joy that you have brought to our lives – may you
always shine and do what you love and love what you do

To the rest of my family –
for the blessing of all their support, fun and wisdom,
and to my learned friend Lucy

To all the CEOs and business gurus that I've interviewed –
for sharing your wisdom from the lessons learnt along
the way; it's a gift to us all

To my publishers (notably Tim and Zoe) –
for being such a great team of whip-smart, open-minded
and lovely folk

To all of you reading –
for picking up this book and reading it today. I hope you
find this book helps you inspire those around you to
move mountains

Preface

This book is for those ambitious people who wish to make a massive difference in the wonderful world in which we live – those who wish to inspire and help those around them. It's for those who want to live a life of passion and to achieve remarkable results along the way. It's for the people who want to stand out from the crowd and rise to the top of their game. It's for those that are fed up of weak, dictatorial, self-absorbed leaders or just plain average leaders, and who instead wish to raise the bar and be great themselves.

This book is for both seasoned, experienced leaders who are smart enough to know that learning never stops – that the pursuit of leadership excellence is a lifelong activity – and for newly appointed leaders eager to learn good leadership habits from the start. It's for those who want their team to achieve *exceptional* results, not average results, and it's for leaders of massive companies as well as leaders of tiny (but ambitious) companies.

Essentially, this book is for those people who are hungry (I'm not talking about a desire for cake), who seek to tap into the awesome power that *great leadership* brings.

If this is you, then I'm honoured to have such a mighty fine person of this world holding this book right now, and I will do my best to exceed your expectations in the pages to come.

Introduction

What do the greatest achievers on the planet do differently? What do world-class CEOs and billion-dollar entrepreneurs do differently? What do the greatest leaders, who inspire intense loyalty within their team, do differently? And what do the world-class organisations, which thrive and win in their market time and time again, do differently? Answering these questions is what this book is all about: sharing those differences – one by one.

There's nothing like learning from those who have actually succeeded, who have rolled up their sleeves, fought in the battleground of business and won. These are the golden empirical lessons from actually *achieving* success, not just *talking* about achieving it. After all, the best teachers are those that have already been where you're trying to go.

As such, the success habits and principles in this book have been drawn from the hundreds of exclusive interviews I have conducted with i) the world's most famous CEOs, ii) entrepreneurs who have created multi-million (some even multi-billion) dollar organisations from scratch, and iii) the most recognised and respected business gurus on the planet. The book delves into the themes and repetitive success habits that define all of the leaders I've interviewed – those that are common to them all.

The list below, while not exhaustive, includes those who are cited most frequently in this book:

World-class CEOs/C-suite

Sir Stuart Rose, Chairman, Ocado and former CEO,
Marks & Spencer

Sir Terry Leahy, former CEO, Tesco

Jacqueline Gold, CEO, Ann Summers

Robert Senior, CEO EMEA, Saatchi & Saatchi

Ronan Dunne, CEO, O2

Allan Leighton, former Chairman, Royal Mail and CEO, Asda

Greg Dyke, Chairman, the Football Association and former
Director General, BBC

Olaf Swantee, CEO, EE (Orange and T-Mobile)

Simon Calver, former CEO, LOVEFiLM

Philippa Snare, CMO, Microsoft

Markus Kramer, Global Head of Marketing, Aston Martin

John Studzinski, former Global Head of Investment Banking, HSBC

World-class entrepreneurs

Stelios Haji-Ioannou, Chairman, easyGroup

Michael Birch, Cofounder, Bebo

Richard Reed, Cofounder, Innocent Drinks

Mike Harris, Founder and former CEO, Egg and First Direct Bank

Tim Waterstone, Founder, Waterstones

Aaron Simpson, Cofounder, Quintessentially

Philip Rosedale, Founder, Second Life

Ed Wray, Cofounder, Betfair

Sahar Hashemi, OBE, Cofounder, Coffee Republic

Jon Moulton, Chairman, Better Capital

World-leading business gurus

Tom Peters, US management guru

Brian Tracy, author, *How the Best Leaders Lead* and *Eat That Frog!*

Daniel Goleman, author, *Emotional Intelligence*

Richard Koch, author, *The 80/20 Principle*

Edward de Bono, author, *Six Thinking Hats*

Ken Blanchard, author, *The One Minute Manager*

Professor Philip Kotler, business guru, Kellogg
School of Management

Douglas Spence, UK business guru

Professor Richard Scase, author, *Living in the Corporate Zoo*

Drayton Bird, marketing guru

David Allen CEO, author, *Getting Things Done*

The book also draws upon insights from other leaders that I have not *yet* interviewed (forever the optimist, I confess) but have studied, including the likes of Indra Nooyi (Chairman and CEO of PepsiCo), Sheryl Sandberg (COO of Facebook), the late Stephen Covey (internationally bestselling author of *The 7 Habits of Highly Effective People*), Jack Welch (former CEO of General Electric), Marissa Mayer (CEO of Yahoo!) and Jeff Bezos (founder and CEO of Amazon) to name just a few.

How was I able to secure exclusive interviews with these world-class leaders?

I've always had a bit of an obsession about learning what it takes to win and what it takes to succeed. So much so, that, in 2007, I quit the safety of being a Regional CEO, with over 500 people under my management across six different countries (many thought I was crazy, and I probably was), in order to set up LeadersIn, a business that is dedicated to interviewing and sharing wisdom from some of the greatest leaders in their field. Some of the interviews were held in our studios, some in front of massive audiences, but all the interviews were focused on one thing: What leadership wisdom could these trailblazers share? I'm eternally grateful to my guests for sharing their wisdom.

The aim of each interview was to find out first hand what has made these folk stand out from the crowd, enabling them to rise to the top. I figured that if I could find that out, I could share the formula with the world and help everybody get ahead.

That's the purpose of this book ... to share that formula.

Why does this book have three parts – self, team and organisation?

At any point in time, a leader has three roles to play, not just one. Many leadership books focus on the single discipline of leading and motivating teams. However, for leaders to be able to transcend averageness and attain greatness, they must have mastered two other keys roles: leading themselves and leading their organisations.

Leadership is like a three-legged stool – and like a stool, you need all three legs to be secure in order to be a great leader in business today. The three legs of leadership are:

- *Self-leadership:* knowing and managing *yourself* to achieve exceptional results and ensure that you can coach others to do so too
- *Team leadership:* learning how to lead and build world-class *teams* that deliver outstanding results time and time again
- *Organisational leadership:* learning how to lead and build world-class organisations that become the gold standard in your industry

Regarding the organisational leadership component, some people say, 'That's the job of the Chief Executive, not me.' Not true. If you're a leader of a team, by definition you work in an organisation, not a silo. As such, you should always be aware of the traits of world-class organisations so that you can influence your own organisation to head in the right direction. Furthermore, if you're a great leader in a poor organisation, then you're like an emperor in a rowing boat (if this is the case, you should either become the CEO and change things, shout upwards until others change things or get off the rowing boat before it becomes the *Titanic*). Plus, one day when you become top dog (or more formally, the CEO – if that's the path you want to take), knowing what great organisations do, as opposed to average ones, is going to be essential knowledge to draw upon.

Makes sense to me. My fingers are crossed that it makes sense to you too. This book *will* help you succeed at all three legs of leadership:

The three parts of *The Book of Leadership* and the
three 'legs' of a world-class leader

A note on the chapters of this book – why so flipping many?

Each chapter of this book is dedicated to one key habit that will enable you, your team and your organisation to get ahead. Yes, there are a lot of chapters; indeed, I'd love it if we could turn this book into *one* habit – a kind of panacea, if you will, or even just three habits, eight habits or 12 habits to ensure your leadership success. However, the bottom line is that there are many essential habits and great leaders are aware of all the tools for success available to them.

We could have focused on just Part One, Two or Three. Yet doing so wouldn't have given you the full picture, and omitting some habits, or even parts thereof, for the sake of reduction is futile. Indeed, this is the first leadership book that aims to provide you with everything that you need to know about all three core aspects of leadership. As such, it's the all-inclusive and extensive nature of this book that differentiates it from others, and, most importantly, its core value to you. That is why there are 38 chapters – *all* are important and *all* will aid you in your journey to great heights.

There are a few ways to read this book

That said, I agree, 38 *is* quite a big number, so you might decide that one of the three parts of the book (self, team, organisation) is more important for you right now and so start there, or you might look down the list of chapter headings and say to yourself, 'I've mastered this, but I suck at that' and jump straight to the chapters that interest you (if you can do that, it implies that you know your strengths and weaknesses, so congratulations – that's one of the first habits of successful leaders), or finally, if you'd like to read this book from start to finish, then that's one mighty fine way of reading it too.

Inspired scribbling in a book, *is* a good thing (forget what you were taught at school – well, not *everything*)

If you're a fan of the 80/20 Principle (if you're not, then hopefully you will be after reading chapter 9), then you'll know that about 20 per cent of any resource brings 80 per cent of the value to you, so, although this book is packed full of wisdom and every word is of critical importance (obviously!), it's a great habit to always pinpoint the content that really sings to you. Circle it, scribble around it – whatever you do, just highlight it. Then, when you review this book, you can quickly glance at what you previously deemed important. As you may know, repetition equals retention, so reviewing books frequently and finding the key messages (as determined by you) is a phenomenal technique.

At the end of the day, however you read it, I hope, from the bottom of my heart, that you'll find the content of this book strikes many chords with you and also helps in your (and your team's) quest for excellence, happiness and success.

Finally, just before we begin – the billion-dollar question: Are leaders born or made?

This book was going to omit this question. However, I have been convinced by *Psychology Today* to include it. After all, as it says on their website: 'This is the most frequently asked question about leadership'.

I would have thought that, as this has been debated since the Sun Gods, it would have been definitively answered and put to bed with the lights out by now. But no, I can guarantee that as you read this, in some windowless fluorescent-lit meeting room somewhere in the world, this question is still being hotly debated. So let's nail it before we even begin.

Who started the born/made debate?

The origins of this debate go way back to Vince Lombardi, who was the Head Coach and General Manager of the Green Bay Packers back in the 1960s (for those whose national team plays football with a round ball, the Green Bay Packers are a US team playing in the National Football League). He declared: 'Leaders are made, they are not born. They are made by hard effort, which is the price which all of us must pay to achieve any goal that is worthwhile.' This claim has been hotly debated ever since.

So, is great leadership about skills that can be acquired, or is it *really* dependent on your inherited genes? I'm going to start with Jack Welch, former CEO of General Electric, who once told American TV channel MSNBC, 'I am often asked if leaders are born or made. The answer, of course, is both. Some characteristics, like IQ, seem to come with the package. On the other hand ... you learn other leadership qualities at work – trying something, getting it wrong and learning from it, or getting it right and gaining the self-confidence to do it again, only better.'

Great leadership is vastly more about habits than your DNA sequence or inherited genes

Warren Buffett, CEO of Berkshire Hathaway, told students at the University of Florida, 'If you really want to have them [qualities and habits of great leaders] you *can* have them. They're qualities of behaviour, temperament and of character that are achievable; they're not forbidden to anybody.' You see, Mr or Mrs Average Manager can become Lord or Lady Inspiring Leader. How? By developing leadership habits. As the bigwig Aristotle once said, 'We are what we repeatedly do, excellence then is not an act, but a habit.' Like your decisions, your habits define who you are today. The good news is, you can *learn* how to form better habits, and you can *learn* how to make better decisions – and therefore you can improve your leadership quotient and ability.

In my interview with Daniel Goleman, author of the internationally bestselling book *Emotional Intelligence*, he pointed out to me that, because of neuroplasticity (the brain's ability to change and adapt as a result of experience), habits can be changed at any age – the key is 'repeated experiences'. An old habit has a strong neural pathway in the brain. The reason the pathway is so wide is that you've been strengthening the pathway between your neurons through repeated use. Harry Chugani, MD, Chief, Paediatric Neurology Director, Professor of Paediatrics Neurology and Radiology, Children's Hospital of Michigan (who might have the longest job title in the US), likens this repeated action to a highway system: 'Roads with the most traffic get widened. The ones that are rarely useful fall into disrepair.'

So the good news is it's possible for you to adopt *all* the habits in this book (optimism, future focus, strategic thinking, catching people doing things right, decisiveness), or any other habits that you wish: you just need to decide to adopt (or drop) a habit and then stick at it until it becomes ingrained in your brain. For example, the ability to focus and not get distracted is a habit. As Daniel Goleman told me: 'Attention is a mental muscle. It's like going to the gym: if you go to the gym and you lift weights, every time you do a repetition you strengthen the muscle that you're working. Attention can be strengthened in the same way.'

After all, *if* leadership qualities couldn't be learnt, a) what's the point of this book, and b) shouldn't we just wait for the next life and hope that we're born leaders not followers? (I'd say that's a risky strategy, although I know a few people who appear to be banking on it!)

The 'born' argument isn't really grounded in reality

Very often, those who believe in 'born leaders' have in mind an image of a leader that is based on stereotypes, films or ill-conceived truths – a leadership 'type' that is based on fantasy, rather than the careful study of reality (take a look at the *Forbes* list of the world's top 100 leaders for photographic evidence of this misconception). Fictional attributes of a leader sometimes include traits like tall, good-looking, extrovert and, even, in some countries, 'rides a white horse'. If this *is* what leadership looks like, then, yes, the case would be closed. Genetics, along with horse-riding ability, would rule the day.

But I ask you this: were Gandhi and Mother Teresa great leaders because of their looks, height or any other genetic factor like 'extroversion'? Nope – it was because they both stood for something; they had a vision and purpose that moved people. Furthermore, if we look back to leaders in history, or the modern era, it's proven time and time again that great leaders have *learnt* to become great leaders, or have been moved (by a purpose) to become great leaders. Was Nelson Mandela born with his purpose of correcting inequality in South Africa? No – he found a purpose during his lifetime that lit him up so much inside that he couldn't help but be a great leader.

Let's look to you for further evidence. Ask yourself, if you could be led by any leader on the planet (an historical figure or a person who is alive and kicking today), who would it be, and why? I bet on your 'why-I'd-want-to-follow-them' list, you'd probably have attributes like integrity, authenticity, intellect, incredible results, strong values, passion, amazing vision, reputation, courage, ability to inspire a great team ... You probably *wouldn't* have things like height, looks, extroversion (or any other genetic factor). As Warren Buffett said: 'I could have been better looking; I could have been a much better athlete. So what? ... You play the hand you get, and you play it as well as you can.'

The only exception to this, and where the born argument has a case, is a little thing called IQ. However, as Daniel Goleman also pointed out, when it comes to IQ, you just have to be average or slightly above average to reach the very top of your industry. In fact, Daniel says you just need to be 'one deviation above normal' on the IQ scale. So don't worry, you don't need to be Galileo, Newton, Einstein or Gates to be a great leader, you just have to be 'smart enough'.

Ultimately, leadership isn't about your genetic make-up – leadership is about results. Brian Tracy told me once, 'The number one job of a leader is to get results' (it's worth pointing out that many leaders forget this fundamental truism) and the great thing about results is that they are subject to the law of cause and effect: if you do X (habit A) then you can create Y (favourable result) – and results are good-looks blind, age blind, colour blind, loudness blind and everything else blind. The only thing results depend on is what you do – your habits.

I hope I've convinced you that the source of world-class leadership is great habits rather than DNA and when babies are born the question should still remain; 'Is it a boy or girl?', and not 'Is it a leader or follower?' After all, that's what passion, integrity, lifelong learning, serving others, strategic thinking and hard work are all about. Cultivating those qualities is what will help you to become a great leader, and that's what this book is all about. I truly hope you greatly enjoy the pages to come.

PART ONE

SELF Leadership

it all starts with *you!*

Why does a book on leadership, which is all about getting results through others, start with you?

In my interview with Daniel Goleman he observed that, 'Leaders get results through *others*.' So, if that's the case (and it is) then why on planet earth are we starting *The Book of Leadership* with SELF-leadership?

Well, it's a universal law that to lead others you need to be able to lead yourself first. The Bible says it beautifully: 'If the blind lead the blind, both shall fall into the ditch.' So, if you want to stay out of the ditch and manage and lead a high-performing team and/or organisation, then the first thing that you need to have mastered is yourself (knowing that self-mastery is a life-long pursuit, we'll forgive you if you haven't reached 'mastery' status yet). Plus, there are some personal habits and characteristics that all leaders have in common, and so it's worth spending some time to make sure you've absolutely brushed up on those. After all, as Indra Nooyi (the Chairman and CEO of PepsiCo and, by the way, one of the best leaders on the planet) pointed out, 'If you want to improve the organisation, you have to improve yourself.'

The other thing about 'self' is the obvious connection with the essential leadership responsibility of setting an example. What you think, feel, say and do will be amplified to your team, and what *you* do, *they'll* have a tendency to do. So, if you have no self-control, or haven't mastered the basics of self-leadership, then the entire team may as well join Jane's team down the corridor – they'll probably fare better there. You don't want that, in fact you want the best folk in Jane's team (and probably Jane herself for that matter) knocking at your door. So let's begin with the most important person in all of this leadership malarkey, and that's *you*.

1

Leadership starts with a love of what you do

'[Leadership] has to start with a love of what you do – a passion, a commitment to the cause.'

Robert Senior

As a leader your first responsibility is to find a job, an industry, a profession, an environment, a team, *anything*, that you love. When you love what you do, you'll quite naturally adopt great leadership attributes; you won't have to force them through conscious effort – you'll just acquire them unconsciously.

You have to be inspired by what you're doing and where you're going, otherwise you won't be able to bring people with you on the journey. Nobody's going to want to follow you to Nonchalant Land. If you love what you do, then you'll have passion. This passion fuels great leaders, enabling them to speak with conviction, and thus appeal to the heart of their followers. (Great leaders appeal to the heart *and* the head, not just the head.)

Daniel Goleman pointed out to me, 'The word "motivation" shares its root with the word "emotion": both come from the Latin word *motere*, which means "to move".' The most inspiring leaders *do* move us. How? With their emotion and passion. It's this passion that makes them unstoppable and makes their teams unstoppable too. It's this passion that has fuelled them to achieve remarkable results, inspire their teams and annihilate any obstacle that might get in their way.

Frankly, if you don't care, you won't bother: on encountering your first obstacle you'll put your speedos on and go to the beach – probably not the sign of an engaged leader. As Steve Jobs said, 'The only way to do great work is to love the work you do.'

Leaders who love what they do work harder, but don't see it as work

Donald Trump's son, Donald Trump Jr, told CNBC that his father said after hiring him: 'Love what you do; if you don't, you'll never do it well ... so if you don't put in that extra time because you don't really enjoy it, I'll know, and I'll fire you like a dog.'

That's a pretty harsh way of making the point, but it's 100 per cent right. The greatest leaders do put in the hours, they do work *hard* – and hard work *is* needed for great success, but here's the key difference: they don't see it as work – they see it as a passionate hobby, so why wouldn't they put in the hours, if that's what they get out of bed for?

In my interview with Jon Moulton (one of the greatest private equity guys in the world), he said: 'I have absolutely no problem knocking out 15 hours a day when I'm enjoying myself, which is most days!' Please note, he said '*most*' days! As Tom Peters, author of *In Search of Excellence*, said to me, we all have some 'shitty days at the office' ... but it's the majority that count – the balance. This love for what they do is why über-successful people who 'make it' financially, continue to work. Why else do you think both Warren Buffett and Bill Gates are still working? It's a pretty sure bet it's not because they need the money to keep the heating on this winter. Conversely, if they hated it, they would stop immediately – just like the lottery winners, perhaps! They'd be gone from their offices, without a trace ...

This reminds me – if you're trying to find out what you'd love to do, then ask yourself: if you won the lottery tomorrow, then what job, despite your millions, would you still turn up to do? (Okay, yes, you'd be able to take a month or two off work, and, yes, you can arrive to work in whatever car, plane or helicopter you wish.)

If your answer is 'Umm, I'd stick with my day job, but rather than drive to work, I'd land on my company's roof,' then congratulations, you're one of the 13 per cent of us who might want to begin their leadership journey with chapter 2. Conversely, if it's not your current job, then commit to beginning your search today.

Love and charismatic leadership go hand in hand

I know this lovely guy called James. James normally speaks in a monotone voice that is guaranteed to send you off on the wildest daydreams. James couldn't excite a Labrador puppy. Six months ago I sat next to James at a dinner party and James was different – very different. When I asked James, 'How are things going?', he was undeniably radiant in his response. His answer engaged the entire table (due to remarkable unconscious vocal variety and projection) and he even caught the eye of a few ladies in the room (a first, I believe). What was the difference? He'd launched a business that he loved. The passion came through and he'd stumbled across this thing called charisma.

Charisma (when used properly) is a great asset in leadership (we have a chapter on it), but *anybody* can acquire it through a single discovery: finding out what they are passionately drawn to do. This, more than any other factor, turns average folk into inspiring leaders.

As Mike Harris, the founder and CEO of Egg and First Direct Bank, said to me, 'Enrolling other people in your own enthusiasm is the essence of charisma in my mind. You have to be able to do that in good circumstances and in bad. People have to listen to you and be energised by you, not listen to you and be depressed by you!'

Let's park leadership for a second; there's something much more important to consider: your life!

There's another reason that finding what you love to do is so important – and it's a somewhat important thing called your life! When I interviewed the management guru Tom Peters, he didn't beat around the bush when he said: 'If you piss away the work hours, you have quantifiably pissed away your life.'

Over a lifetime, you'll spend more waking hours at your workplace than you will anywhere else (unless you're in the habit of nodding off at work). In fact, as Brian Tracy, the US success guru, reminded me in our interview: 'The average executive spends about 2,000 hours a year at work.' That's a lot of hours, so why would you spend it on something you don't enjoy doing? Indeed, what Confucius said a while ago (well, about 2,500 years ago in around 490 BC) has become a cliché, but still holds true: 'If you find a job you love, you'll never have to work a day in your life.' It's really worth bearing this in mind. I don't mean to be alarmist, but the stakes really are quite high.

Yet how many people do you think have actually listened to our man Confucius?

How many people do you know whose eyes light up when they talk about what they do at work? Unfortunately, most people's eyes don't light up when they talk about their jobs. In fact, I was recently at an engagement party where I met a guy called Zac (not his real name to protect his only income stream) who, when talking about his work, looked me straight in the eye and said, 'There are two things I like about my job: leaving at the end of the day and the paid holiday.' I thought he was joking – unfortunately he wasn't. To give you an idea of the scale of the problem – according to a 2013 Gallup study, 74 per cent of employees in the US are actually 'unhappy' at work. In fact, only 13 per cent of people are actively 'engaged' in their jobs, emotionally invested in their work, or helping their organisations improve (leaving a whopping 87 per cent who aren't engaged, let alone loving what they do). Eek!

In many countries, companies use the word 'compensation' for the money they pay their staff at the end of the month. The word 'compensation' is defined by Oxford dictionaries as: 'Something, typically money, awarded to someone in recognition of loss, suffering, or injury.' Sheesh – how miserable is that? Work sounds as painful as chewing a wasp!

One of the reasons so many people are so miserable is that they're overmanaged (told what to do) and under-led (inspired to do it). It's certainly a contributing factor. Gallup also did a study which revealed that the number one reason great people leave organisations is their boss. So yes, leadership really does matter. (As the author of a leadership book, I *would* say that, but remember: there are not enough great leaders in this world. By being one, you can change the stats above.)

With so many miserable people about, some of whom get promoted to leadership positions, no wonder we have so many nonchalant leaders hanging around. If you're a grumpy, unhappy git who sees their pay as 'compensation', you might have a shot at barking orders and 'managing' others, but you'll be an awe-inspiringly rubbish leader. Why? Because you're missing a vital component: inspiration.

Let's check you out for a second

When you're at a dinner party and somebody asks you that inevitable question: 'So what do you do?', do you answer it with rhapsodic enthusiasm and excitement? Or do you answer it with dread, or, even worse, with apathy and indifference, eager to get on to the next subject even if that subject is waste management systems in Angola or something equally as unappealing (at least to most of us)? If you're impassioned and animated when you answer, then that same energy is coming across to your team, your new hires and your customers but if you're not, then your weariness also comes across to all. You see, it's really hard to be a great leader if you just don't really give a 'shoe'.

Warren Buffett once said, 'I tap-dance to work' and it's this passion for his specialism that explains why great people line up to be led by him. That said, I admit that that's the gold standard. But if you *don't* tap-dance to work, but rather take reluctant steps filled with drudgery and regret, then what? How do you turn that on its head and start loving what you do? Here are a few proven ways to find your passion if it's eluded you so far.

Get into the habit of trying new things

It's simple. You learn through trial and error. In fact, as we'll discuss later in this book, everything, when it comes to success in business *and* life, is achieved through trial and error.

Let me explain using the example of music. Imagine for a moment that you'd never listened to music before and that you've been tasked to find out what music you love. Would you a) speak to friends about what music they love, b) read about music and the history of music, or c) put on the radio and try listening to lots of different music, until you found some that you loved? (Answer = c).

It's exactly the same with your career. Throughout your career you should try to move around a lot and try lots of things, speak to a lot of people and research – until you find what you love. Sir Stuart Rose, former CEO of Marks & Spencer, told me that when it comes to searching, 'Because now we do live in a global world ... a fast-moving world, it is important for people to go and get different experiences.'

Ask yourself the right questions

When I asked Brian Tracy how people can find their ideal career, he shared with me an exercise that he does with all his audiences: 'I get them to idealise, to imagine they have no limitations – to imagine that they can wave a magic wand and make their future perfect in every way.'

So if you had a magic wand and could do anything, or £100 million already in the bank but you had to do some form of work, what would you do? Make a list, but don't let your mind edit your thoughts. Don't let Captain Inner Sensible say: 'What? ... you've got no experience in that, you've got to be having a laugh!' or 'What? ... Don't even think about it, bozo', or 'You're a total muppet, you can't become the CEO one day – you'll do well if you just don't get fired and people don't laugh at you'. The purpose of this list is to find your heart's desires, not to find out how persuasive your inner critic is (like most, I'm sure they're exceptionally talented, but once in a while tell them to go bother someone else).

Armed with this list, commit to researching the top items on it as soon as you can. Try to do something every day: read an article, call a knowledgeable friend, sign up to an evening class – just do something. With momentum, you'll be amazed at the results you'll see in just a few weeks and months. Other searching questions (if that didn't really cut the mustard for you) include:

- What job would I love to tell people I'm doing at a dinner party?
- If I could become the world authority on one subject, what would that be?
- Is there any department I'd like to try out?
- What job would stop me hitting the snooze button in the morning?
- What environment do I love being in? (For example, do you love working on your own or in a team? Do you love or hate travel? Matching up your environment with that which brings you pleasure is another great transformational tactic for happiness.)
- Which 10 companies would I love to work for?
- Which industry sector, cause or purpose do I really care passionately about?
- At the end of my life, what would I love to be remembered for?

The answers to any of these questions provide clues as to which way you should start looking.

If you're saying, 'Yes that's all very well but I've got bills to pay, Sunshine, I can't just quit and follow my love!', then what?

Indeed, I empathise – we've all got bills to pay. Things these days are pretty expensive – housing, commuting, schooling – in fact everything ending in 'ing' seems to cost a flipp*ing* fortune.

Many critics of the 'do what you love' advice point out that it's all very well, but (and it's a big but) your passion *must* pay. This is obviously true – in the same way that Cuba Gooding Jr shouts, 'Show me the money' to his agent in the film *Jerry Maguire*. We do all need money as well as a job that brings about a state of Nirvana, so keep looking until you find something you love to do but that *also* covers the bills (or, even better, far exceeds covering the bills). For example, if your first real passion is looking after Tweetie, your pet budgie, then this might not get you on the *Forbes* Rich List, or any list, other than welfare.

This isn't to say you shouldn't follow unpaid passions too. If you do what you love and there's no money there, you'll have a hobby and potentially an unpaid leadership position (nothing wrong with being a leader of the local gardening club), but you need one that pays you well too (assuming you haven't just won big on Red 28).

With this in mind, when looking for a leadership career you are passionate about, there are *two* questions to ask yourself:

i) Is what I do (or am about to do) something that I could love and
   passionately enjoy and passionately lead others in too?

ii) Does what I do (or am about to do) reward me financially for the
   lifestyle that I seek for me and my family (and/or pet budgie)? And
   what are the chances that following this pursuit will lead to
   necessary financial reward?

If the answer to the first question is a resounding 'yes', but the answer
to the second is a resounding, 'the chances are a one-in-a-million', then
don't take the bet. You've found your career when you can tick both of
these boxes, not one or the other.

But back to the bills: if you are very apprehensive about the potential
financial implications of following your passion, there are ways to explore
what you would really love to do, without giving up the safety net of a
monthly pay cheque (for now, at least). Here are a few suggestions:

Get a hobby

If your list from the exercise on p. 11 includes something like, 'I want to
become a photographer', then hold your horses. Before you quit your
day job, I'd encourage you to try photography outside of your primary
job. You might find you suck at it, or that you can't make a dime from it.
Or you might find the opposite. This is why hobbies are so damn important – and also why they're so crucial to finding a way out of your current
situation (if you're in this predicament).

So, do you have any hobbies right now? Remember, hobbies *can* lead
to careers. The problem with hobbies is that they can sometimes get
pushed aside as non-urgent and get buried under normal operational
stuff. The key, like everything important, is to segment time for them and
be strict at honouring the time you're willing to commit to pursuing
them.

Experiment within your organisation

If your list includes something like 'I want to try marketing', then, again, hold your horses before you quit your day job. If you like your company, but are bored in your position, then what about trying a secondment in the marketing department, or signing up for a marketing project?

Far too many people think that a lateral move (i.e. into a different function) is not 'career progression'. This is career folly. Experience in different functions gives you a wider perspective and a wider experiential base to draw upon. So, not only could you find your new passion, but it will help you in the future, whichever team, department or organisation you lead. The greatest organisations (like Facebook) encourage inter-departmental moves and even inter-company moves and the vast majority of the CEOs that I interviewed have spent time in many different departments. In addition to giving them the opportunity to find the department that suits them best, when they get to the top, they'll know quite a few of the departments they lead, inside out.

Do your research

If your list includes something like 'I want to try the media sector' or 'I want to work for Google', then, once more, don't be hasty. Before you leave your current job, spend some time in the evenings to network your way into finding out more and go for informational interviews with people you might know in the sector.

Finally, as with all goals, apply the strategic-thinking exercises discussed in chapter 28. By applying extraordinary thinking to get what you want, you will stand out from the crowd – and standing out matters.

When you test a role, give it some time and put your whole heart into it

Brian Tracy told me: 'Whatever job you have to do ... throw your whole heart into what you're doing and you will find out very quickly if this is the right work for you. If it's not, you won't get any excitement or happiness from it, so then change.' This is true, but you should also remember to work at what you're doing long enough to give it a proper shot; after all, things get more enjoyable when you get better at them. Indeed, Brian Tracy went on to remind me of the truism, 'Work is never fun until you're good at it.'

Going even further: don't forget that mastery can lead to passion

Aiming to become a specialist and expert at what you do is a noble and rewarding pursuit. By following this path you'll create great value, you'll demand the respect of those around you (important as a leader) and the professionals in your industry (good for hiring), your pay will go through the roof (good for holidays and nice things) and guess what? You'll probably start falling in love with what you do (good for your leadership career). So don't forget that putting your head down and becoming very, very good at something often leads to developing a love and passion for it, so whilst you're on your journey it's worth just becoming very good at what you do.

To expand this idea further, ask, 'If I could be the world authority in one thing then what would that be?' At some point the greatest leaders on the planet either consciously (or unconsciously) have declared their area of expertise and made it so. Declaring a niche and owning it can lead to great fulfilment.

Failing all of the above, just take the leap – you won't know until you actually try it

Again, until you *try* the things on your list, you'll never know a) if you actually enjoy it, b) if in fact you're any good at it (another rather important ingredient for success), c) if you can get paid for it (also rather key for a fulfilling career). Before you quit your day job you might want to establish this, or have a bit of an idea ... it's not always possible, but if it is, that's best.

If it's *not* possible, but you're really being pulled to something, then you might want to take Sahar Hashemi's advice to 'leap and the net shall appear'. Life's too short not to take a few risks – it's like walking down a corridor of closed doors: you'll never really know what doors are there for you to open until you've gone down the path – you just have to trust that doors of opportunity will open.

Let's take the pressure off: you have to love what you *do*, not necessarily love your product or industry

Don't forget that many of the greatest business leaders are in businesses that are widely perceived as 'blank stare industries' (i.e when you tell people what you do, you get a blank stare), such as chemicals, logistics, cement, or information management. They might not *love* their product (it might be odd falling in love with widgets and screws, or cement itself), but are in love with the whatever it is that they do in their specific role. For example, a marketing director might be passionate about the art of marketing (or indeed the leadership opportunities that come with the role) rather than the particular product they're marketing. Sure, the ideal scenario would be to match passion with the product or wider industry, but it's not absolutely necessary.

When I interviewed Stelios Haji-Ioannou (the Founder of easyJet and Chairman of easyGroup) he told me, 'Taking on the big boys is what I do for a living'. Stelios is driven by the love of the David and Goliath fight, not necessarily the aeroplanes (easyJet), offices (easyOffice), vans (easyVan) or any other product that he has in his portfolio of companies. He loves business and, of course, leading his companies to success.

I'm not saying that it's goodbye to everything that you don't enjoy

Some people take this advice of 'I must do what I love' a little too far, and they refuse to do anything that doesn't make them ecstatically happy. This makes you remarkably unemployable – and a pain in the derrière. For example, you might not enjoy doing performance reviews, but as a leader that's still part of your job. The key, though, is to make sure that the vast majority of your time is spent on the things you really enjoy, otherwise, what's the point?

At the end of the day, if you're not inspired, then do something about it ... anything, but do *something*

The bottom line is, if you turn up to work day after day nonchalant and apathetic about what you do, you're going to be one heck of a nonchalant and apathetic leader. Conversely, if you're inspired, you'll be inspiring. So if you don't love what you do, it's not too late to do something about it. All you need to do is take action. As Sir Stuart Rose told me: 'If you tell me 87 per cent of people are unhappy at work, I say 99 per cent of [those people] do bugger all about it. Do something about it.' So, if you haven't found what you love yet, then this single goal should become a priority until you have found it. It's never too late. It doesn't matter if you're 25, 45, 55 or 75 – start searching now. Plus, as we have shown, leaders are made when they find their love, not when they settle for what they don't – so if you haven't found what you love yet, keep looking. As the legendary Steve Jobs said in his commencement speech at Stanford University, 'Whatever you do, don't settle.'

The idea in brief:

- *If you want to be inspiring, it helps to be inspired in the first place*
- *Great leaders work hard, but see their jobs as more of a passion/hobby than work – how passionate are you when describing what you do?*
- *Impactful leaders appeal to their followers' hearts, not just their heads, so passion helps*
- *Don't waste your life on anything other than what you love*
- *If you don't love what you do, find your passion through trial and error – there's no other way*
- *When you do what you love, charisma and charismatic leadership will follow*

2

Exude energy – know what lights your fire

'Every successful company, every successful team, and every successful project runs on one thing: energy. It's the leader's job to be the energy source that others feed from.'

Tom Peters

One thing that all the business leaders and CEOs I've interviewed have in common (and all great leaders throughout the ages) is that they have *remarkable* energy and drive. As the leader, you're the source of positivity and energy for your team; somebody has to instil an abundance of positive energy and create a can-do attitude – and if you're the leader, that's high up on your job description.

We all know that we catch bugs and colds off people – that's a given – but we also catch energy off people too. Think back to a time when your whole team was feeling low or flat, and then somebody walked in, challenged the team or just exuded energy – and suddenly everybody was infected by this enthusiasm. Upbeat, or downbeat, mood is very contagious. This is why energy and enthusiasm are so important in leadership. It's another reason (one of many) why grumpy-git leaders are usually woefully ineffective. Why? We catch their mood.

In my interview with Daniel Goleman, he echoed this idea:

> A number of studies … show that if a leader of a team is in an upbeat mood, people in that team catch that mood, and performance goes up, decision-making gets better, creativity improves. If the leader is in a downbeat mood – critical, angry, frustrated – people pick that up and performance goes down. So there's a direct relationship between leaders' moods, teams' moods, and performance. Once you understand that, you see that a leader must start leading by managing himself or herself first, because it's going to affect everybody else.

But where does this energy come from? Having spoken to some of the most driven CEOs and entrepreneurs in the world, it has become apparent that, as well as having a positive disposition (covered in chapter 19), there are eight key drivers fuelling them all. Some have one dominant driver, others have a blend of some or all of the eight and you'll be exactly the same. The key is to know which *your* core drivers are, and then keep them in the front of your mind to fuel you forward.

Driver One – to help and enable others (usually your customers or individuals in your team)

The drive to help and enable others is, thank goodness, quite common. Many people feel most alive when helping those around them, or fighting to correct an injustice in the world that causes suffering to others. History is scattered with folk like Mahatma Gandhi, Mother Teresa and Marie Curie – hats off to them.

If you have this driver, however, it doesn't mean you have to solve a global injustice or run a nationwide charity (although hats off to you too if that's your calling) – it's also a primary driver behind many of the world's greatest business legends. This driver manifests itself in two ways in a leader: the first is a genuine desire to help your customers by meeting their needs, and the second is a genuine desire to help the team you lead; both are equally powerful and lucrative business drivers.

Talking of some of the higher profile leaders with this driver, each year *Forbes* publishes a list of the world's billionaires. I hope your name is on there one day (along with mine, of course!). Recently, Steve Forbes wrote an article alongside the list, entitled 'They Succeed by Meeting Your Needs'. In the article Steve points out that many of these leaders became billionaires because of an obsession about putting their *customers'* needs first and doing whatever they could to serve them (see chapter 30 for more on customer love).

For example, Facebook founder Mark Zuckerberg (who according to *Forbes* is worth $19 billion, as of September 2013 (that's not enough to live on, of course, but it's a very good start)) is obsessed by enabling his users to stay in contact with friends and loved ones. Similarly, Niklas Zennström founded Skype because he wanted to help millions of people around the world speak to their friends, family, colleagues and loved ones via video, for free.

Like all great business leaders, both Mark and Niklas are *always* asking how they can help us reach our unmet needs and how they can better serve us as their customers or users. As a result they're wildly successful (as leaders, business people and as philanthropists).

If you have this driver you're more likely to be a *Servant Leader*. In my interview with Ken Blanchard, the author of *One Minute Manager*, Ken pointed out that some of the greatest leaders in the world are what he calls 'Servant Leaders'. They see themselves as servants to their team and their customers – as such, over time, they become great leaders.

If you have this driver you're also more likely to *genuinely care* about your team – and they will feel it. Sir Richard Branson echoes Ken's point: 'Having a personality of caring about people is important. You can't be a good leader unless you generally like people. That is how you bring out the best in them.' For example, over at Facebook they survey their team by simply asking: 'Does Facebook care about you?' It's a really powerful question. If the answer to that question is 'no' too many times, then, guess what, people won't feel cherished or an important part of the community/ecosystem and, bang, they're gone to a new shiny start-up, or New Competitor Inc.

If you want to use this driver to energise you as a leader, two very useful questions to ask are:

- How can I help my customers, delight them, and answer their needs?

- How can I help the individuals on my team be the best they can be? After all that's my job.

If you frequently think of these two questions (arguably the two most important questions a leader can ask themselves), and respond accordingly, then you will take the focus off yourself and onto serving others. As Stevenson Willis said, 'It is only when you serve others without regard for self, will honour, respect and lasting success be found.'

Driver Two – a core purpose/an ideal vision of the future

Some leaders source their energy from a meaningful mission (a core purpose which moves them), an ideal vision of the future or the goals that will lead to the fulfilment of the aforementioned two. Let's look at them:

Mission

Many maintain that before World War II, Winston Churchill had been just an average political leader, arguing that it wasn't until he found the purpose to 'defend Britain and win the war' that he became great. The purpose became his driving force and awakened the dormant leadership talent within him. So ask yourself: is there any umbrella purpose that you passionately care about – and can fight for? (Hopefully *not* a war, but something bigger than you – see chapter 16 for more on the awesome power of having a clear mission.)

Vision

Some leaders (Steve Jobs, for example) spend time picturing an *ideal* vision of the future, and this vision becomes so captivating that they become obsessed with turning it into a reality. These are the visionary leaders who love innovation and the opportunities that the future has in store. They have a compelling vision and create a map to get there, then get buzzed by seeing it manifest itself as reality.

As Brian Tracy told me: 'The key to success is future orientation. That means top people – the top 10 per cent of people – think about the future most of the time – and they use a concept called "idealisation" (another blisteringly powerful energy source).'

Goals

Some leaders adopt the very powerful habit of goal-setting: they visualise the ideal future, write down their goals (both personal and professional) and commit to doing whatever it takes to achieve them. Great leaders often get addicted to this habit and the success and endorphin rush that comes from goal attainment (if you're going to have an addiction this is up there with the best). As goal-setting is so important, I have dedicated a whole chapter to it (chapter 26), so for further reading, head there.

Driver Three – proving the (ignorant and annoying) naysayers wrong

Some leaders love to set 'stretch goals' or a lofty vision of the future, and then wait to hear the words: 'You can't do that . . .' Then, blast off, they *have* to prove the naysayers wrong. People without this driver might say, 'Phew, thank goodness you told me before I wasted my time trying'.

Sir Richard Branson is a perfect example of someone with this driver. In an interview for *Esquire* he said: 'My interest in life comes from setting myself huge, apparently unachievable, challenges and trying to rise above them.'

Believe it or not, back in the 1990s Donald Trump was heavily in debt and close to bankruptcy. Talking to CNBC about his fall from grace, he said, 'It's a very bad feeling when you're the hot boy in town, and all of a sudden you're reading stories on front pages that maybe you're not going to make it. I think *that*, more than anything, fuelled my enthusiasm or my energy to get up and prove people wrong.'

Back to you: so, have you recently been told 'it won't work' or 'you're not good enough', or not been given finance for an idea because it would never work (Ed Wray when launching Betfair, which was valued at over £1 billion when the company floated in 2010), or even been fired from a job (Tim Waterstone was fired from WHSmith before launching Waterstones and selling it back to his former employer for a fortune)?

They say 'success is the best revenge' – it's a great feeling when you prove the naysayers wrong.

Driver Four – a love for what you do

Some leaders just love leading so much, or love what they do so much, that it's enough for them to be driven forward tirelessly. However, as this has already been discussed in chapter 1, I won't spend any more of your valuable time on it here, other than a reminder, borrowed from George Eliot: 'It is never too late to be what you might have been.'

Driver Five – the love of working out a strategy to beat a competitor and then winning the race (the gamification of business)

Some leaders get their buzz out of naming a competitor (often one that's much, much bigger than they are, or dominant in a market) and then setting out to make sure that their (sometimes tiny) company goes about out-thinking, out-manoeuvring or, in fact, out-anything them – just to ensure that they overtake and rule the day (these leaders can be lovely, cuddly folk; it's just that winning is what they love). These folk often love being the David in the David and Goliath story, and their eyes light up when they say, 'My job is to work out how to lead this company to become number one in our industry, right now we're one-hundred-and-fifty-third [or whatever]'. They love the thrill of winning (or developing the strategy to get them there) so much that this is what fuels them, and as Simon Calver, former CEO of LOVEFiLM, reminded me; 'There's nothing wrong with a bit of gladiatorial spirit.'

In fact, very often entrepreneurs go into business in pursuit of the buzz that comes from overtaking complacent giants. As I mentioned earlier, Sir Stelios Haji-Ioannou, the founder of easyJet, said to me in my interview with him: 'Taking on the big boys is what I do for a living, and I keep doing it industry after industry – and it has never failed me.'

Business is like a game of chess (hence our front cover) and, indeed, it is great fun. Money is just a by-product of how well you're playing the game – it's never the game itself, merely a way to keep score. The thrill of out-manoeuvring the enemy can, in fact, fuel an entire team and organisation. Tim Waterstone, founder of Waterstones, told me that companies are happiest when they have an enemy and that 'the whole team gets behind trying to drag down the enemy'.

So, if you're fuelled by a desire to beat the competition, embrace that. Set up everything as a competition. Have fun with this. As long as it stays at a healthy level, then name the competitor, go forth and conquer (ideally an external competitor, not poor unsuspecting Gloria across the corridor from you!).

Driver Six – a fear of failure/insecurity

Many great leaders are insecure. They aren't insecure in terms of their strengths (leaders are very sure of the value they bring to the table, see chapter 3 for more on this) but they are insecure about success and driven by a fear of failure. As a result they are driven to create enormus success/wealth around them. Indeed many great leaders have had difficult or humble upbringings, sometimes surrounded by poverty. Sir Terry Leahy (who grew up in a prefab house on a council estate in Liverpool) told me: 'If you don't have much by way of background, you're probably insecure', and when I asked him if he was driven by a fear of failure, he replied, 'Without question – and I think that's pretty common.' Sir Stuart Rose said something very similar when he told me: 'What I have got is a massive fear of losing – and that's probably what's driven me.'

If you're insecure, or driven by the fear of failure then, as long as it doesn't get out of hand, it's a great catalyst for energy – and congratulations on having it. As Jon Moulton, Chairman of Better Capital, said to me, 'A lot of the wildly successful people are actually quite unbalanced.' It's a huge asset.

Driver Seven – a love of risk and adrenalin

Some great leaders are actually adrenalin junkies and they love the adventure of business. As we all know, sometimes it's quite scary leading a team into the unknown, but it provides a great buzz. Although these leaders might enjoy taking risks, they always differentiate between dumb risk (where the downside is significant compared with the upside) and smart risk (where the upside is significant compared with the downside). They feed off this balance between risk and reward – and they know that great results come from new adventures.

It's interesting to note that some leaders also love the adrenalin rush of hyper-growth, last-minute crises and super-quick decision-making. If you're throwing this book up in the air and saying, 'That's me, baby' (or words to that effect), just remember that a love for the adrenalin rush leadership can bring is a great asset, but make sure you've got some folk around you who balance out your thrill-seeking nature – hyper-growth, for example, isn't always the right strategy, that's why complementary teams work best.

Driver Eight – the pursuit of money and wealth

Want to be super rich or even just pretty well off? That's great. *However*, it should not be your primary driver (which is why it's bottom of the list). You see, if you make money *the* thing (for you as an individual or for the organisation or team you lead), it's like a dog chasing its tail; it just goes around and around in circles, never fully satisfied. Make money *a* thing, but not *the* thing.

In fact, in the vast majority of cases, using money as a sole motivator will lead you to unhappiness and a rather low bank balance. Far better to choose one or more of the other major drivers and then see the accumulation of wealth as a by-product of these.

You might find that just one of these drivers is driving you, or a few, or all of them – whatever the case, let yourself be driven! Whatever lights a fire under your bottom and spurs you to action is a wonderful thing. Find out what makes you feel alive or tingle with excitement and embrace it. Energy and drive, especially as a leader, are everything. Why? Because they spread like wildfire amongst your team.

The idea in brief:

- *Energy and drive in leadership are everything, they're what others feed from*
- *Providing the right 'energy' is in (or should be in) the leader's job description*

- *Whatever your energy driver is – whatever lights your eyes up, recognise it and love it – it's a powerful asset. Ultimately, whatever ignites a match under your bottom is a good thing; know it and keep it front of mind when energy is low*
- *Don't make 'I will make a lot of money' your primary driver (although as a goal it's fine) – money should come as a by-product of your other drivers*

3

Focus on building extreme strengths, not fixing weaknesses

'If you've been focusing on your weaknesses rather
than your strengths, you've inadvertently been
sabotaging your own progress.'

Jürgen Wolff, author and creativity coach

All the CEOs, millionaire entrepreneurs and world-famous management thinkers that I have interviewed have been acutely aware of their
natural strengths and equally aware of their natural weaknesses. This
might sound obvious, but what's more remarkable is what they do with
this knowledge: they insist on spending time on their strengths, and
they do diddly-squat about their weaknesses. As the German-American
publisher John Zenger once said, 'Great leaders are not defined by the
absence of weakness, but by the presence of clear strengths.'

You're *weak* at the things you're weak at, so it's illogical to do those things

We're very often conditioned at a young age, usually from the earliest days at school, to overcome our weaknesses rather than discovering and maximising our natural, in-built talents; to focus on improving our D and C grades instead of taking our A grades to the next level. In adulthood this thinking results in low wages, slow cars and uninspiring leaders. We need to change this conditioning.

Philippa Snare, the CMO of Microsoft, said in my interview with her:

> I remember going to school and permanently being asked to work on things that I wasn't very good at, because I had to get better at my weaknesses and build on my gaps and the areas that I wasn't so strong at. I didn't realise why I didn't like school so much, until one of my first leaders in the private sector, Duncan MacKillop, asked me: 'Why would you work on your weaknesses? There's a reason why they are your weaknesses!' And then I realised, Yes! ... that's the most ridiculous thing. Ever since then I've been very strength-based and seek to find out what I'm naturally good at and interested in.

Tim Waterstone, the founder of Waterstones, put it bluntly when he said, 'It's a mistake to do that which you can't do.' It's as true for you as it is for Kim and Tim in your team. The fact is, it takes a lot more energy to go from being poor at something to competent, than it does to go from naturally good at something to becoming exceptional – and the pay-off for the latter is far, far higher.

The world rewards extreme strengths not mediocrity (improved weaknesses)

It's far better to become a world authority on one or two areas (natural strengths) than become average at all things by working on your weak areas. The world doesn't really reward mediocrity, but it overcompensates for strengths. It's the same for you, the individuals on your team, and entire organisations. Maximise your strengths, turning them into extreme competitive advantages. When you do, the value you bring the world will increase exponentially.

One caveat: if you (or those around you) identify a weakness that, in order to be excellent at what you do, does require improvement (at least to an adequate standard), then of course you should work at improving those areas. There are times when you are only as strong as your weakest link.

Confidence comes from an awareness of one's strengths

Great leaders are confident. Why? Because they're very sure what value they bring to the world (their strengths) and they know their weaknesses don't matter. You don't have to be better than everybody on your team at everything; in fact, *they* have to be better than *you* at what they're doing. Matthew Key, former Chairman and CEO of Telefónica Digital, told me: 'Know your strengths and know your weaknesses. Once you know that, play to your strengths and get people around you who help you on your weaknesses.' You just have to be confident in the value you bring, and that could be two or three key attributes: inspiration, vision, public speaking, future thinking, people development, hiring, attracting talent, coaching, strategy, execution – whatever it is, know it and augment it.

The bottom line is, if you want to be a great leader, it's essential to be exceptionally sure about what you're good at – it brings you the confidence that you need in order to lead others.

So back to *you*: what are *your* strengths and weaknesses? (No Google answers, please)

'What are your strengths and what are your weaknesses?' is a great, but underrated, interview question. It sounds so amateur, but it really is a great question. Yet, the problem is that it's become so widely used that everybody has Googled the textbook answer to it. So that's all you hear, from *everyone* (when what you actually want to hear is an authentic response). So, unless you really probe the interviewee to test authenticity, it's now a worthless question. But, for your own leadership ability, it's an essential question to ask yourself and to know the authentic answer to.

All great leaders spend some time on introspection and reflection, so grab a piece of paper and write down your five to 10 greatest strengths on the left, and then your five to 10 greatest weaknesses on the right (if you have more, or less, of either that's fine). As a leader, this insight, and the self-awareness it brings, is the foundation for everything: who you hire and how you lead. Have you made the lists? Great. (If you didn't do it, I understand – I've been there too and missed exercises in books, but make sure you can at least mentally list a few before you move on.)

The secret to success is this: do the things on the left and, where possible, avoid the things on the right. Success couldn't be easier.

So, I'm curious – how did you find writing your list of strengths? During leadership training sessions I used to ask people to stand up and tell the group their strengths. What a lot people did was to whisper their strength under their breath and then immediately go a delightful pink. How sweet, yet how uncommercial. This vital list is the value you bring to the world; it's your commercial weight. You should be proud of your strengths – from now on, sing them from the rooftops.

To work on your strengths you need to avoid your weaknesses by:

a)   Delegating them to your team or a consultant, or *anybody* that will take them off you. The Chairman of the last company I worked for called me the CDO – the Chief Delegation Officer! Nice title ... I did work hard on my strength areas too, though, I promise.

b)   Just simply not doing them (the beauty of saying no). Try to refuse assignments where you have to focus mostly on your weaknesses. Why would you do something if somebody else would be far better at it? By taking it upon yourself, you're setting yourself up to be mediocre, and mediocrity is not what great leaders do.

Finding your strengths and weaknesses

If you found the previous exercise tough and you drew a lot of blanks, then how do you find your strengths and weaknesses? The best way is through trial and error (see the previous chapter) and then getting feedback on your efforts. Here are three great ways to find your strengths through *real* feedback (on your skills as a person or as a leader):

Feedback from results

Like everything in life, nothing speaks like results. If you do whatever it is you want to do and you get good results, that's a sure bet you're onto something. Results are the ultimate meritocracy. They don't discriminate against anything other than incompetence. So God bless results – good or bad. Please do bear in mind, though, that when you're new to something, you will suck at it. That's quite normal. Think about the first time you walked: you fell over a lot, but it's a good thing you didn't quit trying. It's called the learning curve (see chapter 11 to find out more about this and its importance), so don't quit too early, especially with regard to leadership.

The key is to stick with something long enough to find out if you have a natural talent. If you continue to be lower than average at it despite practice, work, coaching, hours and everything else, it's probably time to think, Umm … this ain't for me. The other indicator that you're a natural will be whether you love something when you try it. It's a good indicator, although it's not definitive. I love singing, yet I ain't getting in any choir! (In fact, the only time that I've ever been fired was from the church choir at the age of 12 – no warning, no notice period and no pay-out btw.)

Feedback from your friends, family and work circle

The easiest way of finding your strengths and weaknesses is by doing what is called a low-budget 360-degree feedback review. A GPS device relies on four (four!) satellites to give you an accurate location and it's exactly the same for individuals. You need your own opinion thrown in with others to give you an accurate diagnosis. Simply email your friends, trusted colleagues and family (or anybody who you feel knows you very well) and ask what they see as your top five strengths, as well as what they see as areas that you should definitely avoid (a nice way to say weaknesses). Your work circle is particularly great, because your colleagues – be they your boss, your peers or your subordinates – will be less concerned about the emotional impact on you than your friends or family. In fact, some might love to have the opportunity to tell you the truth – and then some! After you've received this feedback, look for patterns in the responses you get. This feedback is also vital in finding out how you can be a better leader; learn to hunt it down.

Feedback from 'Truth Sayers' (wherever they may be)

There are some people in this world that will just say it how it is. They could be friends, family, consultants or friends of friends. Essentially these people feel that they have a higher calling in this world to tell the truth, the whole truth, nothing but the truth, so help them God. These people always prioritise delivering the absolute truth over any negative impact (or emotional devastation) it may cause the recipient. Think back to when you messed up on something; they're the folk that say, 'Yes, dude, you royally screwed up.' They say it how it is. Once you've found them, don't *ever* – even if you're tempted to – delete them from your phone. They're worth their weight in gold. Ask them about your strengths and weaknesses, but don't sulk; it's so unbecoming, and it's just feedback.

Remember – get everybody on your team aligned to their strengths, not just you

Focusing on strengths is a success mantra for all great leaders and this thinking transfers to their teams too. You have to free your team up to allow them to do what they're great at. As John Studzinski, former Head of Global Investment Banking at HSBC, put it, '... maximise their strengths and make their weaknesses irrelevant.'

Ensuring that everybody in your team is focused on their strengths and not their weaknesses is exceptionally motivating for your team. You'll inspire great followers because nothing is more motivating for your team than your making sure they spend time on their power areas – and nothing increases results for you and your team as much as aligning tasks with strengths.

The idea in brief:

- *We all have natural strengths and natural weaknesses – love your strengths, make your weaknesses irrelevant*
- *You'll never be a success by trying to improve your weaknesses*
- *Great leaders focus on turning their natural strengths into colossal strengths – i.e. become world authorities in what they're naturally good at*
- *Have the courage to say no to operating in your area of weakness for too long*
- *360-degree feedback is one of the greatest ways to improve your leadership skills and general business skills – so look for patterns in response*
- *When building a team, be acutely aware of their individual strengths and weaknesses too – it's a habit of great leaders; be 'strength-driven' in everything you do*

4

Be committed: don't do your best – do whatever it takes

> 'There's a difference between interest and commitment.
> When you're interested in doing something, you do it
> only when circumstance permit. When you're committed
> to something, you accept no excuses, only results.'

Art Turock

Too many leaders, teams and individuals around the world aren't achieving their important goals (personal or business) because they preface their intentions with a ridiculously overused phrase: 'I will do my best' or 'We'll do our best'. These phrases are more likely to be the mantras for losers not leaders. To achieve your goals you should never be non-committal; when the going gets tough, you'll default to: 'We tried, but we couldn't do it.' If you let this language slip in and become prolific, you'll be overtaken by people, teams and companies that *are* willing to commit.

As the leader you have to use the right language when communicating. You have to show that you're committed to achieving your own goals, and the goals you set your team. If you show the team (through verbal or non-verbal cues) that you're not actually that bothered about your goals or achieving your vision, your team will pick up on that level of commitment and, if you're not that bothered, they won't be either.

Imagine for a moment that you're an investor. Who would you be more likely to back with your cash – somebody who said: 'I'll do my best to achieve it' or someone who said, 'I'll do whatever it takes to achieve it'? Yes … absolutely: you'd put your money behind the committed genius behind the second phrase, every time. Similarly, which do you think is the better response as a leader, or the better response from a team member? The answer is, 'whatever it takes', every time.

The core difference between the two responses is commitment. The greatest leaders and most successful people in the world are those that identify their own, their team's, or their organisation's most important goals and *commit* to doing whatever it takes to achieve them.

What would you do if you had to achieve your goals this month because somebody had a gun to your head?

I admit this is a dramatic example, but I think you'll agree that conversations about holidays, checking social network updates, together with the language of 'I'll do my best', would go out the window. Your results, productivity and time management skills would go through the roof. In fact, I can guarantee that, for that period of time, you'd become one of the most productive people/teams in the country.

So, therein lies the answer to effective leadership. No, not holding a gun to the head of anyone on your team (it might work for a short time, but you'll have a *significant* retention issue the next day) but total, 100 per cent commitment to achieving your goals, come what may.

If you and your team *had* to achieve your goals, here are eight things you might do differently:

You'd deploy strategic and creative thinking

I cover the power of thinking extensively in chapter 28 but I will just mention it very briefly here. High achievers schedule time for creative thinking – not just on their problems (problem-solving), but on goal attainment too.

To trigger this creative thinking all you have to do is sit down (alone or with your team) and write your goal at the top of a blank sheet of paper and challenge yourself to come up with 30 things you could do to achieve your objective. Very often, 10 or 15 will be obvious, while the next 15 will take some creative juices. Yet the magic very often lies in the last 10–15 – and, magically, the impossible becomes possible. If you're committed to achieving something, then you'll think differently.

You'd go outside your comfort zone and take a risk

If you *had* to achieve your goals, then the fear that you might feel by undertaking even the most courageous tasks would become just part of the day job. For example, standing up and speaking in front of 500 people would be easily digested if you knew you had no other option.

You'd put your focus externally on doing whatever you had to do, not internally on your own self-doubt, personally limiting beliefs or inner critic – you'd shut those voices up straight away. And if your own team had the same attitude, then they would think and behave the same way. Productivity and results would soar!

You'd be willing to make sacrifices

It's true that if you want to be successful then you do have to make sacrifices. If you had to achieve a big goal and you're all running late – then, yes, you'd work late. You'd even give up a day on the weekend. You wouldn't care that the weather is a lovely 23 degrees, sunny with a nice south-westerly breeze – you'd just get on with the job at hand. That's fine. As the leader you have to set the example so that your followers replicate this work ethic and go the extra mile, or 50 miles, with you. (By the way, when you're making sacrifices, it's important to put your focus on what you are getting as a result of doing the work (career success, or whatever), as opposed to what you're not getting (the chance to enjoy the weather!).)

It's not about working late every day and every weekend, but if you've got to hit a target by a certain date, or you're trying to get Microsoft as a new client, then sometimes, yes, you have to do whatever it takes.

You'd show great self-discipline and demand it in others

> 'Self-discipline is the ability to make yourself do what you should do, when you should do it, whether you feel like it or not.'
>
> **Elbert Hubbard**

If you had to achieve a goal, then procrastination would go out the window and self-discipline would be alive and kicking. Having the habit of self-discipline and instilling discipline in those around you is an essential part of leadership. If you have the self-discipline to stay committed to your goals no matter what, then you can instil this in others and soon you'll become the stuff leadership legends are made of.

You'd fire those around you that are holding you back and you'd genuinely love those that can help you get to where you want to go

This might sound cutthroat, but you do have to be ruthless about firing people who slow you down, and equally appreciative and loving towards those who can help you get to where it is you're trying to go. We discuss this in detail in chapter 25.

You'd show great urgency in everything you do – no time-wasting

If you and your team had to achieve your goal, do you think you or others would take lengthy lunch breaks or check Facebook at work? Nope. As the leader, you have to show urgency in what you're doing. Everything needs to come back to 'Are we wasting time here?' If so, move on. As a leader, show urgency. Time is money.

You'd give no excuses and you'd accept none

Some people have come to me and said, 'We couldn't do it because of X,Y or Z.' Great people don't crumble at the first obstacle. Instead, rather like ants, they just go around the obstacle – they find a different way.

That's a sign that somebody's committed to making something happen. Get your team to think creatively. Don't accept excuses, and don't give out excuses either. As one very wise gentleman (who was only 26 inches tall, bald and pale green) once said: 'Do or do not. There is no try' (Yoda).

You wouldn't be afraid of asking for what you want time and time again

So many leaders don't ask for what they want enough. Yet, as Wayne Gretzky said, 'You miss every shot that you don't take.'

If you had to achieve your goals, you'd keep trying until you succeeded. Your perseverance would soar – and you'd be dogged beyond belief. So this is why commitment is everything regarding your most important goals. You'll be like a pit bull terrier: despite failure or rejection, you won't let go. Sometimes that's what it takes: failure and rejection are often precursors to success. In fact, Sir Stuart Rose said to me, 'If you're not getting rejected frequently, you're probably not trying hard enough. (I must be trying *very* hard!)

The world's most successful women and men heed the advice of George A. Custer, a famous officer in the American Civil War, who said, 'It's not how many times you get knocked down that count, it's how many times you get back up.'

If you agree with me that a rejection doesn't matter at all – then why wouldn't you just ask for what you want more often? You should – whether that's asking somebody to join your leadership team, asking for a bigger budget, asking for a job, asking for a discount, anything – just ask and make it a habit. Even the Bible says, 'Ask and it shall be given unto you.'

When I was a managing director in New York, I hired a new salesman called Brent. Brent was, and I'm sure still is, a legendary sales guy. He was the top-performing sales guy in our office, and probably the entire industry. Why? Because he wouldn't let anything get in the way of him achieving his goals, he was committed in every sense of the word.

I remember Brent's first day in the office. When he arrived at 7.30 a.m., I met with him briefly to explain what the company was all about – our values and so forth. About 15 minutes in, I could see he was a little anxious, a little distracted. A little twitchy, in fact.

Then I figured out the problem – he just wanted to get on the phone to prospects and start selling. So I decided to drop any of the formal introductions around the office, and even dropped the mandatory 'let me show you where the loos are'. I just unleashed him on the phone.

Fifteen minutes later, Brent jumped up from his cubicle and started celebrating – he even started doing 'high fives' with people around him. (None of whom he'd even met yet.) So I ran over to him and, although it's not very British, I did a high five too, and said, 'Brent, this is awesome, tell me the great news.' To which he replied, 'I've just got my first rejection – only 34 more to go, baby.' (I don't think he was actually calling me baby, thank goodness.)

At this point I thought to myself, Hmmm, he's got a screw loose, but after reassuring myself that security was just one call away, I asked, 'Brent, what do you mean by "only 34 more to go, baby"?' He explained to me that, based on his career so far, he'd worked out his conversion ratio and he'd calculated that it takes approximately 35 rejections to get, on average, one yes. So all he had to do was to get on the phone and speak to as many people as he could to get through the 34 rejections, in order to get the one yes. The more calls, the more rejections, the more orders.

What a legend. Brent's amazing attitude and approach influenced the entire sales floor – soon everybody was playing this conversion game – and his approach influenced my leadership too. One of the best tips for leadership is, when pursuing goals, take rejection on the chin, smile (or do high fives) and keep rolling the dice until you get what you want. If you get a no, that's cool, if you get a yes, then who knows how that might transform your situation. Foster this attitude in your team too, and always lead the way. If your team see you getting rejected, then it will show them that it is a characteristic of success – which it is.

A word of warning: choose your goals wisely

Because this 'I'll do whatever it takes' language really does commit you to action, it's advisable to set your goals very wisely. Some things are not worth fighting for, others are; it's knowing the difference. As Greg Dyke, the former Director General of the BBC, told me, 'You can't fight every battle; you have to choose which battles you fight.'

So if something is really important to you, then set it as a goal: commit to this much stronger language. Commit. Fight. Be ruthless. Be dogged. And do whatever it takes. Transforming your language from 'I'll do my best' to 'I'll do whatever it takes' (within the law, obviously) is like changing gear on your car. Actually, forget gears in your car – it's like dumping your car and getting in a four-blade, twin-engine Boeing AH-64 Apache (for the civilians among us, that's a fast attack helicopter). Committing yourself and your team to this language will trigger the unconscious mind and you'll naturally take on all the characteristics outlined in Part One of this book without even trying.

The idea in brief:

- *There's a pandemic of 'I'll do my best' – for important goals, replace this phrase with 'I'll do whatever it takes'*
- *Imagine if you had to achieve your goals. What would you do? Now do it*
- *Great leaders just keep going and going until they get to their end goal*
- *Don't fight every battle – choose the important ones and be dogged about winning those*
- *Commit to a different language and results will flow – you'll become a 'natural' achiever*

5

Action is everything

'An idea is meaningless. An idea is completely worthless. You have to do something about it for it to be worth anything.'

Sahar Hashemi, OBE, Cofounder of Coffee Republic

A few years ago I went on a course in London run by a guy called Robin Fielder, who is a brilliant master of the stage. Around 500 people were in a room attending the course and the day was drawing to a close. For a few hours, Robin had been talking about the power of visualisation.

The course was due to finish at 6.00 p.m. and it was around 5.45 p.m. It was the time of day when everybody's bum was getting a bit numb, energy in the room was starting to take a rapid nosedive and the mind was wandering to lesser leadership topics, like what to have for dinner. Anyway, like all great presenters, Robin was acutely aware of this energy drop. So, suddenly adopting the persona of an eighteenth-century town crier, he woke us all up by shouting at the top of his voice, 'Ladies and gentlemen, hear ye, hear ye! Over the last three hours I've been talking about the power of visualisation. I hope that you've been able to listen and learn about the awesome power of this tool. But now, rather than talking to you about the power of this visualisation, I want to *show* you the awesome power of visualisation.' He then instructed one of the audiovisual folk in the room to turn off all the lights in the auditorium.

As there was no natural daylight, it was pitch-black. Pitch-black, in a room, with 500 other people. A few moments later, there was a spark on stage; it was Robin striking a match and lighting a single candle. The candle flickered up there on stage – one lonely candle with 500 people staring at it. A few seconds later, Robin broke the silence, or more like the trance, and said, 'Now, as promised, I'd like to *show* you the awesome power of visualisation', going on to say, 'Ladies and gentlemen, I want you all to visualise this candle being extinguished through the power of your mind. I want you to visualise this candle going out with *all* of your mental capacity. I'm about to show you the amazing power when 500 people come together and focus really hard on one single objective.' A few seconds passed and he said, 'Here we go … now please, no noise – just the power of your mind.' At that, he was quiet and the entire audience fell silent, all absolutely visualising this candle flickering and then going out. You could feel the concentration.

About a minute later, the candle suddenly flickered more than it had done before, and then, just as quickly, it went back to normal. Perhaps it was just a passing draught, or perhaps we as an audience had caused it through the power of our collective thought. Another minute passed, the candle still flickering away, but nothing notably dramatic. Yet you could still feel the concentration and anticipation in the room – we were all about to witness something amazing, and we were all excited to be part of it.

Another minute passed … and another minute and then a few more. Suddenly a thought came to my mind and that thought was, Oh my, what if this candle doesn't actually go out – that's going to be embarrassing! Anyway, another minute passed, and another, and still nothing – then suddenly, about eight minutes into the exercise, Robin stepped forward out of nowhere from the darkness and, with a massive puff of air, blew the candle out.

The lights came back on.

When my eyes had adjusted, the first thing I saw was Robin on stage with a beaming smile saying, 'You see ladies and gentlemen, it doesn't matter how much you visualise something – *nothing* happens without action! If you want something done you have to *act*.'

This is an awesome exercise, I hope you'll agree. Now, every time I blow out a candle, I always think about the importance of *action*. Yes, it's a bit cheesy – I'm guilty as charged, officer – but it's true.

The best vision, the most inspiring goals and the smartest strategy in the world are all totally meaningless unless you act on them

Many authors have written books on the law of attraction or positive visualisation, and, while these are indeed bedrocks of success, often these books fail to point out that things only happen when you take action – a blundering omission of the highest order. Their poor readers will be staring at their 'visualisation goals boards' or their shiny new visions and mission statements in their company reception and thinking, Huh? How come nuffing is happening? Well, without action, nothing happens. As Allan Leighton, former CEO of Asda, told me, 'Twenty per cent is the strategy, but 80 per cent is putting it into action and doing it.'

Sahar Hashemi (who sold Coffee Republic for millions) said to me: 'Lots of people told me that they thought of the coffee-bar idea at the same time, but why weren't they successful? Because they never actually did it.'

All great leaders have a bias for action

All successful leaders have developed a personal bias for action. In other words, they look for a reason to do something, rather than not do something. Herb Kelleher, the brilliant and famous former CEO of Southwest Airlines, said, 'We have a "strategic" plan. It's called "doing things".'

If the result of that action is failure, so what? As Greg Dyke told me, 'If you do something big and it fails, that's all right – that's part of life.' Similarly, when Bill Clinton was asked by *Fortune* magazine what attributes all great leaders have in common, he said: 'Trying and failing is far better than not trying at all.' If something succeeds, then you'll have massive benefits; if it doesn't, then so what? As long as you've weighed the upside and the downside and the upside is greater, and the downside won't cost you the farm, just do it. There's a massive power in just getting started! As Karen Lamb said, 'A year from now you may wish you had started today.' Time will pass – don't have regret caused by inaction.

Don't be held back by perfectionism

The more action you take, the more shots you'll take, the 'luckier' you'll then get and the more goals you'll score. But if you wait for all the moons and the stars to be aligned before you take the shot, you won't get much stuff out there and you won't try a lot of things. Yet it's only by trying many different things that you can discover what actually works.

Facebook has posters on their walls saying 'Done is better than perfect' – a reminder that action and getting stuff done is an essential precursor to success. CEO.com quotes Mark Zuckerberg as having said, 'You are better off trying something and having it not work and learning from that than not doing anything at all.'

So be known for action and demanding action in those you lead

I'm sure you'll know a few people who make up their mind to do something, but absolutely diddly-squat actually happens. Conversely, you might know people who seem to get things moving even before they've made their minds up. As we know, leadership skills come from habit creation, so, when you've decided on something important, either in your personal life or your business life, get into the habit of taking action on it *straight away*.

So how do you commit to action? Well, it's always worth remembering what the masters have said before us: in a speech Martin Luther King Jr said, 'Take the first step in faith. You don't have to see the whole staircase, just take the first step.' By taking action, you create momentum, and once you have created momentum, further progress becomes much easier. As Henrietta Mears said, 'It is difficult to steer a parked car, so get moving'. Some people act like they want to reach their important goals by the age of 128 – don't be one of them: remember 'someday' isn't a real day of the week.

The idea in brief:

- *Don't make the mistake of thinking visualisation is enough to attain your goals*
- *Nothing in life is achieved without meaningful action*
- *Develop an action bias and instil it in your team's behaviour*
- *Do something about your most important goals every single day – this builds momentum, and momentum is everything*
- *The more action you take, the luckier you'll become*
- *Build your own personal brand as somebody who takes action straight away*

6

Foster courage – feel the fear and do it anyway

'The principle that one should feel the fear and do it anyway is absolutely crucial for success in any domain of life. If you're held back by your fears you'll never get anywhere; you'll never try the new thing, the golf swing, the whatever it is, but in order to progress you have to fight through your fear.'

Daniel Goleman

Fear is a gift from God. We need fear to survive. It's one of those evolutionary things that have enabled us as a species to stick around so long (i.e. fear prevents us from entering a dark cave hosting a vicious sabretoothed cat, to give you a prehistoric example).

But not all fear is justified, so leaders have to learn how to differentiate between a good risk and a bad risk. Entering the cave probably isn't a good risk (justified fear); launching a new product that might futureproof your business probably is (unjustified fear). For leaders, the antidote to fear is courage. Courage is *not* an absence of fear; it's feeling it and doing whatever it is despite the fear.

As a leader, you need to build your courage quotient. There are times that your courage reservoir will be called upon. It takes courage to:

- make the right decision, even if it's not a popular decision
- speak at the next company meeting with 500 people
- lead your team into the unknown. As Ralph Waldo Emerson said, 'Do not follow where the path may lead. Go instead where there is no path and leave a trail'
- set an unbelievably exciting and ambitious vision despite highly articulate naysayers
- go back to the board of directors four times to get a yes because your instinct is telling you you're right (when Matthew Key was CEO of O2 he did this in order to get the Millennium Dome sponsored to become the O2 – see chapter 14 for more on this)
- fire somebody who is much-loved but underperforming
- launch a new product into the market with no real indicator it will work
- resolve conflict in your team head-on
- encourage your team to disagree with you and speak openly
- keep fighting for what you believe in – even if it goes against the current corporate assumptions.

All of the above are things great leaders need to just get on and do – but remember, if you get all churned up on the inside, then that's a great feeling – it means you're pushing yourself, pushing your limits, pushing out of your comfort zone and doing the right thing. So don't freak out, tap yourself on the back and go full systems blazing. As Mark Twain said, 'Courage is resistance to fear . . . not absence of fear.'

In fact, leadership is all about courage and getting comfortable with feeling uncomfortable. It's not just important – it's essential. After all, your team will be watching you, and nobody wants to follow a wimp. The good news is that courage is a habit that can be strengthened. As Jacqueline Gold, CEO of Ann Summers, told me, 'Challenging your fear is what all successful business people do.' As the leader it's your job not only to be courageous yourself but to develop this beautiful attribute throughout your team and organisation.

Half the problem is we're programmed at a young age *not* to take risks

Do you remember your mum or dad dropping you off at school and saying, 'Have a great time today. Oh, and take a lot of risks today, please?' No, you always, always hear mums and dads saying, 'Have a great time today. Oh and be careful, please.'

As you were a child, your parents were rightly protecting you, but as an adult, this protection can hold you back from facing the challenges that will help you become a great leader. Everything that's new is inherently risky. And if you don't do anything new (new hires, new products, etc.) you stagnate – and therefore doing nothing is actually the biggest risk of them all. It's time to acknowledge that a certain amount of risk is good – and it's time to fall in *love* with the feeling, and the rewards.

Some people say, 'Oh, I'm not a risk-taker – that's for those nutter base jumpers or for those trainer-wearing, blue-haired entrepreneurs.' Not true. We're all risk-takers. If you weren't a risk-taker you wouldn't leave the house in the morning or get on a train – or, in fact, do anything. It's about increasing your risk quotient and taking more (and sometimes a lot more) *smart* risks.

What is smart risk vs dumb risk?

To establish which risks are worth taking, leaders with courage simply ask themselves:

a) What's the right thing to do? (Not 'What feels easiest?') They then
    choose to do the right thing, no matter how they feel on the
    inside.
b) What's the upside vs the downside? If the upside is greater than
    the downside, they'll do it (in their personal and professional
    lives). If the downside is too big compared with the upside, they
    won't proceed. Sir Terry Leahy said to me, 'I've always avoided the
    risks that asked me to bet the entire farm.' If the downside of the

risk might bankrupt you, or the entire organisation, you really, really want to avoid those risks, i.e. you don't want to put everything on Red 28. But very few risks involve those stakes. Conversely, if the upside is great and the downside insignificant (something utterly trivial like embarrassment or rejection), then, as Nike says, 'just do it'.

How do you start strengthening the risk-taking muscles – and building courage?

Get into the habit by taking a risk every day

Eleanor Roosevelt once said, 'Do one thing every day that scares you.' She was absolutely right. I'd encourage you to start taking a healthy risk every day. Do something that stretches you a bit. Perhaps it's going across the room and putting your hand up and saying 'I'd like to lead the next company meeting', signing up for a public-speaking course or asking your boss for a new project. Whatever it is, learn to love that feeling of taking a risk (it's addictive) – the results will be remarkable. Adopt the mind-set discussed before of 'I'll do whatever it takes to achieve goals.'

As we discussed in chapter 4, if you had to achieve your goal because somebody had a gun to your head, you'd take the risk and do the right thing. Sometimes you have to override your preferences and wishes and do the right thing – even if it's a billion miles due north of your comfort zone. Just ask, 'What's the right thing to do?' and do it.

To give you an example of this, Sir Terry Leahy, the former CEO of Tesco, who led an organisation with over 300,000 staff and was passionate about face-to-face communication, is extremely reserved. As such, he would have frequently found himself feeling the fear and operating outside his comfort zone. When I asked him about this and how he managed, he just said: 'I was painfully shy, but I just had to take a deep breath and get on with it.' He had the courage to do what needed to be done. So the next time that you're thinking, Oh my, I don't want to do that – it's outside of my comfort zone, then remind yourself of Sir Terry's words: '[just] take a deep breath and get on with it.'

Focus on the advantage of doing what you're about to do, not the short-term fear

In life you get what you focus on: if you focus on the good, you'll get more good; if you focus on your anxiety, you'll get more anxiety – so when you're carrying out a courageous decision, embrace those feelings and decide to put your focus on the long-term upside of doing it, not your short-term nerves.

Remind yourself that feeling fear means you're on the right path

All the CEOs and billionaire entrepreneurs that I've interviewed recognise that feeling fear is directly linked to better results. John Studzinksi said, 'I'll always look for a way to get out of my comfort zone.' Virginia Rometty (CEO of IBM) is quoted as saying, 'I learnt to always take on things I'd never done before. Growth and comfort do not coexist.' So just remind yourself that this is a habit of highly effective people – and just do it.

The bottom line is: fear should elicit self-praise in you, not panic!

Have the courage to fail

'You shouldn't be scared of failure; if you're afraid of failure you'll never push yourself. You learn a lot more when you get things wrong than when you get things right.'

Ed Wray

Leaders who are afraid of failure become paralysed – and so do their teams. They stop hiring, they stop innovating and they stop asking for what they want. If you allow some failure, you'll have far greater levels of success.

The world's most famous basketball player, Michael Jordan, once said: 'I have missed over 9,000 shots in my career. I have lost almost 300 games. On 26 occasions I have been entrusted to take the game-winning shot, and I have missed. I have failed over and over and over again in my life. And that is why I succeed.'

So from this day on, fall in love with courage: enjoy the calculations that go into weighing up the upside and downside of risk, the adrenalin rush and fear that come when executing the risk, and bask in the glory and riches that come from making courage one of your personal leadership attributes – it's a great leadership differentiator.

The idea in brief:

- *Feeling the fear and doing it anyway is critical in any domain of life*
- *Recognise that some fear is justified and some isn't*
- *Remember that feeling fear means that you're about to either learn or take a leap forward*
- *We have to condition ourselves (and our team members) to take risk – it doesn't come naturally to adults*
- *Overcome fear by focusing on the benefits of doing something and remembering it's what high achievers do*
- *Avoid risks that bet the entire farm*
- *Take a risk every day and learn to love the feeling*

7

Relationships are at the heart of great leaders

'Strong Relationship-building Skills = +50 IQ points.'

Michael Porter

Many business gurus sermonise that people are your most important asset. If this is true, then relationships are vital. Leadership, as you know, is defined as getting results *through other people.* So people are at the heart of leadership. As such, the better your relationships, the more valuable you'll be as a leader. The wider and the deeper your relationships, the more powerful and influential you'll be. One of your biggest assets in business (and life) is the number of people that you know who think of you in a favourable light.

Unless you're living on Pluto, I don't need to tell you about the global shift of business, wealth, power and opportunity to the East. In Asia and the Middle East, everything in business is based on relationships – far, far more so than in the West. If you speak to any CEO who has been successful in China, they will all confirm this to be true. For example, Aaron Simpson, the Chairman of Quintessentially (who placed their

Head Office in Hong Kong), told me, 'You need to give face time, but also build the trust – a lot of people in emerging markets rely on a handshake and looking into your eyes.'

But, wherever you're based right now, your business network is without doubt one of your most important leadership assets. Like any asset, your network is worth building, and the way to do this is through your relationships.

It's the obvious and the not-so-obvious people in your network who can help you on goal attainment – take the example of a young chap called Bill Gates

In the very early years of Microsoft, Bill Gates, then a rather floppy-haired techie 20-something, was able to secure IBM, as a client, a deal that proved absolutely pivotal for him, and Microsoft. This led to him becoming one of the most famous business leaders in history, and to Microsoft becoming one of the largest companies in the world.

So the question is: how did the young Bill Gates manage to get a meeting with John Opel, the CEO of IBM, in the first place? Yes, you guessed it … it was his mum. Bill's mum was a wonderful lady called Mary Maxwell Gates. Bill discovered that his mum was on the same board of directors as John Opel. So he asked her to introduce them. She did, and that introduction changed his future.

By the way, in the coming years, Mary Gates went to many meetings with Bill to help swing deals. Can you imagine that? 'Hi there, Mr or Mrs CEO of XYZ company. I'm Bill Gates and this is Mary, my mum.' Genius.

So I confess this is a rather crude (albeit very cool) example of how your network can help. Your mum might not be on the board of your ideal client, but this shows that you never know who you know already or who you might meet for the first time today who knows the people you need to know and changes the entire course of your career, financial outlook, happiness and life.

I'm not saying you have to turn into some golden schmoozer – and you should always be genuine and authentic; but you *must, must, must* take a genuine interest in other people and prioritise building relationships and engaging with the world beyond your team from this day forward.

Core benefits of your network

As a leader, you have to get out of your office and spend time with people. That's where your customers, your future customers, other department heads (internal), your suppliers and your future hires are; it's where your business intelligence is, and where your future partners will come from – everything.

But there is also some less obvious value inherent within a leader's network. Your network will help you to:

a) Find out what's really going on in the rest of the business via an informal route (as Allan Leighton calls it, the 'CEO Radar' – see chapter 36). You should always spend time with people that are outside your team – this gives you different perspectives of the business.

b) Get apolitical opinions of what you're doing. Sometimes leaders are surrounded by 'yes' men and women. People outside the organisation are far less political and are likely to give an unbiased, agnostic and apolitical opinion. In fact, Sir Stuart Rose said to me, 'You should build a team of people, outside the business preferably, and, in fact, I would say, exclusively, outside of the business, that you can take for a beer and say, "Look, am I being a complete numpty about this?"'

c) Get referrals from people you trust. There's no way better to find out who's good, what companies are good, what suppliers are good or anything else, than through your network. A recommendation from a trusted contact is always best.

d) Hire great people (members of your network). If you have a talent gap in the future, your network is a cheaper and more effective way to hire than by using a recruitment company.

e) Get things done. Many mergers, acquisitions and partnerships result from a strong network so again, you're more likely to get transformational results through an extensive group of people you know.

f) Get information when you need it. There is a famous saying that goes, 'the most important thing in life is not knowing everything, it's having the phone number of somebody who does!'

An example of networking in action

Some people ask me how the brand-new media company I launched was able to secure partnerships with companies like *Harvard Business Review*, *Wired*, Schroders and many others of that ilk. The answer is nothing smarter than: I identified the ideal partners; I took the time to meet with them; I took the effort to invest in a relationship with them; I made sure they knew we were a great company, that we had integrity and that nobody in our team had three heads.

I then invited them to our studio interviews free of charge; I showed them our product/service; I introduced them to the rest of my team; and, *most importantly*, I found out their goals and aspirations and took a genuine responsibility to find out if there was anything that I, or the company, could do to help them achieve their goals – and then took action. As such, this relationship grew with trust and openness and it just naturally evolved.

Remember, the best way of building a relationship is to take a genuine interest in the other person or business and help them to achieve their goals – it's about spending time on the relationship and investing in the people. For example, sending hand-written cards (birthday, Christmas, Hanukkah, Eid, Diwali or any other occasion) to people in your network is a low-cost and exceptionally high-value way to show you care. And during this process, if you become a gimme-man or gimme-woman, you will fail. Relationships are always built on a genuine desire to help the other party – in business and especially in leadership. It takes time and effort, but it's worth it.

Expanding your network

I'm not going to go into all the ways that you could develop and expand your network (conferences, people you bump into at the bus stop, work colleagues who are not in your team, suppliers etc.) but I will say that it's essential that you get into the habit of spending a significant amount of your time starting and building relationships.

If you think that somebody is smart, with the right personality, then make sure you get to know them – even if it's staying in touch with James, your star performer who's just quit to set up a yoga retreat. You never know when they might want to come back, and when you might have a gap to fill.

Deepening your relationships ... and developing them

Like all great things, relationships need work and nurturing. If a guy sees a girl in a bar, he doesn't just walk up to her and say, 'Will you marry me?' – unless perhaps he's a tad hammered ... In the same way, you wouldn't just walk up to somebody and say, 'Will you give me a job?' or, 'Will you buy this, please?'. So start small and cultivate your relationships over time.

The other key to building relationships, as mentioned above, is when you're with someone, don't just talk about the gossip columns and other trivia (not that you do!), but actually talk about your goals and aspirations (as well as theirs) to have more meaningful conversations. If you want to get to know someone, it's about being open and revealing more than you would in just small talk. It's about being authentic, being genuine and being yourself.

The idea in brief:

- *Your network is one of your greatest business assets so, like any asset, find time to build it*
- *It's a fact of life: more things get done through networks than anywhere else*
- *Networking opens up opportunity but also imparts information*
- *Who might you know who can help? Remember, Bill Gates asked his mum*
- *Take a genuine interest in other people and prioritise building relationships over time*
- *Be authentic – talk about your goals and aspirations and think about how you might be able to help others too*
- *Even if you don't feel like networking, do it anyway – you'll get into the flow*

8

You only have to be perfect at one thing

'In looking for people to hire, you look for three qualities: integrity, intelligence and energy. And, if you don't have the first, the other two will kill you.'

Warren Buffett

An ageing emperor in the East began to feel his age, so he started thinking about the best way to find a worthy successor. He called all the youth from his kingdom and said to them, 'One year from now I will appoint my successor to be the new emperor – and it will be one of you.'

He then ordered his generals to hand each young boy a special seed, after which he told them, 'Go and plant these seeds. Return one year from today and I will judge how you have done, based on the quality of the plant that comes from this seed.'

One boy named Anko took the seed home and eagerly asked his mother for help. Together they found a pot that was suitable and planted the seed. Carefully they watered and cared for it every day.

The days went by, then months, but there was no sign of a plant or a shoot – or any sign of life. They began to feel disappointment with the realisation that their plant must have died. When it was time to return to the emperor, Anko talked with his mother and they agreed that the best thing to do was to just tell the emperor what had happened.

All the boys went back to the see the emperor. On arrival the emperor announced: 'Today one of you will be appointed as my successor and the emperor of this great nation.' Anko stood towards the back of the group, rather coy and embarrassed, for he was the only one that didn't have a flourishing plant in his pot.

The emperor spotted Anko towards the back of the room, holding his empty pot, and he ordered his guards to bring him to the front immediately. Anko was terrified, thinking to himself, The emperor will punish me for my failure – perhaps I will be killed or imprisoned and never see my mother again.

The emperor asked Anko for his name and then announced: 'Behold Anko, your new emperor ... He has the integrity that is needed to be a wise ruler over you all. The seeds that I gave you were boiled and would have never grown; you have cheated your emperor and this is why you are not suited for leadership.'

Some people might have looked at the lengthy list of chapters at the beginning of the book and freaked out. But the truth is, to lead a high-performing team, you don't have to be perfect at everything. As we saw in chapter 3, all great leaders have strengths and weaknesses – and they just need to be very strong in a small number of those to win.

But there is *one* trait all great leaders personify: integrity – *they do and say the right thing.* As Dwight Eisenhower, who was the 34th President of the United States, a five-star general in the Army during World War II and the Supreme Commander of the Allied Forces in Europe (yep, a bigwig of his time), once said, 'The supreme quality of leadership is integrity.'

A more contemporary leadership legend, Warren Buffett recently said:

We can afford to lose money, but we can't afford to lose reputation – not a shred of reputation. Therefore I ask the managers to judge every action they take, not just by legal standards, but also by what I call the newspaper test – how would they feel about any given action if they knew it was to be written up the next day in their local paper to be read by their family, by their friends, by their neighbours – written by a smart but unfriendly reporter? And if it passes that test, it's okay. And I tell them that if anything is close to the line, it's out.

It's true that to get to the very top you have to be determined, dogged and sometimes quite ruthless in the myopic pursuit of your goals – however, the world's greatest leaders never put any of this before integrity. Ruthless, yes, but never if it means losing an ounce of integrity. So how can you make sure that you have the integrity necessary to lead a great team? Here are a few prompts.

Do the right thing

When you come across any decision that might tempt you to do the wrong thing – anything that doesn't feel right, is somehow dishonest or lacking in good judgement, or, as Warren says, you wouldn't like appearing in tomorrow's news – don't do it. Always do the right thing.

Many executives disrobed of their finely cut suits and thrown unceremoniously into jail failed the 'do the right thing' test.

Say it as it is

Being honest and admitting that things are not as good as you'd like, or that you've made a mistake, is candid; it's open, and it has integrity. Acknowledging weaknesses or failings is a great sign of leadership – in fact it's one of the most admired and sought-after in the business world today. Never lie, or blame others for your mistakes, even if you think you'll get away with it.

Speaking with candour is as important when you are interacting with your clients as it is for your staff, your boss, your team, your family – everyone. We're living in an age that demands and respects transparency, so get into the habit of just saying things as they are: your feelings, your anxiety, your results – whatever it is. As a result, people will listen to and trust you, and they'll want to work with you. Trust is *everything* in business and in all of our relationships.

Don't overpromise and under-deliver

Don't oversell, and never allow your sales or business development folk to do so either. I heard about a conference once where a sponsor arrived in a lorry with 5,000 bottles of water to give one bottle to each delegate. It turned out there were only 100 delegates.

That incident resulted in a very hydrated group of people, but it also resulted in a seriously upset sponsor. Anybody can sell something once if they lie. The problem is that that customer will never come back and do business with you again. You might have secured one deal, but sacrificed the lifetime value of that potential customer. So, while you should sell the solutions your product offers like the best of them, make sure to stop at serial exaggeration and certainly stop when you lose all sense of reality!

If you say you'll do it, do it

Get into the habit of delivering on what you say – every time. Reliability is a personal brand value that will get you far in leadership. If you say you'll deliver by Friday, deliver by Friday, and if you can't, be upfront about it from the very beginning. If you say you'll be at the meeting at 3.00 p.m., be at the meeting at 3.00 p.m. If you don't deliver, how can you expect the same from those you lead?

Be yourself

Wearing personality 'masks' and pretending that you're somebody that you're not is also lacking in integrity. Be authentic and be real (see chapter 18).

Turn your back on anything that lacks integrity – no matter how lucrative

Never ever work for somebody that doesn't have integrity – at best you'll ruin your own personal reputation and, at worst, you'll end up in jail. If you find out that unethical things are happening in your organisation, leave.

Your own brand and your own reputation is at stake, and, in life and in business, reputation is *everything*. Conversely, if clients and staff trust you to always do the right thing and say it as it is, then you'll build a great reputation for trustworthiness – which in monetary terms is, as Warren Buffett says, 'everything'.

The idea in brief:

- *You don't have to be perfect to be a world-class leader; the only thing you have to be is perfect in your integrity*
- *In business your reputation is everything – without it you'll have nothing*
- *Remember the newspaper test, i.e. what would you do if you knew that what you did would be on the front cover of the newspaper tomorrow? Then do that*
- *If you say you'll do it, do it*
- *Always be yourself*
- *Never sacrifice your integrity for financial gain*

9

The power of 80/20

There is one principle that underpins all success on this planet. All great leaders and great organisations know it well, and they live and breathe it every day. It's a law that was originally developed by an Italian chap named Vilfredo Pareto back in 1906 called 'the 80/20 Principle' – or the 'Law of the Vital Few'.

The principle was really brought to mainstream business when the legendary Richard Koch wrote a book called *The 80/20 Principle*, a brilliant, brilliant book. I'd highly recommend buying it and keeping it under your pillow. You see, the principle of the Vital Few underpins a lot of this book; it's the foundation of everything – and we'll explain it in this chapter.

So what exactly did this suave Italian chap in a tailored suit, Vilfredo Pareto, teach the world?

Back in 1906, Vilfredo was analysing land and wealth ownership in Italy. After a bit of research he discovered that 80 per cent of Italy's land was owned by 20 per cent of the population. He then looked elsewhere in neighbouring countries and found that this imbalance also applied to Greek and French landowners. Intrigued, Pareto hastily searched wider to see if other things shared this imbalance. To his amazement, they did – not just with regards to wealth, but to everything, everywhere.

Essentially the 80/20 law measures disparity, or an imbalance between input and output. It doesn't *always* have to be an 80/20 correlation; the imbalance could be 90/10 (so 90 per cent of the wealth is owned by 10 per cent), or 70/30 and so forth.

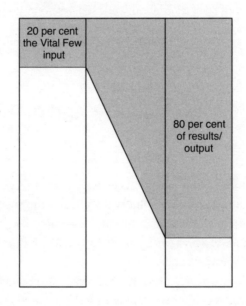

The 80/20 principle applied to input and output

Let me give you a few examples from business and everyday life:

- 80 per cent of your profits come from 20 per cent of your products (e.g. Apple and their iPhones and iPads)
- 80 per cent of your results will come from 20 per cent of your activities
- 80 per cent of your time is spent with 20 per cent of the people you know
- 80 per cent of crime is committed by 20 per cent of the criminals
- 80 per cent of your happiness comes from 20 per cent of your activities (in fact – action point: Make a list now on a sheet of paper of things you love to do that make you happy, and stick it

on your fridge. Then, just make sure you're doing those things
regularly – the more things you do that make you happy, the
happier you'll be)

- 80 per cent of fast food is sold by 20 per cent of the fast-food
  companies
- 20 per cent of the people in your life bring 80 per cent of your
  happiness
- 80 per cent of *complaints* about your staff relate to 20 per cent of
  your workforce
- 80 per cent of *compliments* about your staff relate to 20 per cent
  of your workforce
- 20 per cent of your staff bring 80 per cent of the value to your
  business (hence why headhunters exist)
- 20 per cent of the carpet on the floor in your house or office will
  get 80 per cent of the wear and tear (usually near the door – just
  have a look)

I can hear you shouting, 'Okay, okay I *get it!*' … yes, it applies to everything.

You might also be saying, 'So what? How will using the 80/20 principle make me a better leader?' The key to effective leadership is to be
aware of this disparity and focus on the Vital Few in everything – and,
most importantly, the Vital Few that really matter to you, your team and
your organisation.

So, for example, a few questions might be:

a) What are the Vital Few tasks you do at work which add the
   majority of value? I'd encourage you now to make a list of
   everything that you do during the week and then spot the
   three or four things that you do that have a tremendous
   impact on your job (it could be face time with customers,
   communicating with your team, hiring, innovating etc. but will
   differ for each person) then go straight to your calendar and
   block out time for the most important activities. You'll be
   amazed at the overnight changes in your results. More on this
   in the next chapter.

b) Who are your Vital Few customers? Whoever they are, make

sure you meet them, spend time with them and show them your love. Work out what their current and future needs are; become obsessed by these wonderful folk. (Don't be stalkerish about it, though!)

c) Who are the Vital Few employees in the company who make the biggest difference? Make sure that they're rewarded accordingly, that you know these people personally and that they're being motivated (see chapter 23).

d) Who are the Vital Few employees in other companies that you might want to hire? Start tracking them.

e) Which are the Vital Few products making you a disproportionate amount of money which could be rolled out to other geographical regions (otherwise known as rolling out the winners)? Identify these products and invest in them big time.

f) Who are the key strategic partners that you should focus on to make the biggest difference to your organisation? Is there any third-party company that would be an ideal match for you right now? If so, get yourself or your organisation in front of them. Speaking of which…

A case study of a Vital Few strategic partner at O2: the iPhone

Back in the autumn of 2007, the iPhone was about to be launched by Apple in the UK. All the mobile operators, notably O2, Orange, T-Mobile and Vodafone wanted the exclusivity period and were practically salivating at the opportunity.

Matthew Key, who was the CEO of O2 at the time, won it. In my interview I asked him about it. He said: 'We were part of Telefónica by this time and the first time that we met Apple I actually went to California with the Chairman and Chief Exec of Telefónica and we met the guys from Apple.' So here's the first crucial point: they *all* flew to California for the deal – two CEOs and the Chairman. What message did that send to Apple? Yup, a good one.

Two of the key reasons that O2 won the iPhone contract in the UK was that a) O2 spotted it as an 80/20 opportunity (a Vital Few decision) and b) the company put a lot of time and resources into securing the deal. Why? Because they knew it was important, that it was one of the few deals that year that were going to make a huge difference. The O2 team were, and still are, supersmart (that's why they're one of Britain's greatest business and telecom success stories).

Mastering the 80/20 and being aware of it is exceedingly important to you and your team. I would encourage you to read further on this subject, and there's no better source of wisdom than Richard Koch.

For now, identify the Vital Few in all areas of your life and your business. Focusing on these essential projects will provide you with the leverage that you need to have phenomenal success.

Become quite obsessed by the *leverage* (the few things that will result in a disproportionately large return) that pursuing the 80/20 principle brings you, your team and your organisation. By doing so, you'll find that over time it becomes a tremendously profitable obsession.

The idea in brief:

- *The 80/20 Principle is the most powerful success principle in the world*
- *Vilfredo Pareto originated the principle; Richard Koch brought it to life through his book,* The 80/20 Principle
- *Disparity exists everywhere, so spot the Vital Few in everything and focus on those – a few key deals can make your team and your company fly*
- *Use the 80/20 in business and your personal life (it will improve both)*

10

Time mastery – get the *right* things done, not just *more* things done

'The most precious resource we all have is time.'

Steve Jobs

Time management is, at its heart, not about managing time; it's about measuring the results that you achieve in the time available to you. Sir Richard Branson, Mark Zuckerberg, you and I – in fact, everyone on the planet – have one thing in common: we all have 24 hours available to us in a day (yes, I know you were wondering, that's 1,440 minutes). Nobody can change that (yet). The only thing that you can change is what you do within those hours (or minutes) to radically increase your results – and getting *more* stuff done isn't the answer (although a lot of people mistakenly think it is), but it's about doing the right stuff that gets you far, far better *results*.

As a leader it's critical that you're equipped with exemplary time-management skills (although we've just criticised that as a term, we'll still use it, as everyone else does!). There are two reasons it's so critical: a) if you have mastered this arena, then not only will your output be greatly enhanced, but b) you can set the example for your team to follow.

Then, with your entire team having mastered extraordinary output with the time available, you'll be hard to catch.

Let's explore some of the key lessons about time management that will benefit you and your team.

A time-management revolution – for you, your team and your organisation

Until recently, time-management thinkers were very limited in their thinking. The time-management gurus of bygone eras would stand up on their blocks and preach about how to get more stuff done, anything at all as long as you are doing *more*. Why? Because we were all down the factory mixing iron ore, or working the Spinning Jenny or something (thank God for the digital age). The enlightened gurus of today teach us that it's not about getting *more* stuff done, it's about getting more of the *right* stuff done (think 80/20).

The legendary management thinker Peter Drucker said: 'There is nothing quite so useless as doing, with great efficiency, something that should not be done at all.' Have you ever noticed that some people seem extremely *busy* rushing around like blue-arsed flies in a state of frenetic activity? When you meet with them, they're always huffing and puffing, eager to move on to the next urgent thing. Most of these plum-faced folk haven't distinguished between important and not important, so they'll continue to rush around like blue-arsed flies, but their bank balance will always be quite low, and their contribution to the team will be minimal (apart from noise and distraction as they go around huffing and puffing) – and without a change in tack, they'll never be great leaders. No siree.

On the other hand, all the CEOs that I've interviewed have something in common: they work hard, but they work hard on the *right* things. They know what's important and what's not, so they're chilled, but *insanely* effective. As John Wooden, the US basketball player and coach, once said, 'Never mistake activity for achievement.'

How to identify what's important – your 'vital few'

The Law of Three

In my interview with Brian Tracy, author of *Eat That Frog*, he explained a concept called 'The Law of Three', which is similar to to 80/20 principle:

> The Law of Three says, no matter how many things you do, or how many tasks you do in a week or a month, and that's usually about 20 or 30, there are only three of your tasks that count for 90 per cent of your value. Only three. So make a list of all of your tasks, and ask three magic questions:
>
> 1) If you could only do one task on your list all day long, which one task would have the greatest positive impact on your output? Put a circle around it.
> 2) If you could only do two things all day long, which would be number two? Put a circle around that.
> 3) If you could do just three things all day long, which would be number three? Put a circle around that.
>
> Those are your big three. Everything else is secondary. Everything else can be done by somebody else, or done later, or not at all. Now focus on the three. If you have to stretch to four or five, then so be it, but the key is to know the *most* important (the Vital Few) which have a disproportionate return. Do fewer things, but do more important things, and do them more often and get better at them. If you practise the Law of Three, you will transform your life.

Reflect

Another way to find the vital things is by doing a bit of reflection. Richard Koch advises:

> Sit quietly in a room and work out what's the most important thing that you can do this week or the most important thing that you can do today, and don't do anything else until you've done

it … In most organisations it's talking to a customer, or winning a new customer; it's hiring somebody that's going to make a huge difference, or firing somebody that's detracting a huge amount of value from the team; it's coming up with the new product idea. What you have to do is to say 'What is really, really important and will achieve great results?'

Use a system to prioritise tasks

Another way to single out what's most important, is to use a matrix (in business we all love matrices, so here's some eye candy). This following matrix is an adaptation of the original one given to us by the legendary late Stephen Covey, author of *The 7 Habits of Highly Effective People*.

IMPORTANT

Important & urgent (A1 tasks)	Important & not urgent (A2 tasks)
A1 tasks. These tasks will add long-term value to you and your organisation, but they have to be done imminently, for whatever reason, so are urgent	These tasks will add long-term value to you and your organisation, but they're not urgent because you are being proactive ...

URGENT ———————————————————————— NOT URGENT

Unimportant & urgent (B tasks)	Unimportant & not urgent (C tasks)
Not important as they are not important in the long-term, but they have to get done now!	These tasks are not important as they don't add long-term value, nor do they need to be done now. Examples might include speaking about, or listening to, holiday stories of the Algarve

UNIMPORTANT

An adaptation of Stephen Covey's Urgent/Important Matrix

When something new comes your way, or you're looking at your to-do list, first figure out if it's important (so an A task). If it is, then schedule time for it. If it can be done in two minutes or less then, as David Allen, the author of *Getting Things Done*, says, 'just do it'. If it's a B task, see if you can delegate it and if it's a C task, then just delete it. The secret to success is to make sure that you're mostly working on your most important A tasks while staying out of the gutter of doing Bs and Cs – delegate or delete.

Similarly, if you find one of your team is always focused on low-grade administration stuff, then your job as leader is to help them get back up to the high-value activities. Watching people run around chasing administrative stuff, not achieving anything at all is, as a leader, very painful. (I find it strange that MBA stands for Masters in Business Administration. Who on earth would want to master admin? Shouldn't it be called MBE – Masters in Business Excellence?)

To illustrate the importance succesful folk place on spending time on the Vital Few things that matter, take the example of Bill Gates, who said: 'The key resource you have to deal with is your time, and how you spend your time. I even get Steve Ballmer [then CEO of Microsoft] to look at my schedule and criticise it, to say, "Hey you didn't really need to spend time on this or that." I'm always trying to make sure I'm doing that which is important!' So, like all good leaders, develop a distaste for low-value pursuits.

Block and protect your time

> 'The key is not to prioritise what's on your schedule but to schedule your priorities.'
>
> Stephen Covey

When you've identified the Vital Few things you need to focus on, you need to make sure you schedule and protect enough time to attend to them. Biz Stone, cofounder of Twitter, is famous for blocking off time for the most important tasks in his diary and he's a rather successful guy. In fact, all great leaders do it. If you don't, your time *will* get filled with low-value stuff. After all, as entrepreneur Jim Rohn said: 'Either you run the day, or the day runs you.'

At the beginning of the week reflect on the most important things you can do that week. Most leaders find planning for the week ahead is about the right time frame. Daily planning usually means you're reacting to tasks coming in and therefore failing to prioritise them in an objective way, whilst longer term planning, in this era of dynamism, is not that realistic. Richard Koch suggested that on each Monday morning (or the Friday the week before) you should work out 'the most important things and make a school diary for the week – with your blocks in there. By doing so you'll ensure that you're spending time on the important stuff.'

Prioritise priorities

'If you have three big priorities you have at least one too many and possibly two.'

Ronan Dunne

You may have hundreds of projects and hundreds of tasks, but you really want to have just one, two or three macro priorities. And then always make sure that your priorities are your priority (to measure that, simply count the hours in the week you have spent on them so far). So, for example, a new CEO in a turnaround company might have two priorities:

- Stop losing money. As Allan Leighton said about the Royal Mail, 'If you're losing £1m a day, you need to stop losing £1m a day!' The first job of a company that's losing money is to stop losing money.
- Spend face time with staff and customers to develop a strategy that will enable your company to change course.

It's important to know what your core priorities are. These are the umbrellas that sit above your goals. Leadership, at the end of the day, is about clarity. You (and your people) can remember one, two or, maximum, three macro priorities. If you start stretching to 18 and 19 key priorities then everyone will be running around in a sea of confusion and utter despair. Priorities create the focus necessary to avoid this fate.

Distraction kills productivity – so focus, focus, and focus again

There's one thing that will still trip people up, even if they practise the habits outlined in this book so far. Yes, it's the killer of productivity – distraction. We all get distracted – the key is to realign back onto the task. So here are a few magical techniques to make sure you don't fall prey to it.

The awesome power of saying No, Nope, Nah, Non, Nein, Nej, Nee, Na or 无

In the same way that when you receive a 'no' you shouldn't take it to heart, equally you should be able to give out 'no's in order to preserve your time. Rejection isn't necessarily personal. You have to be quite firm about not letting low-value things creep in, and the way to do that very often is with a clear 'no' – especially when it comes to new projects that are ancillary to your important, high-value pursuits.

Daniel Ek, the cofounder of Spotify, recently told students at Stanford: 'I'd say my dumbest mistake is taking on too much, doing too much at the same time, which never works. Be really, really focused; be obsessed about the few things that matter and say no to everything else.'

Focus on one person/task/situation at a time

Many folk valiantly declare how great they are at multitasking. However, in reality it's much, much better to simply focus on one thing and absorb yourself in that one thing. When you're at work, be at work; when you're with friends, be with friends; when you're with your family, be with your family; when you're visiting an overseas office, focus on that office. In other words, there's so much magic to be had by simply pointing your focus exclusively, like a laser beam, on where you are, who you're with, and what you're doing. You'll get much more done and the recipient of your focus (a person or a project) will be all the better for it. By doing everything, you do nothing. By focusing on everybody, you focus on nobody.

Echoing this, in my interview with Brian Tracy he said:

Discipline yourself to work single-mindedly at that task, no matter what happens. If you get pulled away, keep coming back to the task – like a gyroscope that keeps coming back to centre. Keep on that task, because you have now decided that everything else is a relative waste of time. If you can do that, and develop the habit of doing that, you will double your productivity the first day and then it will just continue to increase for the rest of your career.

Work in 60- or 90-minute chunks of time

We all need rest ... even the hero leaders among us. Our energy during the day ebbs and flows; it's important to recognise this and not to fight it. As the Taoist saying goes, 'When hungry, eat; when tired, sleep.' (Note: I'm not suggesting that you pile under your desk right now, scoff a doughnut and then snore away until the cleaner wakes you with the hoover this evening ... but it *is* important to take breaks.)

For some people, it works to take a mini-break at least every 60–90 minutes. If you're one of them, the best thing to do is to take a timer, set it for 60–90 minutes, or whatever time you have available (but no more than 90 minutes), and then work in a sprint. Take massive action with absolute focus. To make this even more effective, because we all like a challenge, grab a piece of paper and write down what you're going to achieve in the next sprint, then focus entirely on trying to achieve it. You will find that by doing this you can achieve more in that 60–90 minutes than you could sometimes in an entire day. The magic ingredient again? Focus.

When the buzzer goes, take a break – go for a walk, drink some water, run up a nearby flight of stairs, stand on your head, whatever it takes to get your blood flowing; you'll feel so much better when you come back and you'll prepare yourself for the next sprint.

Only check emails at set times during the day

Daniel Goleman in my interview with him said:

> I think one of the most insidious realities at work today is how technology is destroying our ability to focus and get things done. Because every time there is a distractor – you get an email and you feel you have to answer that right now instead of putting it aside and finishing your task – it's going to take a long time to get back; in fact, some studies have shown it's going to take up to 15 minutes to get back to where you were before in terms of focus.

Be aware of this, and don't get into the habit of checking emails every minute of the day. Be proactive and focus on your goals, rather than reactive to what's coming in. Then, when you're going through your email, you'll be much more efficient as you're in that proactive state.

Create massive urgency on your most important tasks

One way to minimise the potential for distraction and boost productivity is to always, always work to deadlines. Why? Because they instil urgency. Urgency is a beautiful thing in performance. In fact, people perform magic under the pressure of a deadline. John Studzinski said to me once: 'People always ask me, "How do I become a successful banker?" And I always say it's the three Ds: Deadlines, Detail and Data.'

If you don't have a deadline, then guess what, as Cyril Parkinson, author of *Parkinson's Law*, said: 'Work expands so as to fill the time available for its completion.' If there's no deadline, that's an awful lot of time. So, whether it's a quarterly goal, a monthly goal, or a daily goal – set them for yourself and your staff and honour the line in the sand.

Don't tolerate badly run meetings

In my interview with Jon Moulton, the Chairman of Better Capital, he said to me very firmly, 'I have absolutely no tolerance for a pointless meeting.' (Oh my, if I were working for him I'd make sure that my meetings were masterpieces of efficiency!)

Jon is absolutely right, time is so precious, and as a leader you have to both convey urgency to your team and set the example through your own behaviour. Don't ever run a badly organised meeting (especially if you're working for Jon) and if you find yourself in one, then tolerate it while you're in it, but afterwards tell the chair about how to improve next time. It's your responsibility to give feedback and set a higher standard.

Chairing poorly led meetings is a habit people need to get out of – it's a colossal waste of both time and money (the cost of paying for the time of those people in the room for the duration of the meeting, multiplied by the number of meetings in the year, equals heaps of wasted cash). By the way, it's probably best to offer your thoughts to whoever was chairing when everybody else has left the room!

A final point on finding discretionary time (TV time) to work on your goals

So far we've talked about time management as it applies to leadership and work in this chapter, but good time-management principles also apply to your personal goals. As Brian Tracy said to me:

> The great discovery of all of human history is that you become what you think about most of the time: top people think about their goals all the time, and surprise, surprise, they create wonderful lives for themselves; average people think about television and sports and socialising, and surprise, surprise, that's what they're doing 10 years from now.

Stephen Covey was absolutely adamant that sometimes leaders waste too much time on low-value pursuits. It's easy to do. In his book *The 7 Habits of Highly Effective People*, he said, 'Too many vacations that last too long, too much TV, too much undisciplined leisure time in which a person takes the path of least resistance gradually wastes a life'.

So the next time you're thinking of watching a rerun on TV, just ask if there's some other important goal that you can work towards (personal ones as well as business). Those 20 minutes here and there add up to years over a lifetime.

The idea in brief:

- *Time is precious, so treat your own time and the time of your team with respect*
- *Time management is about doing the right things, rather than just doing more things*
- *You have to identify the Vital Few things you do*
- *Once you know your Vital Few – block them into your calendar to protect them*
- *Remember, successful people say 'no' more often than other folk*
- *Work in 60–90-minute sprints and take a short break after each one*
- *Recognise that important tasks (A tasks) are those that move you towards your goals*

11

Be addicted to learning, and turn your team into addicts too

'Leadership and learning are indispensable to each other.'

John F. Kennedy

As you're already reading this book, my guess is that I'm preaching to the converted. You see ...

Without a single exception, *all* great leaders share the same habit: a devout commitment to learning

Even Mark Zuckerberg, the CEO of Facebook, is currently learning one of the hardest languages on the planet, not French, not Thai, but, yep ... Mandarin. All great leaders learn, and make learning a lifelong habit.

As you know, I've interviewed some very cool folk through my company, LeadersIn, but one of the most revelatory moments in my career was when I looked at the members who had signed up for email alerts of new content; on the list we had CEOs and chairmen of Fortune 500 companies. I was stunned.

But then, when I chatted it through with my über-smart wife Shaheena, she said, 'Why are you surprised? They've probably got to their senior position because they're so dedicated to learning and self-development – so of course they'd sign up!' And, of course, she's right – even the legendary Sir Richard Branson said, 'I see life as a great lifelong learning experience!'

If you're not learning, you're falling behind

Getting overtaken is easy in a fast-changing world. Our industries and even our companies are moving forward faster than ever in history. If you don't like change, then, unless you find a way to get back to the early 1900s, it's best to learn to love the variety and excitement this volatile era has to offer, and go with the flow.

The moment you stop learning and improving yourself, you do just that, you stop, and if you stop you get overtaken. If you stop going forwards then, because the world is moving forwards so fast, you'll actually be going backwards. Backwards is dysfunctional. Yet, a lot of CEOs get to the top, start barking orders and stop learning. Before long, they're out. The best leaders are always learning, listening and reflecting.

As a leader, if you're going backwards, then the chances of you spotting future trends or taking your team forward is slight. So yes, you have to always learn; I'm not *just* talking about soft skills, but also industry dynamics and changes. Learning and keeping your finger on the pulse of what's coming up is what all the greatest leaders do. But I know you know this already. (If you're intrigued by this 'finger on the pulse' thing, head over to chapter 33 where we discuss the role of futurology in leadership.)

Learning is the best antidote to ageing

'Anyone who stops learning is old, whether at 20 or 80. Anyone who keeps learning stays young. The greatest thing in life is to keep your mind young.'

Henry Ford

Carly Fiorina, the former CEO of Hewlett Packard and first female leader of a Fortune 20 company, was talking to Stanford University when she said:

> I'm older than most of you, so I can say this with some certainty; I see people who are in their 40s, 50s, 60s, 70s or 80s and some people in those age groups are vibrant, and some aren't. A big part of that difference is that the people who keep learning, who keep trying new things, are vibrant – and the people who stop learning, and stop trying new things, are old before their time.

Commit to having a curious, playful mind and to life-long learning and self-development. This will enable you to be vibrant and to change with the industry and the economic winds. If you stop learning, you'll become inflexible like the old oak tree that has its roots so deep in the ground and, despite its size, is blown over by a strong wind – if you're flexible, like a blade of grass, even the strongest winds can't harm you.

How can you continuously ensure that you're learning and looking forward?

Learn from your own actions and observations

There is no better way to learn than by continually doing new things – it's by far the best. Why? Because it's experiential and it sticks (empirical lessons). Imagine if David Beckham had spent his entire footballing career reading about how to take a free kick, but had never kicked a ball in his life – he'd be utterly hopeless. It's when putting theory into your practice that your greatest learning happens. This is why action, taking risk and having a go are *everything*.

So remember, the best way to learn is to get out of your comfort zone and learn by *doing* whatever it is you do. So if you're a speaker, it's speaking. If you're a surgeon, it's operating (I just hope if ever I need an op, I'm not the first in line!); if you're a painter, it's painting; if you're a trader, it's trading; and notably, for the purpose of this book, if you're a leader, it's *leading*! So whatever game it is that you're playing in life, it's playing the one that will teach you the best lesson –

never underestimate the experience of getting out there and taking action. Go, go, go.

In my humble opinion you're reading a comprehensive book on leadership (self, team and organisation). However, and this is *so* important, I'm shouting it in caps: I WOULD NEVER CLAIM IT TO BE EXHAUSTIVE (despite that being possibly good for book sales). This is why it's important to combine the information in this book with your own observations of life, and the lessons you've learnt from your own experiences playing the game. The best thing in the world for you to do is to train your mind to look for lessons everywhere and to develop this into a habit. Ask always, what can I/we learn from the lessons around us every day? Switch on the part of the brain that's looking for lessons. It will bear fruit in your life incredibly quickly.

Commit to spending time on learning, and make it a priority for you and your team

Many people think that they've scheduled time for learning and self-development, but it doesn't take Sherlock Holmes to reveal that they haven't. Usually when people go back to analyse days spent on learning and development, they have to go a long, long, long way back to spot the last time they attended a course, or had exposure to development. You might be different, because you're already reading this book, so a smug feeling can now ensue. Just make sure you're always asking if there's a course to go on, a book to read, a podcast to listen to, a coach to learn from – anything, but just keep going forward.

Get ready for another corny, but wildly accurate saying: 'Leaders are readers'

One year ago, I was interviewing Ronan Dunne, the CEO of O2, and Robert Senior, CEO of Saatchi & Saatchi. The interview was at the London Stock Exchange in front of another 150 CEOs and business leaders. During the interview, I decided to put them both on the spot. I asked them: 'So what did you guys think of Walter Isaacson's biography of Steve Jobs?'

What was remarkable was that, despite these guys running massive companies, they had both read it. Not only that, but they were both able to fluently recall the lessons that they'd learnt from it. Yet, perhaps it wasn't that unusual – it's what great leaders do: learn from other great leaders.

On the subject of reading, Brian Tracy had this to say on his website, BrianTracy.com:

> You can actually earn up to a college degree each year. How? By reading for 30–60 minutes each day you'll be working your way towards becoming one of the most knowledgeable people in your field ... if you read 30–60 minutes each day, preferably in the morning before you start off, this will add up to about one book per week – the average American reads less than one book per year. If you read one book per week, this will add up to about 50 books each year. To earn a PhD at a major university requires the reading and synthesis into a dissertation of about 50 books. So that's the equivalent of a practical PhD in your field every year.

The privilege of teaching

One of the greatest privileges (and responsibilities) of a leader is the opportunity to teach. Without exception, leaders not only teach but also formally, or informally, mentor their followers. By continuously learning, you can ensure that you are in a position to continually share wisdom, thus helping the individuals you lead to develop.

To do this, consciously learn something every day

Carly Fiorina, the magical former CEO of Hewlett Packard, said at Stanford: 'The other important thing [about success] is to keep learning; to learn something every day.' Carly went on to remind us that Darwin said, 'It is not the strongest of the species that survives, nor the most intelligent that survives. It is the one that is the most adaptable to change.'

People who can't adapt to change get thrown out, so never become fixed. From this day forward be willing to learn new things, and to challenge yourself to learn something every day. By doing so, you turn learning into a habit and you'll ascend to the lofty heights of doing what great leaders do.

Two common reasons some folk never commit to learning

1) *Some people think the need to learn is a sign of weakness.* One of the biggest challenges the learning and development functions have within large organisations is to get their very senior leaders to keep learning. Why? Because he or she thinks that they can't be seen to go down to the development centre. They're supposed to know it all already. However, followers are inspired to see their leader learning. It sets an example and it shows that the leader isn't willing to ever get complacent and that they are human too.

2) *They don't take responsibility for it.* Loser leaders say things like, 'My company doesn't have a development plan for me' or, 'Oh I haven't learnt anything for ages because my company doesn't *do* training; they don't even give us a book budget'. Well, if that's the case, make no mistake, it's *your* responsibility to learn and develop your own skills. Never abdicate responsibility. At the same time, if you are in one of those companies that really doesn't invest in people (despite your asking for it) then I'd whisper loudly in your ear, '*Get out quick* before the ship goes down!' It's been shown that some companies don't train their staff because they ask themselves, 'What if we invest money in training this person and they leave?'. But as the Chairman and CEO of my former company used to say, 'The better question to ask is, what if you don't train them and they stay?'

The learning curve – it's always tough at the start

Very often the biggest tragedy of all is when an extremely talented person tries something a few times and then, because their self-perception is that they aren't very good at it, concludes that it's not for them.

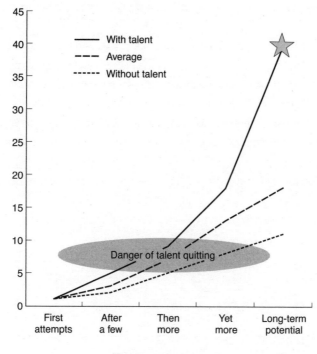

The learning curve

You see, when anybody does anything for the first few times, they'll always be worse than the average person that's performed that task/skill for quite some time. And so the talented person quits because they're comparing themselves with the experienced average. However, as shown in the graph, the key is to keep going (like you did when you began walking!) until you find out whether you have a 'natural' talent in whatever it is you're doing – far too many people give up too quickly.

The idea in brief:

- *All great leaders commit to lifelong continuous learning – it never ends*
- *If you stop learning, but the world keeps moving, it means you'll actually be going backwards*
- *If you're in reverse, you can't pick future trends to ride and lead your team forwards*
- *You'll be vibrant into your 80s and 90s (and beyond) if you keep learning something new every day*

- *Learning from your own actions is the best way of learning (empirical lessons)*
- *Read extensively in your industry, every day (make it a habit) and don't forget to be curious about others too (sometimes what works for one industry can be air-lifted to your own – be the person who connects the dots)*
- *Remember, when you learn something new, you'll always suck to begin with, but you could still be a rising star*

12

Manage your emotions using Emotional Intelligence

'One of the cons of the British education system is that they make people believe that being clever is enough – and it's not.'

Greg Dyke

Emotional Intelligence or EQ (Emotional Quotient) is a relatively recent behavioural model, rising to prominence with Daniel Goleman's 1995 book *Emotional Intelligence*. Since writing *Emotional Intelligence*, he has written many other books and has become a rock star in the worlds of leadership, business, neuroscience and psychology (in order of importance, of course!). I've been lucky enough to get to know Daniel and to interview him twice. Those enchanting encounters form the basis of this chapter.

So first of all, why is EQ so flipping important for leaders?

The first time we met, Daniel pointed out to me that the people who get to the top 10 per cent in their field (i.e. the star performers) get there largely because of their EQ rather than their IQ:

> Study after study shows that in order to be in a top profession, in order to get an MBA, in order to become an MD, or be a top executive, you need an IQ that's about one standard deviation above normal, or higher. That puts you at about 115 IQ. But then, after that, studies show there is no correlation between your IQ and actual effectiveness or success in that particular line of work ...
>
> You see, throughout school, IQ is a huge advantage for grades. But in the workplace, after reaching that criterion level, it has no added benefit and what makes the difference are your personal abilities, for example, how you manage yourself. Do you stay focused? Are you adaptable? Are you self-aware? Can you read other people? Do you know how to get along well? Are you a good team player? Can you be a leader? These all depend on Emotional Intelligence (EQ).

So, if you're a super-genius person with a 170 IQ or something, then I hope you're sitting down when I tell you this: it's not enough – you also need to be streetwise; you also need to have a high EQ.

What exactly is Emotional Intelligence?

There are lots of definitions out there, but Daniel is the world authority and grandmaster, so let's take his as he defined it in our interview:

> Emotional Intelligence refers to how well we manage ourselves and our relationships. There are four key domains. *Self-awareness*: knowing what we're feeling and why we're feeling it, which is the basis, for example, of good intuition and good decision-making. The second part is *Self-management* – handling your distressing emotions in effective ways so they don't cripple you and get in the way of what you're doing ... also mastering positive emotions – getting

ourselves involved and enthused by what we're doing, aligning our actions with our passion. The third is *Empathy*, which is knowing what someone else is feeling, and the fourth is putting that all together through *Skilled Relationships* and *Social Skills*.

For the purposes of this chapter we're going to really focus on self-management. A lot of Daniel's other wisdom will come up in the following chapters, which are more aligned to the team and organisation – and for wider reading I'd strongly recommend all of Daniel Goleman's books.

Self-management is all about how to manage your feelings and your emotions. It evokes questions like, 'How do you perform under high-stress? How do you manage your feelings when you work with somebody you hate? How do you respond when things in your team are not going well? How do you respond and react to an email that annoys the heck out of you? How do you manage and lead in a crisis? How do you perform in pressurised situations when the stakes are really high? If the answer to any of these is 'I get revenge', 'I get angry' or 'I flip out and totally lose it' – you'd better read on …

Can you improve your EQ or are you stuck with what you've got?

If you're reading this and thinking, I'm the moodiest git I know; I make people cry and I don't know why; I've got zero tolerance, I'm impatient with everyone; people work for me because they have no other choice and they need the money; I've fired people before just because I was in a foul mood – then fear not (well, perhaps a little bit), you can change. When I asked Daniel if people could enhance their Emotional Intelligence , you'll be pleased to know he replied with the following:

The good news is that you can improve Emotional Intelligence competencies. They are learnt abilities that build from fundamentals. So, for example, emotional self-control – being calm under pressure – is a capacity that can be learnt; the steps are quite well known. But first you have to want to get better.

As we discussed in the introduction, the key to improving your EQ and your leadership is to master your habits. After all, you define your habits and then your habits define you. We'll discuss the power of habits in the next chapter, but for now let's look at the word ...

Response-ability

As Stephen Covey rightly said: 'You cannot control what happens to you, but you can control how you react to it.' As leaders we all have response-ability – in other words, the 'ability' to choose the best 'response'. The best response is one that will generate the best long-term outcome, not the one with the best short-term feeling of gratification (the 'I'll tell you!' emails). If it's an angry letter you've received, or the economy has collapsed (again) – whatever it is, as a leader you have to choose the right response.

Indeed, if you can't manage emotions and stress then this will play havoc with your decision-making skills. On this, Daniel says:

> It's very clear that there's an interaction between our emotional centres (the centres for distress and alarm) and the prefrontal cortex (the brain's executive centre). This is the part of the brain that helps us think clearly, take in information fully, and respond adaptively; the more alarm the brain is experiencing, the more distressing the emotions, the more crippled the executive centre becomes.

Remember that in life we can choose our responses, but we can't choose the consequences of our response. As they say, when you pick up one end of the stick, you pick up the other end. So choose wisely.

The Traffic Light system

In the heat of an enemy attack (which is how it can feel sometimes), how can you adjust your response to ensure that you're making the right decision? One of the many systems that Daniel shares is one that he discussed with me and mindfulness consultant, Shamash Alidina. It's called the Traffic Light system. This is what Daniel told Shamash about using the image of a traffic light to help you respond in times of emotional distress:

> When you're upset, remember the *red* light; stop, calm down and think before you act. *Yellow* light: think of the range of things you might do and what the consequences would be, and then *green* light – pick the best response.

The day after I interviewed Daniel, I was having dinner with my friend Tamara in a fine-dining Japanese restaurant in London. Like most restaurants in London, Tamara and I were sitting opposite each other, closely flanked on either side by other diners. The couple to the right looked like two high-ranking Japanese business people, and the couple on our left looked like two funky creatives from the advertising or media world.

Tamara ordered chicken teriyaki skewers as one of her dishes. When they arrived she found the chicken had caramelised onto the skewer and wouldn't budge, so she slid her fork down the skewer and started forcefully jolting the chicken to try to get it off. Nothing happened for a few seconds until, in the blink of an eye, all of the chicken pieces fired off the skewer with such velocity that they bounced off the side of the plate, became airborne and landed right in the lap of the Japanese man sitting next to her; six cubes of chicken in teriyaki sauce just sitting there on his suit trousers.

Despite it all happening very quickly, I can clearly remember seeing this Japanese man go through Daniel's traffic light system (whether he knew it or not). His first look was of horror and shock, then anger, then reflection – followed by a remarkably gracious response, thank goodness. If we weren't sitting next to such a gracious chap, *I* could have been on the end of the skewer. But forget the skewer example – check this out ...

The personification of EQ: 155 lives saved in the Hudson River

A leader with incredibly advanced natural Emotional Intelligence is Captain Chesley 'Sully' Sullenberger. Captain Sullenberger was the pilot of US Airways flight 1549 which, on 15th January 2009, five minutes after take-off from LaGuardia Airport and packed with 155 passengers, hit a flock of birds that disabled *both* its engines (Airbus A320s have only two engines). At the time, the plane was flying low at only 3,000 feet above one of the most populous areas on the planet, with no power.

With the aeroplane descending rapidly, the pilot managed to control his emotions and therefore control the situation. With no thrust, he had no choice but to glide the aeroplane. Quickly calculating that he wouldn't be able to turn and make it back to LaGuardia Airport, he contacted a very concerned air traffic control and in a matter-of-fact tone said, 'We're going in the Hudson'. Despite the incredulous response he received from air traffic control, this is exactly what he did: flying south, and at approximately 130 knots (150 m.p.h.), he landed the plane calmly and serenely into New York's Hudson River. All 155 passengers' lives were saved.

His ability to choose his response was remarkable. Here's what he told CBS News: 'The physiological reaction I had to this was strong, and I had to force myself to use my training and force calm on the situation.'

So next time you find yourself in a stressful situation, you might want to remind yourself that it is probably relatively Zen compared with Captain Sullenberger's flight above New York City that day.

The idea in brief:

- *Read Daniel Goleman's work – he's the master at all things EQ*
- *Beyond a certain IQ level, your EQ will determine your level of success far more than your IQ*
- *You must be aware of your EQ and work on improving it*
- *To improve your EQ you must first want to improve it, and then work on changing your habits (next chapter)*
- *Your mood, which is one of the most obvious emotional manifestations in the workplace must be managed, otherwise it spreads*
- *Responsibility is all about your 'ability' to choose your 'response'; you have this ability, it's vital you use it and don't just react*
- *Consider the Traffic Light system to slow down your mouth or your email responses*

13

Deal with stress well – set the example and have at least a bit of a life outside of work

As leaders, managing and dealing with stress, and helping those in our team that are under stress, is a wonderful and important leadership skill to acquire and nurture.

Psychologist Cary Cooper revealed the cost of stress to the economy when he wrote an article for the *Guardian,* in which he said, 'Surveys show that stress is now the leading cause of sickness absence in the UK' and that 'mental health and stress-related absence is costing the UK economy £8.4 billion per annum'.

But it's not all doom and gloom – exposure to some stress is a good thing. A short exposure to stress isn't a problem (in fact short-term stress comes with a boost of adrenalin, bringing short-term advantages including heightened memory, augmented energy and even, according to the charity Mind's website, a decreased sensitivity to pain.) So a bit of stress can be helpful for meeting project deadlines, making speeches, doing urgent tasks etc. – all the things leaders need to do frequently. The problem comes when there are long periods of feeling overwhelmed, i.e. chronic stress. Chronic stress can cause problems in all areas of health – so that's when the red flags should start flying and the sirens should start wailing – and yes, perhaps you *should* be running for the hills (exercise is a great antidote to stress!).

Like everything in life, it's about a balance. On the one hand, if you're too chilled, relaxed and nonchalant, you won't get much done. On the other hand, if you're too stressed you'll feel overwhelmed, freak out, spread negative energy to your team, suffer 24/7, and quite possibly send everybody around you into a state of panic too. I'm guessing that being too chilled isn't a problem for you right now ... so let's look at the too-stressed side of the coin.

The first thing to realise is that if you, as the leader, are feeling stressed or anxious, then your team will be anxious too, because they will look to you for a sense of how they should feel. If you portray a relaxed but proactive disposition then that will be emulated by your team. I have heard people say that you need to adopt the manner of a swan – graceful on the outside, but paddling like crazy beneath. I think it lacks authenticity, but if you have to act it, until you actually feel it, then so be it.

However, acting doesn't solve the problem – masking isn't the best solution. When it comes to actually tackling the problem, then, as Desiderius Erasmus, the fifteenth-century Dutch humanist rightly said, 'prevention is better than cure'. The reason this quote has been flying around for about 600 years is because it's so very, very true – especially when it comes to stress. So let's explore ...

As the leader, what is the antidote to your own stress?

Stress is a very personal thing for leaders – both the causes of stress and what works as an antidote to it. For example, for some leaders, speaking in public brings great joy, while for others it sends cortisol (the hormone released in moments of stress) levels soaring and the leader in question fleeing for the hills in a state of utter panic and angst.

Equally, the antidotes to stress are very personal: for one person, spending 30 minutes sitting and focusing on one's in-breath and out-breath might lead to a state of inner peace; for others it might lead to a state of complete and utter boredom, frustration and lack of action. Everybody has a different antidote. Here's what Daniel Goleman said to me about this:

People really differ in what works for them as a relaxation modality. One thing doesn't work for everybody ... I recommend that people have a method, and the reason is this: what you're doing is training your brain to relax, even under pressure; you don't want to learn [this method] under pressure; you want to practise at home when things are quiet and calm and you can try it out and do it daily, because you're going to need that method in the heat of the day.

One of the methods, for example, is very simple: it's just paying attention to your breath, and letting go of other thoughts; it turns out that that's very effective for most people in lowering your metabolic state, which is to say, to get more relaxed and to stay focused. For other people, deep muscle relaxation will work better, or exercise – but it's different for everybody.

Try different tools and techniques to chill you out

Make a commitment to a period of trial and error to find out what works for you. Try deep breathing; try scheduling a form of exercise that you *love* twice a week; try meditation (there's lot of apps out there); try deep breathing (again); try *anything* until you find something that gives you a break and puts you in a state of relaxed proactivity.

If you take a further look at exercise to reduce your stress (and I suggest you do), then do whatever works for you – what *you* most enjoy. It's individual. For Thomas Jefferson, it was walking, he said: 'Walking is the very best exercise. Habituate yourself to walk very far.'

Take breaks – and rejuvenate

To manage stress you have to rejuvenate yourself. The best way to do this is to take mini breaks of five to 10 minutes every 90 minutes during the day (as discussed in chapter 10), to take Sunday off in full (after all, even God did) and take your holidays. You'll come back better able to do your work each time. Quality will go through the roof, as will your spirits and your results. Also, be a good leader and encourage your team to take breaks and look after their stress. After all, you can't go out for your nice breaks if you're screaming at Kim and Tim for doing the same.

Remember your Circle of Influence and the Circle of Concern

So many people worry themselves silly about things that they can't influence or control – but I ask you, if you can't influence or control those things, why worry about them?

Great leaders recognise that they should only stress about things which they *can* influence. They may be concerned by other factors, but they won't spend one moment trying to resolve them – they're smart enough to know they can't. These two spheres of influence and concern, and how they should be treated, were identified by the late Stephen Covey in his book *The 7 Habits of Highly Effective People*. According to Stephen, the issues we face at work and in our personal lives fall into two categories: the 'Circle of Concern' (things over which we have little or no control, such as the weather), and the 'Circle of Influence' (things we can do something about, like our health, family life or problems at work). If you want to reduce your level of stress, try to let go of the things in your Circle of Concern and be proactive in addressing the things you can control in your Circle of Influence.

Here are some examples of things that are just not worth stressing about – there are other more important things to focus on:

- You're stuck in a queue. There's not much you can do about it, so use the time constructively; don't get stressed (easier said than done, I confess).
- You've screwed up in the past. It's the past – don't stress about things that you can't control.
- The economy is taking a nosedive. It's not something that you can control (unless you're the Chancellor of the Exchequer or Governor of the Bank of England), so just do your best to react in the right way.
- Your company is going through a merger with another company and there will be redundancies. Don't stress, you can't stop it.

Develop interests outside your adrenalin-pumping leadership job

In all my interviews with our business gurus, I started off with a quick-fire round. The quick-fire round was there to get to know our guests on a personal level. They all seemed to enjoy it, and so did our studio audience. One of the reasons we did this was to show that these CEOs and business leaders have passions outside of work, and this actually helps them wind down and de-stress and regain perspective. All of the gurus that we interviewed had passions ranging from their horses (Philippa Snare) through to giving their money *away* through philanthropy (John Studzinski).

As a leader, it's a very good thing to not just set career or business orientated goals, but also goals outside of your current day job. By doing so it really helps you be more productive when you're at work – and your passion and happiness will carry from one to the other.

So let's do a quick spot check on you: grab a pen and score yourself (0 = very dissatisfied to 10 = very happy) on the following wheel representing the most usual aspects of a leader's life and when you're done, connect the dots with a pen:

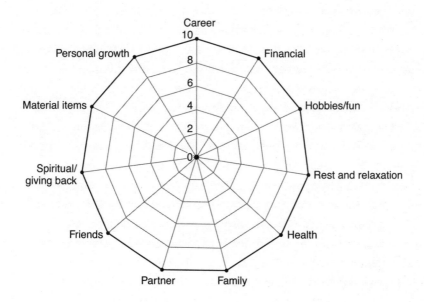

How is the wheel looking? Like a wheel? Probably not, hardly anybody's does. (If it's better than just a dot in the middle, you're already doing better than quite a few!)

So now the key is to:

1) Visualise what 'perfect' would look like in all the core areas of your life (the power of visualisation is a key tool for all leaders – in the words of Zig Ziglar, 'If you can dream it, you can achieve it')
2) Write down two or three important and inspiring goals for each that you'd like to achieve in the next 12 months
3) Write down some immediate action points that can be taken
4) As Brian Tracy told me in our interview, 'Do something that moves you towards your most important goals, every single day.'

By making sure that you, as well as your followers, are well rounded individuals, you won't be such a stress-head, you'll expose yourself to new people, new contacts, new opinions and very importantly you'll have interesting things to say, which means that when you talk to your team, you won't be as dull as dishwater.

May I just ask before we sign off this chapter – what do you think is the most important spoke on the wheel above? Have a look for a second (clue: it's not material items).

Yes – it's health. It's a cliché but it's true; your health *is* your wealth – why's that? Apart from the fact that, yes, if you're dead, your leadership skills will probably not be required, if you're healthy then you'll be more vibrant and have more energy to do your job – and, as we discussed before, leadership is *all* about energy. So why don't you slam this book shut and write down three health goals for you for the next three months? If you do this you'll not only de-stress but you'll live longer and be a lot happier. Even if you didn't slam this book shut, make sure you prioritise health, and ensure you set the example for others in your team to follow – it's about the best thing you can do for yourself and for your followers.

So yes, stress does come with the territory of being a high-performance leader, yet the difference between your managing stress and its managing you is night and day. To go forth and change the world, you need to keep protracted stress at bay.

What about work–life balance? Is it overrated or even achievable?

As we're discussing stress, let's briefly discuss that elusive work–life balance thing. Many leaders think they have to throw it out of the window if they want to reach the top, and drive their staff to do the same. So let's explore some of the key things to consider when trying to strike a balance between work and life.

Work–life integration

Some leaders don't separate work and life – they see their week as a blend of both, not to be formally separated into specific hours allocated to work. This is called work–life integration.

Here's what Sir Terry Leahy told me about this:

> The thing that worked for me was not to try to separate family and work and not to try to get a balance, and it actually just became one thing: there was work and family or family and work. So what that meant was, if I needed to take time off to go to the school, I would; if I needed to work at the weekend, I would. So, in other words, you used all the hours in the week on just two things – family and work.

If that route works for you (and your employer), it's a good thing to do. However, some people love and need that separation between work and life – without it, everything becomes work.

Like everything in life and business, balance takes trial and error – after all, whatever works for you, works for you.

Include your family in the decision-making process

Just as you have a team at work, you have a team at home. It's essential you apply your leadership skills there too – notably, that you communicate openly and honestly and include them in decision-making.

For example, if you're about to close Google as a major account, and that means you have to work your butt off for the months of October and November, then include your family up front and get commitment from them. Including your family in your decision-making is essential for buy-in. Don't just hear, but listen – a lot of the lessons that are shared in this book can be deployed in other areas of your life too, none more so than candid communications, securing buy-in and then making the decision (that's the great thing about leadership – it helps in *all* areas of your life).

Be agile – and know there'll be different demands at certain times

In this day and age everything needs to be agile. There will be some periods in your career when you have to make massive 'life' sacrifices. If, for example, you have a big project coming up that will make your career then make the sacrifice, and for the month of January don't insist on having a work–life balance. Equally, sometimes there'll be a crisis in your personal life and you'll have to sacrifice the 'work' part of the work–life equation.

So don't always seek equilibrium. Sometimes it will be much more 'work', and sometimes it will be much more 'life'. The key is to be agile and recognise that there'll be peaks and troughs. You can't score an A+ on all areas of your life, all the time.

The idea in brief:

- *Leaders do go through some periods of stress (and that's actually an asset, adrenalin helps in speeches and deadlines etc.) but it's the chronic (prolonged) periods of stress that you need to be very wary of*
- *Prevention is better than cure*
- *Keep stress under control by finding a relaxation modality that works for you; it's trial and error – keep searching*
- *Take breaks to reinvigorate yourself*
- *Only worry about things that you can have an influence over, otherwise your stress is wasted*
- *Develop interests outside your day job*

14

Decisions – listen to others, but back your own judgement

'Make decisions, because a wrong decision is better than no decision – you can always go back and change them.'

Ed Wray

Imagine you're the leader in a room with eight colleagues and they're *all* arguing with passion and great intelligence about which way the team should go on a specific decision. Nobody agrees, but everybody is worked up and gnashing their teeth. You're not allowed to run for the fire escape. Whose job is it to make the final decision? Yes – it's yours. Even if you decide to delegate the decision, that is still a decision to delegate the decision.

It's no surprise that leaders have to be good at decision-making. If you're a natural, that's great; if you're not, the good news is you can get much better at it. As we saw earlier, mental muscles are like physical muscles, you can beef them up through repeated use.

First things first: be a leader, not a donkey

I remember years ago seeing an illustration of a donkey standing in the middle of two stacks of hay. Both stacks of hay were easily within reach, but as the donkey never made up its mind which way to go, it died. Tragic. The key here is that if the donkey had turned left or right it would have been fine; indeed, it would have stuffed itself full of delicious hay, survived and prospered. Alas, because it couldn't make up its mind, it perished. Making no decision is always the worst thing to do. As the late British Prime Minister Margaret Thatcher once said, 'Standing in the middle of the road is very dangerous; you get knocked down by traffic from both sides.'

One thing that has come out during my interviews with leaders over the years is that they know that people look to them to make the decisions. And they accept this responsibility. So if you want to be an insanely successful leader, turn decision-making into a core strength of yours.

Making decisions is a leader's job. Indeed, as controversial musician Marilyn Manson said, 'A lot of people don't want to make their own decisions. They're too scared. It's much easier to be told what to do.' Sure, it *is* easier to be told what to do (for some of us at least), and not to have to make decisions. Equally, it's probably easier to follow than to lead; sure, but it's easier to bore people than inspire people, and that's not what this book is about.

This book is about leaders in their field, not losers in their field. Making decisions (like speaking in public, vision-setting and everything else) is what great leaders do. So be the leader, step up and make decisions.

The good news: it *does* come naturally to you

If you ask any group of people what they believe are the common characteristics of leaders, being decisive is always high on this list. You probably agree with that. I remember doing an exercise with a team of managers in our China office and asking them to shout out the traits of leaders. (Chinese people can be the shrewdest and smartest people on the planet, but, as they honour hierarchy so much, brainstorming meetings in China can be quite a tough gig!) Eventually we filled half a flipchart page and the ability to make decisions was right at the top.

Somebody asked me afterwards in a beautiful Shanghai accent:'I'm not a good decision-maker at all – I take ages to decide and even then I get most wrong. Does this mean I'm in trouble, and will never reach great heights?' Some of her fellow colleagues nodded and, knowing that if I nodded too, she might jump straight out the window, I chose a different (and honest) response. I said, 'No, not at all. The truth is that everybody is a natural decision-maker; you just have to awaken it within you.'

Allan Leighton said to me in my interview with him:'Most people are natural decision-makers. We make decisions every day. That door vs that door, that drink vs that drink ... Every day, you get up and decide what to wear. Nobody thinks, Hey I'm going to hang around here for four hours [deciding what to wear].'

Everybody has the ability to be a great decision-maker, but, like everything, it comes with practice. In fact, Anthony Robbins, the famous success guru, says that we all have a decision-making 'muscle'. If that muscle is weak, you'll struggle at every crossroads; conversely, if it's strong, you'll fly through decisions and nail them all – you just have to give the muscle a good workout!

So, if you're reading this thinking, I'm not good at decision-making, then you'll find this good news: all you have to do is strengthen your decision-making muscle by using it more. Start working it out by making small decisions today, quickly and fast. Think, feel, decide and act. Do this frequently and often. Over time you'll find it gets easier and easier and that, as you build your muscle, you'll make decisions faster and get more right. All great leaders and successful people have simply built this muscle, and they use it to their advantage every day.

If you practise on small decisions (those that in a month's time you won't remember making or give two hoots about which way you went) then, when in the future you come to a much bigger crossroads, you won't freak out, you won't jump out the window – you'll enjoy the process and as a result you'll make better decisions. Your new competency will breed in you greater confidence and you'll be seen as a 'natural'.

Why making a wrong decision is better than making no decision at all

In the interview I did with Greg Dyke (former Director General of the BBC), he had the following to say about committing to decisions:

> If you want certainty you're never going to do anything. You can analyse more and that's where I think a lot of very clever people run into problems – you can keep analysing, but just take the decision. What is your instinct telling you?
>
> If you do something big and it fails, then you go, 'That's all right, that's part of life.' The last thing they [members of your team] want – what drives them nuts – is you constantly changing your mind, you doing this, then that. At the end of the day, make a decision. It can be the right one or the wrong one, but make a decision. And don't keep analysing it to death, because the one thing that kills good ideas in the end is boredom.

At least if you make the wrong decision, you'll soon find out that it was the wrong decision and take an alternative route. There's value in that. You'll then, by default, know the other way was the right way. By a process of elimination, you'll eventually be right. Job done. In the words of Arianna Huffington, 'We need to accept that we won't always make the right decisions, that we'll screw up royally sometimes – understanding that failure is not the opposite of success, it's part of success.' Many of the world's greatest companies know this, especially when it comes to innovation and product development (more to follow in chapter 32).

However, if you don't make a decision, then as a leader you can't set a course or a direction. Your team, your organisation and, indeed, even you, need a direction. Reiterating this point, the very cool and slick (which you'd expect if he's running one of the greatest creative companies in the world) Robert Senior, CEO EMEA of Saatchi & Saatchi, said in our interview, 'A rudderless team isn't a team: it's wasted energy; it's just wastage. You have to set a course, and, even if underneath you're thinking, I don't know which way is right, then just flip a coin (it happens, by the way) … anything – at least set a course. It's because everybody needs to know which direction they're going in.'

Go forth with conviction, even if you're not 100 per cent certain it's the right path, at least you're moving forward. As the legendary Sir Stuart Rose said in our interview: 'Doing nothing is not an option. Standing around doing nothing and milling about is why companies go nowhere. You've got to keep moving.'

You can't decide on your direction if you don't know where you want to go

There's another reason why some people find it hard to make decisions and that's because they just don't know where they want to go. It sounds banal, but it's very true. Knowing where you want to get to (goals, vision and purpose) is the foundation of everything. So make sure you know what your goals are, for your life, your team and your company. (If you think you've omitted this vital part of life so far, then please jump straight to chapter 16 which discusses the importance of setting a 'Vision' and 'Mission').

Knowing where you're going also applies to the company perspective. Richard Reed (cofounder of Innocent Drinks), when talking to me about his controversial decision to distribute Innocent smoothies through McDonald's, said that knowing his purpose – 'to make the world a little bit more healthy' – enabled him to make better strategic decisions in the heat of the moment. The question simply became 'Will distributing through McDonalds sell more smoothies and therefore make the UK a little bit more healthy?' The answer was, 'Yes it will.' So the decision was easy. Innocent knew where they were going so it simply became a case of choosing the path that would lead them there.

Once you've decided on a course, don't dither – here's how

Very often people will draw up a list of all the pros of going with Route A and the pros of going with Route B. Then, after months, they decide to go with Route A. As soon as they've made their mind up to go with Route A they start thinking of all the pros that they're missing out on by not going with Route B. This practice could send you into a stress-related early retirement!

The economists call the benefits lost by going with one decision over another 'opportunity costs'; in other words, the costs of not having gone with the other opportunity. You could also call this 'going around in circles' or, as Greg Dyke quaintly puts it, driving people 'nuts'. Imagine a weirdo in a car just driving around a roundabout time and time again; essentially you want to avoid being that weirdo! At some point you have to get off the roundabout and go somewhere – after all, you look bonkers driving around a roundabout: you ain't going anywhere and you're holding up traffic.

From my research, it's clear that once any good leader has made a decision (either using gut, logic or both), they essentially put all the focus on the positives of going that route (opportunity gain), and they tend to forget the other path (opportunity cost). Not only do they forget it, they usually put the decision in a vault. In fact, I know one person who would literally write a decision down on a piece of paper and lock it away in box (it was actually his tuckbox – he was one of those posh boarding-school chaps) as a reminder not to go and revisit that decision. It's a good technique; even if you do this mentally as opposed to literally, it works.

In my interview with Jon Moulton (Chairman of Better Capital, one of the world leaders in private equity), he said, 'The only tip that I would give on decision-making is, having done your best, having looked at the options and taken one, don't revisit it, don't regret it, don't dither about it afterwards. That way, you'll end up very inefficient and you'll do very little.' He went on to point out, 'Better in a business career to take a lot of decisions and get them 80 per cent right than take very few decisions and get 100 per cent of them right.'

Justin King, the former CEO of Sainsbury's, makes the point even more forcefully, saying: 'Always remain firmly attached to a decision right up until the point that you say it's the worst decision you have ever made; it is more damaging to change the decision than stick with a bad one.'

If you make the wrong call and you screw up – that's okay, everybody's done it

That said, I believe if you know that you're heading towards a brick wall, it's better to turn around before you hit it. U-turns are okay, and, in fact, being agile (particularly these days) is a trait of all great leaders and companies. Just don't do it so much that people get dizzy and lose focus.

Robert Senior points out: 'Sure, taking a decision entails risk – but risk is what life is all about. Remember that pretty much all decisions can be reversed.'

The only thing that you *must* do, if you're the leader and you made the wrong call, is to accept responsibility; if it was the wrong decision, don't blame it on your new hire or the intern – let everybody know that it was your mistake and correct it. They'll respect you for it – it's a sign of a great leader; it's not a sign of a great leader to blame Emelia, the new intern!

Besides, at the very end of the day, perhaps this commentary will provide some solace:

'Sir, what is the secret of your success?' a reporter asked a bank president.

'Two words.'

'And, sir, what are they?'

'Right decisions.'

'And how do you make right decisions?'

'One word.'

'And, sir, what is that?'

'Experience.'

'And how do you get experience?'

'Two words.'

'And, sir, what are they?'

'Wrong decisions.'

When the stakes are high, it's not always about speed; sometimes it's okay to take your sweet time

I've explained how the world's greatest leaders have a tendency to make fast decisions and accept that some will be right and some will be wrong.

Very often they do a quick analysis, identify their gut instinct and use this to choose a path and proceed.

Having said all that, there are times when you might want to pause a little longer than usual, gather more data, listen more and reflect more. These are what I call the 80/20 decisions – the Vital Decisions. These are the types of decisions that really, really, matter to you and your organisation – the types of decisions that will still matter in 10 years' time. For example, some of these Vital Few decisions might include: Should I launch my own business? Should I hire this person into my management team? Should we expand our business into the Far East and China? These are the big ones, and as they're 'vital', they deserve more time if needed. In fact, the world's most successful people differentiate between insignificant decisions and the Vital Few decisions – and they will spend more time on the really Vital Few and hardly any time at all on less important decisions.

Sir Terry Leahy told me, '[During my time as CEO of Tesco] I always tried to distinguish between things that didn't matter and a few things that really mattered (or that I thought really mattered), and with those ones you had to be really careful about what you decided.' He went on to say, '[on these decisions] I always avoided rushing to a decision. I think it's not a bad idea, because often when you turn things over, they do become clearer. I never felt the need to make a quick decision.'

So the key, like most things, is spending a bit more time on the very important decisions, but then, like all decisions, big or small, coming down on one side of the fence eventually. After all, sitting on any fence too long gets rather uncomfortable.

But remember: leaders don't always play it safe

Great leaders don't always take the 'safe' decision. If you always play it safe, you might not take anyone anywhere new. If you're a leader who always plays it safe, then remember the words of leadership guru and CEO coach Mike Myatt, 'Leaders whose default setting is "play it safe" are most often doing just the opposite.' Plus, by playing it safe, you are likely to bore the pants off everybody around you.

Which is better, the neocortex or the subcortex? (In English this means 'which is better: intuition or logic?')

When it comes to making decisions, many people just suggest going with what feels right: 'use your intuition'; 'back your gut'; 'what do you feel?'. Others tell you to 'forget that fluffy feeling stuff' and 'use your head – use the block on your shoulders'. They'll say things like 'just put it down on paper' and 'we'll do an analysis and we'll eventually get to the right decision'. So which is right? Well, they're both right: to be really great, all the world's most successful entrepreneurs, CEOs and people use both.

Intuition is a very powerful tool, but you also have to use your head. Don't just 'feel' your way around life, and don't just 'think' around it either. Use both. As Bill Clinton told *Fortune* magazine, 'You have to be able to trust your instinct as well as your intellect.'

In my interview with Daniel Goleman, he had this to say about logic vs feeling when decision-making:

> My advice is both. There's interesting data on that: there was a study that analysed Californian entrepreneurs who have built huge businesses from nothing and they were asked: 'How do you make your decisions?' They all said essentially the same thing ... that they were voracious gatherers of data; they delved into the numbers, they looked at everything – and then they would check it against their gut feeling.
>
> What that means is that their first swipe is on the cortical part of the brain that thinks in words and numbers, and then they check that against their gut feeling. The reason is this: there's a primitive part of the brain at the brain stem, which, as we go through life, gathers decision roles, i.e. when I did this, that worked well; when I said that, that really didn't work well. As we face a decision point, it's [your subcortex] summing up your life experience relevant to the topic, and it's sending you a message. The problem is that it has no connection to the part of the brain that thinks in words; it sends the message to the gut (the GI tract), so when you say 'trust your gut', it's literally true – because you experience a sensation: it feels right vs it doesn't feel right. All these entrepreneurs say they check their decision against that: 'Even if the number looked good, if I didn't feel right I wouldn't go ahead' ... It's feelings and thoughts.

If you're not tapped into both your thinking *and* your intuition, you're not using all the tools available to you. Sometimes it's absolutely fine to go with what simply 'feels' right.

The reason that intuition is so powerful is simply that our conscious mind can only hold approximately seven thoughts at any one time. So it's the subconscious that analyses everything beyond this and then sends the result of that analysis back to you. There's no way you could ever consciously remember or analyse everything you've ever come across or learnt, but your subconscious can. So yes, the ability to tap into both your thinking and your intuition is a serious talent!

This is why the more years you gain in an industry or a function, the more you should use and trust your gut feeling – simply because your mind has gathered more empirical lessons in its incredibly powerful data storage.

Robert Senior summed up this data-gathering and intuition process when he said in our interviews on making decisions: 'Get all this input; now go for a little walk on your own, buy a Starbucks or something – just have a little moment to yourself (to reflect and feel what's right), because you are going to decide, because you are accountable.' In this sentence you can see the dual usage of data analysis and intuition.

In the noisy world we live in, with open offices, commutes and over-crowding, it's often hard to hear the inner voice, yet finding it is crucial when it comes to making astute leadership decisions. So find a bit of time to reflect and think. As Robert says, go and have a moment to yourself – a coffee, a bath, a walk, a run – anything! By doing this, you're more likely to be able to sense when something feels right or wrong based on your emotions (excitement or anxiety, for example). If you give yourself the space to listen to these feelings, they will often lead you towards the right decision. Very often you'll have a feeling that sometimes feels like excite-ment or anxiety; if you listen to this, it's more than often right.

As psychologist Dr Joyce Brothers said, 'Trust your hunches. They're usually based on facts filed away just below the conscious level.'

If in doubt, back your own judgement every time

When all is said and done, listen to your own judgement and back your-self. If you don't follow your judgement and instead go with somebody else's opinion over your own, and in time they prove wrong, you'll always regret going with their opinion. Don't have regrets.

When Matthew Key was CEO of O2 Telefónica UK, he backed his instinct and judgement in a huge way with the O2 arena. Anybody living in the UK will know that, since its launch back in 2000, the Millennium Dome had been a colossal 'white elephant', i.e. waste of space and a laughing stock for all those that owned it.

Despite this, Matthew Key had a vision and an instinct that O2 should sponsor the Millennium Dome and turn it into the world's greatest music and entertainment centre. At the time, O2 was a challenger brand in the UK mobile market and it was a colossal risk both for him (the new CEO) and also for the brand. At the end of the day, he and the company were at risk of becoming a laughing stock like all the previous owners of the building.

In the interview with Matthew he said to me:

> I went to the O2 plc board (as it was then), and I vividly remember sitting in a board meeting presenting this and somebody from the board said, 'So do you want an answer?', and I said, 'Yes please', and they said, 'Well the answer's no', to which I said, 'I'm not accepting no. I'm coming back until you say yes' – which was quite a risky move for me at the time; I was relatively new (as the CEO), but I'm glad I pushed for it because we now look back and what a fantastic venue it's become, and the most visited entertainment centre in the world.

Matthew was turned down by the board not once, but three times. He kept going back. Why? Because he trusted his judgement – he'd done the research and then, most importantly, it 'felt' right to him. Eventually, he got it through.

He went on to say:

> I wasn't financially betting the house on it, but we felt the potential upside more than outweighed the potential downside. Once you've reached that point, trust your instinct. A lot of business decisions are around instinct. You can show me a spreadsheet that proves something or proves something else. Instinctively, do I think it's right? You have to back your own judgement.

In a nutshell, great leaders weigh up the upside vs the downside, and if they feel excited about it, it's a sure bet they'll hit 'go'. In this case, the O2 went on to become one of the telecoms industry's biggest marketing and customer successes – and indeed it *is* the most visited entertainment centre in the world. It's a good job Matthew didn't listen to the naysayers on the board.

Just don't forget your team during the process

In my interview with Daniel Goleman, he discussed a concept with me called 'Group IQ', whereby the collective intelligence of the group is always going to be higher than any individual. Great leaders are aware of this and, therefore, always 100 per cent open to the opinions of the teams they lead. These leaders understand that there is always a tendency for facts to reinforce beliefs in one's mind, even if those beliefs are in fact wrong and, as such, always invite those they lead to challenge those beliefs.

Poor leaders don't include their team in decisions pertaining to the direction of that team. That's not pretty – and those leaders end up getting thrown out or replaced. By consulting your team, you'll not only get some wisdom from them, but you'll also get their buy-in – their support and commitment to your decision. The simple act of including them and genuinely listening to their thoughts is what will make the difference between your own lovely team backing you in a blissful, united front, or each of them turning into little 'internal terrorists' and destroying your beautiful plan (okay, I might be overstating it with internal terrorists, but you get what I mean, and I bet you might know a few).

If you have truly listened to the team, but you end up disagreeing with them, as the leader you have to make the decision. That's your job; sometimes the majority vote isn't right. Go with your judgement even if it's unpopular. It takes confidence, it takes courage – and it's what great leaders do.

Warning: there is a massive trap that leaders (particularly extroverts) can fall into – being swung by the last person you spoke to

Yes, you should listen to your team, but if you keep getting swayed by the last person you spoke to, you'll become woefully ineffective as a leader. You can't keep changing course, so this is where conviction in your own judgement is paramount – and your team will respect your conviction, even if they don't agree with the course (more on this in the next chapter).

Robert Senior said: 'I think poor leaders tend to make a decision or talk based on the very last conversation they had. So they're constantly changing their view, based on the last person they spoke to. It's unwitting – it just happens. I think strong leaders talk to a lot of people, get a lot of feedback, but then decide.'

On a similar point, Sir Terry Leahy, who claimed to be an introvert and shy (although you'd never tell in person), points out that he has a significant advantage when it comes to decision-making, because introverts look internally for guidance. As such, they're more consistent and less swayed by the millions of opinions and views out there in the world. So if you're an introvert, congratulations; if you're an extrovert, just be aware of this potential danger, or, as that saying goes, 'be the wind; don't be blown around by the wind'.

You can't please all the people all the time. Some folk get caught up in trying to please everybody with a decision. You can't, it's never going to happen – there are always going to be people who don't like a decision and speak loudly about it. But remember, there's also going to be a fanbase that loves your decision. I always find this quote from Pulitzer Prize-winning journalist Herbert Swope useful for remembering this: 'I cannot give you the formula for success, but I can give you the formula for failure, which is: to try to please everybody.'

The idea in brief:

- *Don't be the donkey – it's better to make the wrong decision than no decision at all*
- *We're all natural decision-makers – some of us just need a lot more practice*

- *Remember, it's okay to take your time when making Vital Decisions*
- *Weigh up data, do some research, speak to your team – have a left-brain fact-finding phase first then combine this with intuition to reach your decision*
- *Consider the upside and the downside – make sure that the upside is (significantly) bigger than the downside*
- *Don't bet the farm – avoid decisions that will risk everything you've got*
- *Consult with the team on the bigger decisions and really listen to them – don't fake it*
- *Give yourself space to make the final decision – go for a walk, a coffee, a bath – and then see what feels right (right brain)*
- *Have the courage to make a decision; remember that the majority vote isn't always the right one – have conviction in your beliefs and sometimes take a risk*
- *If your decision is wrong, admit it and head back for the U-turn; don't be stubborn and crash into a wall if it's avoidable*
- *Above all, make a lot of decisions and know that all great leaders make mistakes once in a while, but the majority of your decisions will be right, and, at the end of the day, that's all that matters*

15

Be confident, not arrogant

'I rarely encounter self-confidence problems in my
work with CEOs and potential CEOs. It is almost
impossible to make it to the top level in a multibillion-
dollar corporation if you do not believe in yourself.'

Marshall Goldsmith

In an article for the *Harvard Business Review*, Amy Jen Su and Murial
Maignan Wilkens describe confidence as a trait possessed by everyone,
a 'dynamic emotion that, like a physical muscle needs exercise to grow
stronger'.

Daniel Goleman concurred with this when he told me, 'It's like going
to the gym: if you go to the gym and you lift weights, every time you do
a repetition you strengthen the muscle that you're working; [mental
muscles] can be strengthened in the same way.'

For those of you that are reading this book chapter by chapter, you
might be beginning to see a pattern emerge: all the habits of successful
leaders can be developed and strengthened. That's good news.

When it comes to leadership (and life, in fact), confidence is a beautiful, admired and wonderful asset; arrogance on the other hand is an ugly, abhorred and nasty little liability. Yes, you want to come across to the world as being aware of your abilities and your strengths, but you don't want to come across as a total doorknob. So, it's important to be aware of when extreme confidence can lead to extreme arrogance.

As one repels and the other attracts, it's worth spending a moment on the essential differences. Master Arrogance would say:

- I'm so good that I've got nothing else to learn
- I'm better than other people; they're useful to me but inferior
- I'm always right; nobody else knows better than me

If you develop any of the above symptoms, it's time to get help. Master Confidence would say:

- I'm good at what I do, but I'm always open to learning, and learning from others
- I'm better than some people at what I do, but other people have greater strengths in other areas; I respect everybody for their strengths, including myself
- I'm often right, but I'm aware that I'm sometimes wrong and I listen to other people

If you have confidence, you'll aim higher and expect greater things

You tend to get in life what you expect and what you believe. So, if you believe that you deserve great things, then they will come to you. If you believe in yourself (and the value of your core strengths), you're more likely to set higher goals for yourself and your team. As such, the old confidence thing really is integral to great leadership.

When Brian Tracy talked to me about self-confidence, he said:

The amount that you like and respect yourself determines the entire quality of your life. It determines the goals you set and how big they are. It determines how much you believe in yourself, which in turn determines how much you persist in your goals. It determines how much you like other people and how much they like you back.

So the psychology of achievement is based around this concept that the more you do the things that make you feel good about yourself, which is: setting goals, working towards them, treating people well, learning, taking good care of yourself – all the positive things that you do – these will raise your self-esteem, your self-image and all improve the quality of your relationships with other people and enable you to have a wonderful life.

From a leadership perspective, your followers want to see that you're confident in where you're going, what you're doing and your ability to get the team and the organisation from point A to point B. (Although you might need to fake this confidence at first, you should work at building authentic confidence, which is much more powerful. Authenticity is always supreme.) Reverend Hesburgh, the President Emeritus of the University of Notre Dame, once said: 'You can't blow an uncertain trumpet.' The Reverend was right.

Building confidence as a leader

The great news is that confidence can be built in you and in your team. There are a few tactics for boosting confidence usually focused around acknowledging and celebrating competence. Here are a few of the most potent ways to boost confidence in yourself and in the individuals on your team while at all times avoiding it tipping into arrogance.

Be competent

Competence and confidence go hand in hand so a great confidence-building exercise is to write down all the things that you're good at or very knowledgeable in. Whenever you lack confidence go back to this list and remind yourself of that which you do very well.

Identify your unique strengths

As we discussed in chapter 3, knowing your strengths is essential. When you do, it builds confidence. When people lose confidence, they compare themselves unfavourably to others, i.e. they look myopically at the strengths of others and then say internally, 'I don't have that strength, so therefore they are better than me,' etc. Replace that with, 'Yes, they have those strengths, but I have a whole suite of other strengths; we're all born with different strengths and weaknesses.'

Celebrate successes loudly – bask in your successes for a moment (and then drive forward again)

Another great trick is to convince your subconscious mind of how successful you are by looking for and celebrating every single success you can (and getting your team doing the same). The more your subconscious mind hears success, and absorbs the emotion attached to it, the more convinced it will become in your future abilities. As such, the subliminal messages your conscious mind receives from your subconscious will be based on positive self-belief thereby creating a vicious cycle upwards.

Be 110 per cent yourself: 'Never leave your personality at home'

Many times people try to be somebody they're not or dilute their true personality to conform to corporate stereotypes. We're going to discuss authenticity in chapter 18. However, make no mistake, you have to give yourself permission to be yourself. Love what you love, hate what you hate – and say what you think. As Olaf Swantee, CEO of EE, said, 'Never leave your personality at home.' Your personality is what makes you unique – better to be 100 per cent of yourself than a diluted version of somebody else. Love your idiosyncrasies – they're what make the world an interesting place and you unique. The world, and especially the business world, can be far too 'samey', so be yourself and be confident in who you are.

It's not narcissism to admire your own strengths and character

It's worth pointing out that it's okay to love yourself and to admire your strengths, your personality, and who you are ... why not? As Oscar Wilde said, 'To love oneself is the beginning of a lifelong romance'. So look for your good qualities, look for your strengths, your unique personality, your interests – all this makes up you; you may as well love them all. Admire the different qualities of folk in your team too.

Step up

If an opportunity comes your way, never, never, never turn it down because you don't feel qualified. Become an opportunist and step up to the challenge. If you're unsure, simply take a deep breath and say, in your best Latin, *'Aut inveniam viam faciam.'* Or, if you don't speak Latin (like me!) say, 'I shall either find a way or make one'. If you lack confidence when taking on a challenge, then, as the saying goes, just 'fake it 'til you make it' – just don't not do it.

Challenge limiting beliefs

We are often held back in life and leadership because of false, limiting beliefs we have about ourselves: we believe we're not smart enough, not old enough, not young enough ... These beliefs can have an adverse effect on your attitude and confidence. If you feel you're being held back by a belief, write it down, challenge it, recognise it's a belief and not the truth and replace it with a more (at risk of sounding a little 'airy-fairy') empowering belief. Then proceed to hunt down facts to support that new belief – it will be easier than you think to find facts to support and strengthen your new, positive outlook.

Also, who talks to you, more than anybody else on the planet? Yes *you* do. Be aware of the inner chatter going on in your head and make sure you opt for the confident/bold/reassuring voice as opposed to the negative grouch.

And if you're being authentic, don't be hypersensitive to the opinion of others

People that are self-conscious are often overly worried about what other people think of them – as such they have an acute internal focus (and often dialogue). Decide from this day forward to take the focus out of your own head and put it towards your goals, or whatever it is you're trying to achieve, and care less about what people think of you. As Allan Leighton said, 'Leadership is not a popularity contest'; it's about results and just being yourself.

In fact, *be like tofu*. Tofu doesn't care if you like it or not, nor does it try to change to make people like it; nor should you. The bottom line is that in this world some people will like you, and others will not. So just be yourself and then appreciate those that do like you, and when it comes to the ones that don't like you, then, as Robert Sutton, a Professor of Management Science and Engineering at Stanford University, once wrote, you might want to 'practise the fine art of emotional detachment, or not giving a shit!'

The idea in brief:

- *The more positive your self-image, the higher goals you'll set for yourself in life – and the higher you'll go*
- *Self-confidence and self-image are everything, so work at it*
- *You can't have insecure leaders in a business; it gets complicated!*
- *Give yourself permission to love yourself*
- *Confidence comes with competence, so always focus on your strengths and your accomplishments*
- *If you're being you, and people like you, great; if they don't, practise the fine art of emotional detachment*
- *Celebrate success; it's great for the subconscious and subliminal messages*
- *Be 100 per cent authentic and never leave your personality at home*

Congratulations on getting to the end of Part One. Now, that's you sorted, let's move on to your team and your organisation ...

PART TWO

TEAM Leadership –

building and leading world-class *teams*

Before we launch into Part Two, let's remind ourselves of the *why*. Why bother with leadership? Why not just become high achievers, star performers, superb sole agents or anything else where success just comes down to individual ability? If we did that we wouldn't have to bother with this leadership malarky; we could forget about all the psychobabble, emotional intelligence and hassle that comes with managing and leading others. After all, we can count on our-selves, but who knows about others – they're human and they're wild cards.

The answer lies in leverage.

Leadership taps into the beauty of *leverage*

Ronan Dunne, the CEO of O2, told me of the moment when he realised the power of leadership:

> We can achieve a lot more with the impact we have on those
> around us than we could ever achieve on our own. I remember
> when I worked in the City, I joined a team and wanted to impress
> everybody – so I worked Saturdays and Sundays, just so that I could
> help the team get ahead.
>
> Then I worked out that, unless I could invent an eighth day [my
> impact and output was limited to my individual input]. So, I worked
> out that it would be much more effective if I focused on impacting
> on those around me, so they could be more effective. Surprise,
> surprise, it was a real transformation for me; to have the most
> impact, it's not what you can do, it's what you can influence others
> to do.

Indeed, as Daniel Goleman told me so succinctly, 'Leaders gets results through people.' Even if you work every hour that God sends you, your output will be limited. Yet, if you can inspire a team of people, and if they also lead a team of people, then all of a sudden, your output becomes exponential.

It's all about the leverage and scale leadership brings. Think, for example, of the impact Sir Terry Leahy had when he improved the output of more than 300,000 staff at Tesco. It's because he influenced so many that he became an icon of British business.

The monumental economic value of leadership

It's the inherent leverage of leadership that makes such a massive difference to bottom-line success. After all, if leadership didn't have an impact on the bottom line, then the term would have faded out by now in Big Business. Has it? Quite the opposite, in fact.

Let me elaborate on how leadership through scale creates phenomenal value to any organisation. Imagine you're the Chairman of the Board of Directors for a company called Nice 'n' Tasty Chocolates (you can see why I'm not involved in branding companies!) and you and the board have to appoint a new CEO. What do you think the bottom-line impact will be of hiring one of the following two leaders?:

1) Faith, an inspiring leader who encourages people to go the extra mile, can hire great talent to join her, is focused on the customers' needs, sets the right strategy and executes on that strategy to perfection, and is able to keep star performers.

2) Matthew, an uninspiring manager who fosters a culture of 'I'll do the minimum I need to just so as to not get fired', is autocratic, doesn't innovate, doesn't get buy-in from his team, sets a stupid strategy, takes martini lunches, and has high turnover of talent in star performers.

What would the difference in their performances be over three years (not a bad innings for a CEO)? Ten per cent, 25 per cent, 50 per cent? Well, let's say Nice 'n' Tasty Chocolates has a revenue of £150m and profits of £30m. After three years, assuming a 20 per cent drop in annual profits by Matthew and a 20 per cent increase by Faith, the profit swing is £12 million in year one, £24 million in year two and £36 million in year three. That's a combined variation over the three years of £72 million in profit, not revenue. Imagine if the above scenario was applied to a major FTSE 100 or Fortune 100 company. Perhaps it goes some way to explaining why £778 million was wiped off the value of Tesco the day Sir Terry Leahy announced his retirement. Repeat, the same day.

There is colossal economic value in leadership and this isn't just applicable to big companies. For smaller or start-up companies, the economic value of great leadership vs bad leadership can be even greater. On the one hand, the business could grow by 20 per cent, attract investment or be acquired; on the other hand, it could easily drop 20 per cent – and a 20 per cent drop (because sometimes margins can be tight) could mean lights out.

It's because of this impact that good leadership is so, so valuable and why:

- in the private sector, leaders are able to get paid a fortune for success
- in the public sector, or charity sector, great leaders are so incredibly valuable to those they serve

The bottom line is, because of this scale and its ability to touch many lives, great leadership is needed across the world. So let's get on with it. Just before we do, let's do one warm-up exercise:

Ask not what you can do to be a better leader, but what you can do to inspire followers

If I was asked to encapsulate the messages of all the chapters found in Part Two into a single concept, it would be the following: How do I inspire people to want to follow me? Instead of asking, 'What can I do to be a better leader?', ask, 'How can I create willing followers?'

Greg Dyke, former Director General of the BBC (now Chairman of the Football Association, is one of these leaders with an army of 'willing followers'. To give you an insight into their fierce loyalty, when he resigned from the BBC following a dispute, staff across the country left their broadcasting posts and went out on to the streets to march in support of him (and it was a freezing cold and bitter, rainy English day in February).

In my interview with Greg, I asked him how he inspired such loyalty from his employees. What did he do differently? The quick answer is that, 'We spent years letting them know that we valued what they did.' Valuing others is an integral part of good team leadership, but of course there's more to it than that and much of the wisdom Greg shared with me is included in the pages to come.

But for now, let's think back to the exercise we did in the introduction of this book, in which we listed attributes of leaders we admired. Ask yourself the following: 'If I could work for anybody on the planet – a historical leader or a leader alive and kicking today – who would that be, and what are the characteristics that I admire so much?' (For the purposes of this exercise, you can't name yourself!) Take a moment and jot down their name, and some of their characteristics . . .

Great. This list provides some of the key attributes of great team leaders. Going forward, where possible, simply decide to adopt those habits/characteristics yourself. I hope that most of the attributes on your list will be covered in this section, but, if they aren't, doing those, as well as embracing the habits in the pages to come, will enable you to inspire a team to go above and beyond.

16

The two leadership titans:
'Vision' and 'Mission'

'Good business leaders create a vision, articulate the vision, passionately own the vision, and relentlessly drive it to completion.'

Jack Welch

Welcome to one of *the* most important chapters in this book

Many would argue that vision and mission are what leadership is all about – defining them *and* achieving them. (Unfortunately you can't just define them, Blu-Tack them to the wall, and then bolt for the nearest British Airways flight to Tahiti to let others do the work – although I'm sure some do.) With all the pressure to perform on this chapter, I hope I don't get writer's block and become all tied up in verbal knots. Here goes ...

Why is it so important to bring out the big guns: Vision and Mission?

The vision and mission bring a higher meaning to the work people do. As such, the leader should be in a position to frequently remind their team of its mission (or, in other words, the team's purpose or the value they bring the world) and the vision (the beautiful picture of what it will look like when they get there). Both should be inspiring and pull people out of the daily grind by reminding them that there is something bigger that makes their hard work worthwhile – noble even.

Let's park 'mission' for a moment and look at a story that illustrates the motivational power of vision (if you've heard this before, then please forgive me – but it illustrates the point very powerfully):

> In 1428, three stonemasons were working in Florence when an inquisitive visitor came along and asked them what they were doing.
>
> The first stonemason, who was despondent and uninterested, grumbled, 'What does it look like I'm doing? ... I'm cutting stone.'
>
> The second stonemason, though slightly less despondent, responded with a deep sigh, 'I'm building a part of a dome for some new building or something.'
>
> The third stonemason replied with a smile and excited urgency, 'I am building a beautiful cathedral that will be seen across the whole of Florence and will be used to glorify God for centuries to come.'

Whose fault is it that the first two weren't aware of the bigger vision? Although I wasn't in Florence in 1428, so can't answer for sure, the vast majority of the time it's the leader's fault for either not having a vision in the first place or not communicating it effectively.

If you're the leader, it really is your job to make sure everybody is equipped with a vision and a mission, otherwise you won't get the discretionary extra work inherent when people feel good about what they're doing and have purpose. It's a fair bet to say the third stonemason took fewer sick and personal days off work than the first two. A strong, well-communicated vision helps in all areas of the business, even absenteeism. As it says in the Bible, 'Where there is no vision, the people perish.'

Echoing this, James Kouzes, in an article for *Harvard Business Review*, wrote: 'Being forward-looking – envisioning exciting possibilities and enlisting others in a shared view of the future – is the attribute that most distinguishes leaders from non-leaders. We know this because we asked followers.'

To be a leader – you must lead people somewhere ...

'Leadership is about going somewhere. If you don't have a vision, how do you know where you're going?'

Jesse Lyn Stone

I'm sure I don't need to point this out, but the word 'leader' has the word 'lead' within it, and the word 'lead' implies that you're taking people somewhere; it implies a forward destination, which is why leaders do, to an extent, need to be forward-looking.

Taking your team forward takes vision – a vision for the future. Great leaders will usually they have strong and clear opinions on macro-future trends facing their industry, and where their visions for their teams and organisations sit within those trends. If you don't know your vision, where exactly are you leading your people? And if you don't know your mission (the *why*), then you don't really know the value of taking people there.

As Ken Blanchard once said, 'The greatest leaders mobilise others by coalescing people around a shared vision.'

So why do so few companies have a crystal-clear vision and mission?

There are many reasons, but the main one is that most leaders haven't got the foggiest clue what the difference is between a mission statement and a vision statement, and they are afraid to admit it! If this is you, your secret is safe – and welcome to the club; it's a *massive* club – in fact, it's such a big club that it probably needs its own mission and vision statement. But even if leaders *do* know the difference, there's a whole host of other reasons that they may not have been brought to life. Let's just look at a few of the most cited reasons why this valuable piece of paper with the mission and vision might be hidden under the Mars bar wrappers in the boss's second drawer:

- The leader is so impressed by the mission and vision statements which they developed, they deem them worthy of the highest strategic value and so keep both a secret from the organisation (you'd be surprised!).
- The leader thinks that if they talk about their vision they'll come across as fluffy – and so instead choose to bark orders about results and costs.
- The leader did a big launch, but nobody came.
- They did a big launch, but as the statements weren't cocreated with people in the company, they got no buy-in from the people on the front line actually doing the work.
- The vision and mission were written by the leader, but were so ridiculously out of touch with reality that the team would be better off doing without them.
- The vision and mission are so full of MBA jargon that nobody understands a word apart from the business degree intern.
- The leader wrote the mission and vision statements, and tested the statements on some of the staff, but the staff looked so bored that the leader decided not to spread the low energy any further. (A wise move.)
- The leader wrote the mission and vision statements, and tested their statements on some of their staff, but when the staff heard them they laughed so hard and so hysterically that the leader lost confidence and dumped the whole idea.
- The leader failed to connect the vision and mission for their team to the values of the larger organisation and as a result they never got off the ground.

Let's say you've circumvented all these common mistakes and you have a mission and vision for your organisation. There is now another test: does your team actually know what they are?

You might be thinking, Oh, sure they do, so let's test it. When you're back at work, grab five random folk and say to each shell-shocked person: 'Hi, I'm doing an important leadership test – are you able to tell me both the vision and mission of our organisation?' If they can, well done. But even if they can tell you, then just before you pass this chapter and collect £200, the final, final test is … when they tell you, do they speak with passion and gusto, or do their eyes glaze over or, even worse, does their whole body slump over in utter apathy?

If you nodded at any of the above or failed the second part of the leadership test, then congratulations, you've come to the right spot.

So let's clarify – what is a mission and what is a vision?

Mission

A mission statement should:

- define the purpose of an organisation – *why* we're doing what it is that we do
- encapsulate the value that the organisation brings to the world (a big one for hiring and retention)
- answer three questions: *what* it does; *why* it does it and *who* it does it for

Here are some real-world examples of mission statements:

To build a place where people can come to find and discover anything they might want to buy online

Amazon

Make natural, delicious food and drink that helps people live well and die old

Innocent Drinks

Organise the world's information and make it universally accessible and useful

Google

To refresh the world. To inspire moments of optimism and happiness. To create value and make a difference

Coca-Cola

Vision

A vision statement should:

- present a compelling vision of the future, usually five to 10 years from now
- be an inspiring mental picture that creates something specific for people to rally around and to aim for
- be specific so that people will know when the vision has been realised

Here are some real-world examples of vision statements:

A computer on every desk and in every home

Microsoft's vision (set by Bill Gates in 1980)

To develop the perfect search engine

Google's vision currently

To become the most competitive enterprise in the world by being number one or number two in every business in which we compete

General Electric's vision under Jack Welch

A world without Alzheimer's disease

Alzheimer's Association

We choose to go to the moon in this decade

John F. Kennedy (declared on 25 May 1961 and accomplished 20 July 1969)

Now let's talk about some best practices in creating these simple but all-powerful statements.

How to create a mission statement

Keep it nice and short

Remember, your mission statement is a declaration of your very purpose for existence – the value you bring to the world. If you notice it starts to resemble the front cover of *The Times*, then it's turning into a *user manual* not a *mission statement*. It's essential to keep it short – simply so that it can go viral; in other words, people can remember it easily and pass it along easily.

Use everyday language

When writing your mission statement, use the language that your team and your customers use on a daily basis, otherwise it's just MBA-speak, which, while making your board of directors salivate with excitement, will only baffle your front-line staff and your customers.

Show the value your organisation brings to the world

Make sure that your purpose is an inspiring purpose, i.e. it's based around the value that you bring to your customers and the wider world. This will help to make your employees feel good about the work they do, especially when asked what they do at dinner parties!

Conversely, saying your purpose is ... wait for it ... 'to make a lot of money for our company's owners' might inspire the owners, but nobody else (okay, it could also inspire the owners' wives or husbands too).

If you look at Innocent Drinks, its purpose is to 'make natural, delicious food and drink that helps people live well and die old'. That's very cool! I'd be proud of saying that. Making a ton of money is a by-product of having a meaningful vision and mission; it's never *the* vision and mission in its own right.

Mention those whom you love – your customers

Most organisations (well, the profitable ones anyway) exist to serve customers and are dedicated to meeting their current needs and their spoken or unspoken future needs. As such, the customer deserves to be mentioned in the mission of the company, or at least for it to be written around the value you bring them. After all, they are paying your bills.

How to create a vision statement

The vision must be inspiring, not factual or dull (as 85 per cent are)

Make the vision something that people are excited to achieve (like John F. Kennedy's) – make it a stretch. In doing so, it will imply the need for innovation and creative thinking (always good for the smart folk hanging around). A good test is, if it makes people yawn, shred it. After all, our overthinking, scheming Italian friend, Machiavelli told us: 'Make no small plans, because they don't have the ability to stir the soul.'

Spend some time on imagining and dreaming the ideal future too. As author and activist Gloria Steinem said: 'Dreaming, after all, is a form of planning.'

Again, like your mission, it can't just be about making money. Olaf Swantee, the CEO of EE (the biggest mobile network in the UK, which includes Orange and T-mobile), said in my interview with him:

> It is important to create a single vision for the organisation. It cannot be just a financial goal, saying, 'Our goal is to hit seven billion pounds – now let's print the t-shirts, and put it on all our baseball caps.' That type of vision just doesn't motivate the employees – top management maybe, but not employees. To get the employees behind your plan there has to be something more – a compelling vision and purpose.

Keep it simple and clear – 'a very simple tune to whistle'

Again, like missions, nobody remembers long visions – not even the CEO. If your vision is so long that you have to go and look it up before reciting it, you're missing the point. As Tim Waterstone, the founder of high-street bookshop Waterstones, told me: 'Your vision has got to be very clear, and the articulation of the vision has got to be very, very clear – to your staff and to the public. It's got to be so clear that everybody understands it. It's the secret of great politicians that they have a very simple tune to whistle.'

When creating your vision/mission statements, include your staff/team and then keep working until you're all 100 per cent confident in it

There's no point in having a vision and mission that nobody rallies behind. You will be able to get much greater buy-in from your team if you include them in their creation. So work with your team on developing the statements (and, whilst you're at it, you may as well do the all critical organisational values too – see chapter 35 for more about values). Keep working on them until you become passionate about them, only then will you a) be certain of the validity of them, and b) get real buy-in from the organisation/front line. Without that, you'll have diddly-squat in the way of buy-in.

Once you have your vision and mission – keep it front of mind

Whatever you decide about your purpose and vision, be it a cure for Parkinson's, to be number one in your market, to be the best at serving your clients – whatever it is, having found it, keep it in the front of your mind. By doing so, you'll be able to remind people why the hard work was worth it, and also to spur you and your team to greater things: you'll remind Joyce in accounts payable that she's *not just* processing invoices, but she's finding a cure for Parkinson's (or whatever the vision is). In other words, whatever it is – remind people they're not just cutting stones, they're building cathedrals.

Using vision and mission during times of change

A very powerful time to use your vision and mission is during difficult times. On this, the wonderfully whip-smart Carly Fiorina (former CEO of Hewlett Packard) told Stanford University's eCorner:

> As people go on in their lives, they're afraid of trying something new. Change is always resisted because people are afraid. If you are trying to drive a company or an organisation or colleagues through change, you have to know that they are afraid. You have to know the only way you can help people get over their fear is to give them a vision of something that's worth striving for, and worth taking a risk for.

Understanding, clarifying and communicating where you want your team to go, and the value they bring to the world by getting there, really is one of the most important things that you can do as a leader.

Finally, why don't you think about creating a mission and vision statement for yourself? As we saw in chapter 2, having a clear vision and mission can be as powerful on an individual level as it is for your team or your entire organisation.

The idea in brief:

- *To lead your team to a picture of the future is the most important job of a leader*
- *Remember to identify the 'cathedral' in what you do, and remind people of it every day*
- *The mission statement reminds people of the 'why' behind coming to work and results in discretionary effort*
- *Mission is the purpose of what you do*
- *Vision is a picture of what you want to achieve in the foreseeable future*
- *Make both moving, emotive and succinct and keep them alive for your team and throughout your organisation*
- *Having a living and breathing mission and vision isn't just management speak – it's a powerful force that can attract and retain your best people*

17

Charisma is attainable by all, not just a few

'Enrolling other people in your own enthusiasm is the essence of charisma in my mind.'

Mike Harris

Lots of people talk about the importance of charisma. They're right to. It is a very powerful tool. For leaders, it helps to engage an audience; it helps to get your message across; it helps you to gain willing followers; it helps you to hire talent; it helps you to retain talent – in fact, it helps with everything. The bottom line is: people prefer listening to and engaging with charismatic leaders.

Thankfully, charisma isn't magic dust only a few of us can possess; it too is subject to the law of cause and effect, i.e. if you do *this*, you can attain *that*. As such, it's attainable and available to us all.

Before we talk about how to get in on the charisma action, I have a business health warning for you: charisma is a powerful weapon but, like all weapons, it *can* backfire. So yes, you should make every effort to develop charisma, but you and the team around you should also be aware of its potential unintended consequences.

Charismatic leadership backfires when two things happen:

1) **The leader falls in love with the short-term popularity charisma brings and forgets about the long-term popularity results bring**

    Great leaders have charisma, but they also maintain an external focus: they put the focus on the vision, on their team, on their customers, on their results, on anything but themselves. In leadership *real* popularity should come from the results you bring (and charisma helps you bring those results), but not from charisma alone. Indeed, inspiring management consultant and author Peter Drucker said: 'Effective leadership is not about making speeches or being liked; leadership is defined by results, not attributes.'

2) **The leader has the wrong strategy and/or is immoral (think Hitler and Attila the Hun)**

    In this situation, the leader's charisma overpowers and silences other objecting voices, and so this leader gets their way, even if their course is immoral or wrong, because they're able to move the 'masses' to want to follow them wherever they're going. Supporting this point, Christian Stadler and Davis Dyer say in *MIT Sloan Management Review*, 'If your company is heading in the right direction, a charismatic leader will get you there faster. Unfortunately, if you're heading in the wrong direction, charisma will also get you there faster.'

So yes, bringing to life the charismatic person inside you is a good move. It's a powerful weapon in your leadership armoury, but just remember: a) don't fall in love with your own charisma – you'll still get fired if you have oodles of charisma but no results, and b) as Greg Dyke said to me: 'Nothing matters if you haven't got the right strategy – we're all buggered.' With these small business health warnings out of the way, let's focus on how you can increase your charisma.

How to up your charisma quotient

The good news is you don't have to do *all* of the below, but just a few will help you to up your charisma game (the only mandatory one is the first).

Be charming to all – not just a few

When a charismatic leader walks into the building, he or she is *as* engaging to the people on the front desk and the random selection of folk they share a lift with, as they are when they meet the CEO or Chairman of the Board. Why? Because they know that everybody, absolutely everybody, is an essential part of making the vision of the business a reality, and that everybody is worthy of respect, thanks and praise. Let me illustrate this point with the following account:

> An MBA graduate told me that her business professor gave everyone in her class an unexpected test in the last term of business school. It was one of the final tests that they were going to have to take before leaving to use their knowledge in the outside world.
>
> This graduate was conscientious and supersmart, and so she breezed through all the questions until she got the final one: 'Please give the name of the woman who cleans this lecture hall every morning, every lunch and every evening.'
>
> All the MBAs had seen this woman cleaning every day, but nobody could answer this final question. They knew what she looked like, but nobody knew her name, her life story or anything about her. So everybody handed the paper in without a single student answering the final question.
>
> At the end of the class the graduate asked the professor if the final question would go towards the final mark. The professor said: 'Of course! In your careers as leaders in business you will meet many people on your travels. But remember that everybody is significant. Everybody contributes in their own way to the goal of the organisation – they all deserve your attention and respect. By the way, when you see her this evening, her name is Helen.'

Never forget: politeness, respect, kindness and good manners are the bedrock of charisma, but also leadership success. Greg Dyke shared a similar message in my interview with him:

> If you walk in and you ignore the receptionist and you never say
> hello to the security guard, that's the story people will tell about you,
> and that's only negative. On the other hand, if you walk in and chat
> to everybody, say hello, go to the canteen and sit down with people,
> then that's the story people will tell about you – they'll say you're
> one of them. That's what it's all about – after all, we're all on the
> same side and we're all trying to go to the same place.

Lose your inhibitions (get out of your head and have an external focus)

A powerful tactic to build your charisma right now is to simply 'throw' your focus from yourself (the internal focus of being in your head) to being 'out there' (external focus). Don't engage in wishy-washy inner conversation, such as thinking about what you're going to say next or asking yourself, I wonder how am I doing, I wonder how I'm coming across, do I look silly in this tie, or with this handbag? Or even, did I defrost the chicken for dinner tonight? Instead, focus your mind on the person in front of you: focus on that conversation. It's a fact that you can't have two conversations at once without rapid diminishing returns on both. So get into the habit of just putting the focus on who's in front of you – and letting them feel the magic of attention.

I met with the Dalai Lama in Sweden (okay, okay, it was more of a 'shook hands with') and when I was standing in front of him I noticed that, for the time I was with him, I had 100 per cent of his focus and attention: he smiled, maintained eye contact, touched my arm, leant in and looked genuinely pleased to be meeting me. Master Charisma. Okay, so it wasn't just me – he had the same warm expression when he met the bloke after me, but hey, that's what charismatic leaders do: they focus on whoever they're with.

Taking it up a notch, when charismatic leaders are with their team, they're fully with their team; if they're at home with their kids, they're playing the clown role 100 per cent and being with their kids; when

they're on holiday, they're on holiday – and when they're with their customers, they're with their customers, putting themselves in their
customers' shoes, 100 per cent.

Be interested (and interesting)

Related to the above, but slightly different (because it's more of a long-
term play too), is the point that great leaders take a genuine *interest* in
you (not just in the results you achieve) – they want to know more about
you personally.

They take an interest in what drives you, what makes you unique,
what your motivations and aspirations are and your personal circumstances (i.e. family, background and so forth). And their interest is
genuine. By putting their focus on you, and building a genuine interest
in you, their charisma quotient goes through the roof. Nothing beats a
genuine interest in others – nada, zip. By doing this yourself, you'll also
become a much better listener, and you'll retain facts about the person
that you're with … they'll sense the curiosity.

Have enthusiasm and energy

There is a proven connection between enthusiasm and charisma. There
are a few signs of enthusiasm, notably: animation, wide vocal variety,
hand movements, energy, storytelling, eye contact, movement – all the
traditional characteristics of people with charisma. So how do you
awaken the enthusiasm within?

The first element is to have a genuine, palpable passion for whatever
it is that you do. The second is to let that enthusiasm come through in
your interaction with your team and infect them with energy (see chapters 1 and 2).

As we discussed way back in chapter 1, the most important thing you
can do to be charismatic is to really love what you do. You certainly
shouldn't be impartial, uninterested or even bored by what you do. So
if tomorrow morning you look in the mirror and say, 'I'm really not
inspired to go to work today' and if that goes on for a week, or a month,
then you might want to consider solving the problem, after all, it's hard
to be charismatic if you don't really give two hoots.

Smile

Time magazine mentioned that one of Nelson Mandela's most powerful leadership attributes was his 'incandescent smile'. I'm sure you can visualise his beautiful smile now ... got it? How charismatic is that! Why did he have this smile? Because he was enthused by life. So let's prove right now that you have one of the most important leadership qualities there is: I want you to give this page a *massive* incandescent smile (even if, like me, you're not absolutely sure what incandescent means). So go on, 1. 2. 3 ... Smile! Done it? Go on ... do it, smile – *there* it is! I can feel the charisma; I can feel the leadership quality.

No matter how tense things get, charismatic leaders never forget to smile and never forget their sense of humour. As you know, the Chinese are one of the greatest enterprise nations in history, and they have a proverb that says: 'If you cannot smile, do not open your shop today'.

Have the finest manners

Charismatic leaders know that manners maketh the leader. They're always themselves, but they always excel in the dying art of manners.

Compliment – but only when deserved

Insecure people don't compliment other people, conversely, confident and charismatic people do, so always look for the good in the person you lead – and let them know you see it. A genuine compliment goes a long way, so use them liberally, but don't overdo it – great leaders only compliment others on the things they see that they genuinely like – they're not sycophants.

Share something about yourself (deeper than just small talk)

It's essential that you talk to your team about things that are more meaningful than the weather. Heck, I'm an English boy – I love talking about the weather, but if you really want to truly get to know somebody, you have to take an interest in them (beyond their opinion of the week's weather and scandals in the tabloids).

As such, you should reveal something about yourself – an opinion, how you feel about something, a lofty goal, a wish, a little-known fact, an embarrassing story – anything that relates on a personal level. Critically, it also gives the recipient the permission to do the same. That's how you have a deeper connection. By the way, I'm not saying get too heavy straight away – that wouldn't work either, but it's a balance.

Use colour in what you say (humour, stories, quotes, wit and anything else you can to bring colour to your message)

Ronan Dunne said in our interview, 'My job is chief cheerleader and storyteller.' Like Ronan, great leaders use a few communication techniques, including stories, (appropriate) jokes, metaphors, quotes, sayings, terms – anything to illustrate a point.

As they're readers (remember, leaders are readers) and as they're learners, they always have a library of interesting facts, perspectives, opinions, insights from smart competitors and so forth to draw upon when they are looking for ways to communicate a message in a powerful, memorable way. Warren Buffett is reported to have a file of jokes stored away with his financial charts over in Omaha. As well as being a gifted investor, businessman, philanthropist, he's also a billionaire, stand-up comedian in the making – you can see it for yourself over on YouTube! So if you come across a humorous anecdote, funny quote or witty remark, it's not a sad, geeky thing to have a file that captures these.

Leaders also try to have a colourful voice (pitch, pace, pause and all that). Some, like Margaret Thatcher, have even gone for voice coaching – and it's not a bad thing to do. However, bear in mind a) you'll get what a coach is trying to teach you if you just talk like you do when you're telling a story to a friend at a bar (enthusiasm changes everything), and b) a lot of people I know need to go for listening coaching not voice coaching! That said, it's certainly got its place – as has, of course, public speaking (we'll elaborate on this more in chapter 26).

Very importantly ... have fun

If you're having fun, what happens? You'll display all the aforementioned charismatic traits automatically and people will be attracted to this playful side of you. Don't get me wrong, you need to take your leadership role and your team's results seriously, but you can avoid taking yourself too seriously, and have fun along the way. If you want another opinion, ask Richard Branson what he thinks about having fun! In his book *Screw It, Let's Do It,* he wrote, 'As soon as something stops becoming fun, I move on.' Perhaps more of us should do the same.

The idea in brief:

- *Charisma is a useful leadership tool*
- *Be charming to all, not just a few*
- *Lose your inhibitions and be present and focused on the moment*
- *Be enthusiastic about what you do and communicate that enthusiasm to your team – enthusiasm and charisma go hand in hand*
- *Get into the habit of smiling*
- *Be willing to share something about yourself*
- *Have fun: it's the best way to come across as charismatic*

18

Authentic leadership – the power of being 110 per cent you

'The single most important factor in leadership is authenticity, i.e. are you really who you are. The danger is as people go up the chain they start becoming what they think managers should be, as opposed to who they are – and that's a disaster.'

Greg Dyke

People talk about leaders having great charisma, but they also talk about great leaders having presence. While, as we discussed in the previous chapter, charisma is more about how a leader speaks or how they interact with others, presence is defined by how comfortable somebody is in their own skin; it's about authenticity – the fine art of just being themselves.

Without exception, all of the CEOs and business leaders I interviewed were engaging, natural, informal and real and encouraged those around them to be the same. I remember meeting Jacqueline Gold, CEO of Ann Summers, and she was just fun, relaxed, charming, and even cracked some jokes. When I interviewed Ronan Dunne at the London Stock Exchange he was exactly the same: informal, relaxed, quirky, fun, natural ... in fact, just like you and me.

In an article for *Forbes*, leadership guru Mike Myatt wrote: 'Average leaders are viewed as business executives, the best leaders are viewed as great human beings.' This couldn't be more true – authenticity is all about being human and real.

Sir Terry advised people to: 'Just be yourself, this builds trust, and leadership is all about trust.' It *does* build trust. Why? Well, as the people around you are smart (well, they should be smart – if not, dump the rest of this chapter and quickly head to chapter 22), they'll be able to see if you're *acting it* or really *being it*. They'll respect you much more, and trust you much more, if you're real.

Being real – in practical terms

How does it actually manifest itself in real life, this *being you*? It's all about being relaxed, transparent, honest and candid in your communications (see chapter 27), comfortable in your own skin, excited about the things that you're excited by; if you're quirky (join the club) then be quirky; if you love working alone, work alone; if you love surrounding yourself with noise, surround yourself with noise; if you have a passion for funky shoes, wow people with your funky shoes; if you love travelling, go travelling ... just be yourself.

So ladies and gentlemen, boys and girls ... don't hide behind cloaks – you'll be hiding your greatest asset.

Drayton Bird, the advertising guru who was loved by David Ogilvy, 'The Father of Advertising', said in our interview:

> You only come into this world with one thing: yourself. You only leave this world with one thing: yourself. I think in the intervening period, you should do as good a job as you can of being yourself, not of trying to be like everybody else, because if you're like everybody else, what was the point of you existing?

Identify your leadership values – the foundation for your brand

Look at the list of characteristics below and check which ones really come off the page – the ones you would want to be known for. Then circle anywhere from three to six and make them your own; own them.

Accountable	Confrontational	Excellent	Loyal
Accurate	Considerate	Excited	Mature
Action-oriented	Consistent	Expert	Mindful
Affectionate	Controlled	Exploratory	Motivated
Aggressive	Cool	Expressive	Nurturing
Agile	Cooperative	Extrovert	Optimistic
Ambitious	Courageous	Fearless	Organised
Analytical	Courteous	Firm	Original
Approachable	Creative	Flexible	Outgoing
Assertive	Curious	Focused	Passionate
Attentive	Customer-	Forgiving	Patient
Authentic	orientated	Friendly	Peaceful
Being the best	Daring	Frugal	Perfectionist
Benevolent	Debating	Fun	Persistent
Bold	Decisive	Futurist	Personal
Brave	Dedicated	Generous	Playful
Bright	Deliberate	Gratitude	Polite
Brilliant	Dependable	Happy	Positive
Calm	Determined	Helpful	Pragmatic
Candid	Different	Honest	Quality-
Capable	Diplomatic	Humble	orientated
Caring	Disciplined	Independent	Realistic
Charismatic	Dominant	Influential	Reliable
Cheerful	Driven	Innovative	Resilient
Clear	Dynamic	Insightful	Respectful
Clever	Easy-going	Inspiring	Responsible
Collaborative	Efficient	Intelligent	Results-
Committed	Emotional	Intuitive	orientated
Compassionate	Energetic	Inventive	Savvy
Competent	Enthusiastic	Kind	Self-confident
Confident	Even-tempered	Logical	Self-sacrificing ▶

Selfless	Straight-talking	Tough	Warm
Sensitive	Strong	Trusting	Winning
Servant leader	Successful	Trustworthy	Wise
Sincere	Thorough	Truthful	
Spirit	Thoughtful	Valiant	
Spontaneous	Tireless	Visionary	

Once you've got three to six that really sing to you, make sure you're living them every day; this is the essence of your own leadership brand – of being who you are, every day. This is a great exercise to do with your own team members too, to make sure that they're developing their own individual leadership brands.

Why do so many people find it hard to be authentic in a leadership position?

Here are a few common reasons:

They believe that they need to act how they think leaders should act

In my interview with Ronan Dunne he said, 'I think for everybody, leadership is and should be different, because for leadership to be successful it must be authentic.' One of the most important things to remember is that leaders come in all shapes, sizes and personalities. Everybody has their own strengths and weaknesses – it's just about maximising your strengths and playing the hand you were dealt. For example, some people think that extroverts make better leaders, while others say introverts are supremely better. The key, as *always*, is to recognise that both profiles have natural strengths and weaknesses, and like any game player or military strategist, the leader plays to their natural strengths.

Sir Terry Leahy said, 'My message to all the shy people out there is speak up and be yourself and don't try to be how you imagine successful people should be. Don't worry about being charismatic or saying the right things or being seen in the right situations just be yourself – but open up enough so people can see who you are.'

People want to follow people for a whole host of reasons (brilliant brain, results, determination, vision, incredible results, whatever), and it's not, repeat not, about beating your chest and being the loudest – it's just about working out how to get results, and playing the hand you're dealt to the best of your ability to get those results.

So don't change as you climb the ranks. If you've been appointed to a leadership position because of your team spirit, positive energy and open nature, don't turn into a total doorknob by becoming all aloof and superior! The whole team will say, 'Who's *this* guy/gal? Where has the person that we appointed gone?' Remember, leaders come in all shapes and sizes – that's the beauty of leadership.

They believe they can't have fun any more – after all, they're paid more to be dull

Another reason many people struggle to be authentic when they are appointed to a leadership position is that they try to behave in a way they think good leaders *should* behave. I've seen some of my crazy, animated friends put a tie on, go to work and become Captain Borealot. They're boring to their clients, boring to the team and boring to their boss. They leave their personality at home and they conform to what they believe good leadership should look like. As a result, they'll never be described as being 'natural' leaders. Why? Because they're not being natural. They'll also be exceptionally tired – it's exhausting pretending to be somebody else all day.

This is particularly common within large organisations (perhaps less so in small organisations, where the personality is somehow more encouraged – probably because the founder is wearing jeans and a T-shirt and being a big personality anyway!). But whether you're in a small company or big company, great leaders never leave their personality at home or act like a different person in the office ... and they encourage their followers to follow suit (excuse the pun).

You *don't* have to be dull as a leader. In fact, all the CEOs and business leaders I interviewed seemed to be having a blast (whilst being very serious about getting results). This positive energy is contagious. Moreover, it's been proven that having fun at work and making a profit go hand in hand – there's a causal effect and a direct correlation. This is why Sir Stuart

Rose (former CEO of Marks & Spencer) said to me, 'Business should be fun. What's wrong with having a laugh and a joke at work?'

They try to become a clone of the leader they look up to

Don't try to emulate other leaders – Alan Sugar, Donald Trump, Li Ka-Shing – you can never be as good as they are at being them, and they can never be as good as you are at being you. Just like designer clothes, people want the authentic you, not the fake you. You might look the part for a while, but under a bit of pressure and wear and tear, the seams will become undone! People will like you and value you a lot more if you're being real.

They change because they're on stage or in front of a camera

Other circumstances in which leaders feel compelled to undergo a personality transformation is when they get up on stage, or when the red light from a camera goes on and they're being recorded. But the greatest speakers are the ones who are themselves and act naturally wherever they are: up on stage, in front of the cameras, in the lift or in the boardroom.

I've interviewed some of the most successful leaders the business world has to offer and I can tell you that not one of them changed a single bit between when the camera was off from when it was on. Do you think Steve Jobs, a master of the stage, was trying to mimic some-one else or be anything but himself? Nope – he was just being Steve and that's what made him such a great speaker. So despite all the material out there telling you 'How to present like Steve Jobs', *don't* present like Steve Jobs, present like you!

The idea in brief:

- *Leadership is about authenticity; authenticity builds trust – the most important business asset in leading a team*
- *Being 110 per cent you is far better than being a 70 per cent watered-down version of yourself – people love people that are real and comfortable in their own skin, it gives them permission to follow suit*

- *Don't be what you think a leader should be like, just be proud of your strengths and play the hand you've been dealt the best you can*
- *Don't change when you're promoted; what made you successful before is what will make you successful now*
- *Never leave your personality at home; it's your most important asset*
- *Be the same person whether the cameras are on or off*

19

Use extreme optimism and realism to inspire

'A pessimist sees the difficulty in every opportunity; an optimist sees the opportunity in every difficulty.'

Winston Churchill

Leaders take people on a journey

Leaders take people from where they are now (point A), to where they want to go in the future (point B). But the journey to point B might be on very rough terrain; there might be obstacles in your way; you might hit Hurricane Whoever; you might take the wrong path and head down the wrong track for a while ... anything might happen – that's the fun of it; that's why it's so addictive – it's an adventure! So embrace it, don't fear it.

But when something happens or doesn't go your way, it's about how you react that counts. Some of your team, even at the slightest bit of bad news, might become hysterical, lose the plot and proclaim the end of the world is coming – but not you, sunshine! You're the leader; that's not what you do. After all, as you know, you set the example, so if you throw your papers in the air and freak out, everybody will throw their papers in the air and freak out – and that's not the best working environment.

The leader is the one who remains positive about getting to point B no matter what; they take setbacks in their stride; they know they can turn back if they go the wrong way and they're always positive that no matter how many turns or setbacks, they'll get to point B in the end.

Indra Nooyi, CEO of PepsiCo and one of the most amazing people alive today, said: 'If you can get people to follow you to the ends of the earth, you are a great leader.'

But let's forget the end of the earth thing for a moment; after all, a lot of leaders can't even get people to follow them to the kitchenette. So for now, let's take Sir Terry Leahy's definition of effective leadership, which is, 'Leaders get people to go further than they would on their own.'

To get people to go further, you need that positive attitude – to help them when they want to quit, to inspire hope for a better day. Andy Cosslett told me, great leaders 'provide hope that there'll be a better day' and, as Tim Waterstone told me, they 'have an absolute conviction that they'll make it in the end'.

Leaders are armed with both optimism *and* realism

Staying optimistic doesn't mean that you should exist in blissful denial, though. Indeed, if the road is rough, the road is rough; leaders don't pretend or say it's smooth. In fact, they speak with 100 per cent candour about the current situation – after all, they equally value honest and candid communications.

Leadership is about being 100 per cent truthful, honest and aware of the reality – and facing the truth head on. So, leaders don't turn their back on the reality and live in 'lah-lah and clap-clap land'; they're not quixotic and they're realistic about where they are today.

Reiterating this point, Mike Harris, who has built several billion-pound businesses from scratch, said to me:

> Leadership is, in essence, about balance. The one fundamental
> balance a leader has to maintain is between an apparently irrational

belief that you will get to that destination in the end – and you've got to totally transmit confidence in that to everybody around you (yeah, we're going to get there; that is where we're going; that is where we're going to get) – with a totally rational assessment of where we are today. You can't spin it, you can't put it under the carpet, you can't pretend it's not there – so you have to balance that rational assessment of where you are today with the apparently irrational confidence that you will get there in the end.

Of course, as a leader, it's far better to be an optimist than a pessimist, but being a realist with your feet on the ground is equally important. As the leadership guru John Maxwell once said, 'The pessimist complains about the wind. The optimist expects it to change. The leader adjusts the sails.'

How do leaders maintain optimism? They point to a better day

No matter how dire the situation, you can choose where you put your focus: on the pain of today, or on a brighter future. Brian Tracy said, 'Successful people think of the future, most of the time.' And Andy Cosslett nailed it when he said (in relation to the 2008–2014 economic downturn): 'You have to be very focused on today and making sure you're doing what you need to do in terms of managing your costs: thinking about the cash, thinking about your customers … but people also need hope for the future, and they need to know there's a better day.'

So keep inspiring people with how good it's going to be when you get to point B (your vision) and lift the focus from the day-to-day drudgery to the glory of days to come. As a leader, you have to believe your best days lie ahead of you.

Negative people have their place in life, but it's not in leadership

Imagine, after consulting with your team and your superiors, that you've just presented the top three strategic goals that you want to achieve in the year ahead. At the end of the meeting, your boss shouts out: 'What! You think you can achieve those goals this year? You honestly think you and your team can do that? You've got to be having a laugh – you've got to be winding me up. No way, José!'

Let's be clear: from that day forward, your boss's only contribution to the organisation should be to make sure that you, and all the other staff throughout the entire organisation, have a nice hot cup of tea in their hands whenever they feel like one. Leaders have to be realistic but *definitely* optimistic and that's all about attitude. In the words of Thomas Jefferson: 'Nothing can stop the man with the right mental attitude from achieving his goal; nothing on earth can help the man with the wrong mental attitude.'

It's all very well saying, 'be optimistic', but what if you just don't feel it?

What if you start feeling uninspired about the journey yourself? What if you're getting fed up of all the setbacks on the road to success, or to point B? What if your boss is treating you like a second-class citizen? What if you're having a tough time in your personal life? What if your commute was a total nightmare, culminating in you being stuck in the lift for the last three hours, desperate for the loo? Now what?

First, you need to remember that we all have bad days, as the saying goes, 'some days you're the pigeon, some days you're the statue, just live with it'. Second, you have to try, through emotional intelligence, and new habits of focus (below), to stay positive. If we agree with Tom Peters (author of *In Search of Excellence*) when he says, 'It's the leader's job to be the energy source that others feed from', then you can't afford *not* to stay positive. You're the person that has to provide this positive energy and optimism – especially when your team, or when individuals in your team, are feeling down or low in energy.

Note, this doesn't mean that you won't have bad days in the office, but, as soon as humanly possible, you'll shrug it off and get back to a positive state – if not for you, then for your team.

In General Colin Powell's book *It Worked for Me*, he explains how in the military it's drilled into you that in every difficult situation, you have to have a positive attitude. He was told:

Lieutenant, you may be starving, but you must never show hunger. You may be freezing or near heat exhaustion, but you must never show that you are cold or hot. You may be terrified, but you must never show fear. You are the leader and the troops will reflect your emotions.

So how do you keep spirits high, even if you too start having doubts about whether you'll make it? How do you keep your chin up when you face yet *another* roadblock or setback on your path to success?

This is what some of the great leaders do:

They look for the good

There is a powerful principle in life that states, 'You get what you focus on' or 'You see what you're looking for'. To illustrate this idea, try this quick exercise:

Don't read beyond the end of this paragraph for a minute ... Now, look around the room, or the train carriage, or the pub ... or wherever you're reading this book, and look for everything that you can see around you that's red; try to memorise as many red items as you can. Take a moment now; have a look around, and then come back to the book.

Back?

Great.

Now, without taking your eyes off this page, recall everything that you saw that was green.

Unless you're Rainman, it's much harder to recall the green things. Why? Because you weren't looking for green – you were looking for red. You see what you look for.

So, to build your optimism, put your focus on the good, not the bad. By celebrating and rewarding your successes, and seeing the good in all people and situations, you can change your outlook. Over time it will become easier and easier to do this unconsciously, because you'll have conditioned your brain through the power of habit and automaticity.

They reframe their thoughts – who knows if it's good luck or bad luck?

Tim Waterstone looked at the good when he was unceremoniously fired from WHSmith. He couldn't believe it – he was stunned. However, rather than seeing it as a negative event, he chose to see it as an opportunity by reframing his thoughts. (Remember Churchill's quote: 'An optimist sees the opportunity in every difficulty.')

Tim chose not to focus on feelings of rejection; instead, he focused on what he could do with his redundancy money and, with all the time now on his hands, how to launch a competitor to WHSmith. So he launched Waterstones to compete with his former employer, and compete he did – so much so, that 11 years later WHSmith decided they wanted to buy this genius and aggressive start-up company – and they paid a fortune. Tim told me in our interview: 'When WHSmith made their offer, which was a sensational offer at that time, I added one million pounds for the insult of being fired, and, I must say, hugely to their credit, the WHSmith Chairman laughed and added one million pounds to the price.'

Tim is now a multi-millionaire and one happy bunny. Why? Because he looked for the good and the opportunity in a bad situation.

So as a leader it's your job to remind yourself and your team that what seems like bad news or bad luck might actually be the beginning of a colossal and previously unseen opportunity. There's a famous Zen Kōan called 'Good luck or bad luck?' which illustrates this idea very powerfully:

Centuries ago there was an old farmer who had worked his crops for many years. One day his horse ran away. Upon hearing the news, his neighbours came to visit. 'Such bad luck,' they said sympathetically.

'Perhaps,' the farmer replied.

The next morning the horse returned, bringing with it three other wild horses. 'What great luck!' the neighbours exclaimed.

'Perhaps,' replied the farmer.

The following day, the farmer's son tried to ride one of the untamed horses, was thrown and broke his leg. The neighbours again came to offer their sympathy on his misfortune.

'Perhaps,' answered the farmer.

The next day, military officials came to the village to draft young men into the army. Seeing that the son's leg was broken, they passed him by. The neighbours congratulated the farmer on how well things had turned out.

'Perhaps,' said the farmer . . .

As a leader it's paramount that you keep this perspective when something seemingly 'bad' happens to you; you have to reframe it for yourself, your team and for your organisation. After all, who knows if it really is good luck disguised as bad.

They laugh and have a playful outlook

Having a playful outlook and retaining your sense of humour about life is a very powerful and productive state for leaders. Get into the habit of laughing and relaxing, and getting the team to do the same. Remember, there's nothing wrong with fun at work – you can still take your results very seriously. Being in a positive, playful state helps leaders think better (quite an important executive function to hold onto, you could argue).

They have something to look forward to (not just the end game)

Another great habit is to have something to look forward to in the future – for you and your team. Whatever that is – a company outing, an inspirational speaker, a weekly lunch – always have something to look forward to.

They manage stress well

We covered this in chapter 13, so I won't go into detail here, but it's essential that leaders do have a relaxation technique that works for them: it helps them stay Zen in the midst of battle.

They do things that inspire them, and have people around that inspire them too

One of the most powerful techniques for staying positive is (as we discussed in chapter 1) doing things that you love or you are passionate about. This doesn't just apply to your job. If you're positive outside of work it's much easier to carry that positivity with you when you come to work. Here's a great exercise to do to make sure you're as happy as you can be outside of work: keeping the 80/20 principle in mind, list all the activities outside of work that you love to do and which bring great joy and happiness to you. Then just make sure you schedule time for doing those things.

In a similar vein, as every experience you have is logged in your subconscious and therefore has an impact on your positivity, make sure you surround yourself with positive people, watch positive things on TV, listen to motivational tapes – in fact, anything but horror movies or hanging out with Bob who really irritates you (even after having tried to look for green not red in Bob!).

The idea in brief:

- *Optimists are better leaders – fact; so become one*
- *Followers rely on you to be positive, so you have to learn how to be that way, even if you're not feeling it*
- *It's a balance between optimism and realism – on the one hand, world-class leaders are very realistic (even if a situation is dire) and they speak openly about it, yet they're 100 per cent optimistic that they'll get everybody to a better place and reach their destination*
- *Thinking optimistically is a habit that becomes easier the more you do it – it's a muscle that can be strengthened, so if you're a grouch, be optimistic about your prognosis and don't despair*

20

Lead by example – be what you wish your team to be

'We don't just need leaders, but role models.'

Douglas Spence

There are a lot of leaders in the business world who know what great leadership looks like in theory, but unfortunately don't actually put this knowledge into practice. These are the folk who can inspire the socks off you in an interview (when talking the talk on vision, innovation, listening skills, authenticity, talent development and humility) but when you've hired them and they're actually doing their day job, they seem to have gone on a sabbatical to the Caribbean and sent their twin brother to work instead.

Many a CEO has been hired because of their Academy Award-winning leadership chat but fired because of their dismal ability to actually follow through on those inspiring sermons day to day. There's only one thing that counts – what it is that you actually *do*. As Mahatma Gandhi once said, 'An ounce of practice is worth more than tons of preaching.'

If you're trying to encourage a set of behaviours or values, then, as the leader, you *must* live and breathe those behaviours and values yourself. For example, if you want people to speak openly, speak openly; if you want people to receive respect, give respect; if you want to foster courage in your team, be courageous; if you want people to really focus on the customer, be seen to be focusing on the customer; if you want honesty, be honest; or even if you want people on the phone, get on the phone yourself. I can feel myself becoming slightly repetitive, whatever it is, in the words of Gandhi, 'Be the change you wish to see in the world.'

In my interview with Andy Cosslett he told me: 'Leadership is a mirror; if you do something, then your people will do the same thing; they just reflect it.' Matthew Key (who was CEO of O2 at the time) gave me another example of this:

> We have a saying in our organisation called 'Shadow of a leader' ... people watch what you do and how you behave. For example, when I go into a call centre or a retail store, I know that people will be looking at everything that I do, so if I happen to ring up one of our staff and say thank you for a job well done, all the managers in the business will see that Matthew Key has done that – and they will replicate it; they will copy that behaviour – and soon everybody will be catching people doing things right.

When you start walking the walk (standards, behaviours, values, or anything else you seek) your team will follow suit. This is how transformations happen and corporate culture *can* change – even in massive organisations. Defining your values and then living them through *example* will define you, your leadership and your organisation more than any other strategies in this book.

If you say something is important, but you don't *show it* in your actions, it's a disaster as far as leadership is concerned.

Here is an example of a disconnect between supposed values and actions. A few years ago, a supplier was trying to win our business in Germany. The managing director of the company heard that I was going to be in town and invited our marketing director and me out for dinner. For the first 15 minutes the MD saw the predinner spot as an opportunity to sell himself, the company, its product and the values of his organisation.

He spoke of a 'genuine love' for his customers and staff, 'an openness between parties and a mutual respect in all things' and 'a genuine ability to listen to his customers and seek to understand their bigger corporate objectives'.

It was music to my ears. I was taken in. Then all of a sudden he said (loudly): 'OY!' to a waitress walking past, and snapped, 'Are we invisible? Haven't you seen us here? Go and get us the menus.' He then turned back to me, turned his snarl into a smile and was once again charming.

Was this the same guy that was preaching mutual respect a few moments before? Was this the guy who was advocating respect to all stakeholders? Yes it was – but luckily I had seen the *real* him, before it was too late. He never got a cent of our business, but he did pay for dinner – and I made sure he paid the waitress a good tip!

The saddest thing about this MD was that he had had another junior member of his team there with him. What kind of example was that? If you've got a boss like that, get out before they influence you! As CEO EMEA of Saatchi & Saatchi, Robert Senior told me in our interview: 'When leaders are interviewing leaders they take them to a restaurant just to see how they behave. I think politeness in leadership is essential – I just don't understand what's clever about rudeness; it's so demeaning and I don't see the point.'

How to live your own leadership values

As the leader, you need to become a physical manifestation of the values that you deem are important. It's as true whether you're in the office or when you're on your sofa at home (especially if you're a parent!).

If you see a leader whose behaviour is congruent with the values or the behaviours that they're seeking, then it's beautifully inspiring for followers; if you see a leader whose behaviour isn't, it's quite repugnant. Between you and me (and the other readers), there are simply not enough inspiring leaders in the world – we need more ... You have the opportunity to be one of this group, and all you have to do is define a set of values (your own, your team's and your organisation's) and then demonstrate those values through your behaviour and the way you live your life. As John Quincy Adams (who we all know was the sixth President of the United States, or at least we do now!) said, 'If your actions inspire others to dream more, learn more, do more and become more, you are a leader.'

The idea in brief:

- *People remember you more for what you do than what you say – so even if you've got good leadership chat, it's futile unless it's turned into action*
- *If what you say and what you do lack congruency then you lack credibility*
- *Define your values, and then live them every day – and consider them at every decision*
- *Every interaction with any stakeholder is a great opportunity for you to reinforce your values and set an example*

21

Build a really, really hot team

'Having a disproportionate amount of talent is a great business strategy.'

Robert Senior

Ray Kroc, the guy who bought McDonald's from the McDonald brothers and turned it into a global empire once said, 'You're only as good as the people you hire.'

If you're a great leader with a dysfunctional Neanderthal-like team (well, if you were great you'd have already replaced them by the time of reading this), you're not going anywhere fast. If what Daniel Goleman told me in our interview is true (and it is): 'Leaders get results through others', then your people are your engine, and it doesn't take Paul Allen (cofounder of Microsoft) to work out that if you've got a low-grade engine, you'll get low-grade results. Your team is what defines you.

As Tom Peters said in our interview: 'At the beginning of the day, in the middle of the day and at the end of the day, you are as good as your talent.' He also reminded me that, 'When it comes to the importance of talent, sports managers get it, symphony conductors get it, but sometimes Big Business doesn't get it.'

Tom's right: if you were the manager of a football team, you'd *know* that you're only as good as the talent out there on the field; yet, often in the world of Big Business, the obvious link between the amount of talent you have and the amount of winning you enjoy is sometimes forgotten. Forgotten by many, yes, but not all. Make no mistake that in the minds of the greatest leaders and greatest organisations on the planet, it's never forgotten; the war for talent is alive and kicking. They focus on talent: spotting it, hiring it, keeping it, developing it and, if, God forbid, talent in their team or company should ever leave, staying in touch with it.

This is also why a leader who inherits a team (through mergers and acquisitions, promotion or whatever) often has many sleepless nights in fear that they're going to inherit a mediocre team, because that, in turn (until individuals are turned around or moved on), makes *them* mediocre too. The one trait you'll always find in great leaders is that they never abdicate, or rarely even delegate, the responsibility of having a great talent pool in their team. After all, talent is right up there in the Vital Few quadrant (see chapter 9).

So, as the leader, from this day hence, be totally and utterly obsessed with talent in your team. Here are some tips on how to surround yourself with the best team you can:

Hire people who are smarter than you

Yes, I know that might be tough – although I know some people for whom it should be a walk in the park ... Some leaders don't want to hire people who might turn out to be better than they are – just in case they turn out to be so good they might take their job.

Not one of the CEOs I interviewed ever thought like this. The leader's job is to build a great team, and they *have* to be better than you in the areas that you're hiring for. As Tom Peters said during our interview: 'If you are the boss, you are not paid to be the best sales person, the best accountant or whatever; you're paid to develop the best sales person, the best accountant.'

Echoing this, Ronan Dunne said: 'The people around me are much better at their jobs than I could ever be.' Ronan knows full well that, as the CEO of O2, he has to hire in or develop experts around him – and then simply delegate to these trusted people. As Ronald Reagan (fortieth President of the United States) put it, 'Surround yourself with the best people you can find, delegate authority and don't interfere.'

In my interview with Tim Waterstone he told me: 'Great leaders are really good at hiring people around them who are much better than they are in certain areas. Branson is an example of somebody who hires people who are much better than him in certain areas.'

The way to avoid hiring non-threatening employees, or what Steve Jobs called 'preventing the bozo explosion', is to always recruit to improve the average. If you always ask yourself the question, 'Am I improving the average by hiring this person?', you'll always hire well.

Regarding the idea that they might nab your job – if you're doing your job as the leader and hiring great people, you'll have great results; if you get great results, you'll get higher responsibility. You won't get moved out, you'll get moved up. You *will* however get moved out if you surround yourself with muppets who will never challenge you. Muppets are great to watch on TV, but they're not going to create economic value and, as their leader, nor will you.

Hire grade-A talent, not B or C or any other letter

Philippa Snare, the CMO of Microsoft, said in my interview with her: 'If you've got great leaders, you'll attract great talent: As attract As, but Bs attract Cs. As soon as you hire grade-B people, then you're in trouble.' Simon Calver (former CEO of LOVEFiLM) said bluntly, 'Never hire grade-B people in your management team.' Why is that? Well, great people are attracted to work for great people, not Mr or Mrs Remarkably Average. So, apart from the fact that grade-B people will produce grade-B results (or worse), in the future, if they start hiring for you, then they'll only attract other grade-B people (or worse) to join the team. As don't like working for Bs. As Steve Jobs once said, 'A small team of A+ players can run circles around a giant team of B and C players.' Amen to that.

Don't ever discriminate on anything but brains

Sir Stuart Rose told me: 'You need a good mix of people; you need thinkers, you need doers, you need people that are geeks and you need people that are generalists, you need people that are followers, you need people that are leaders, and it's getting that balance right that's the most important thing.'

The best leaders, or in fact anybody that's worthy of the title 'leader', don't discriminate on anything apart from, as Allan Leighton put it, 'the best brain for the job'. As such, they always have a beautifully rich diversity of age, gender, ethnicity and everything else in their teams, and these teams always outperform those that don't.

Anybody in this day and age who doesn't hire somebody on anything other than ability to do the job is living in a bygone era – indeed, it's most likely that their business will soon be confined to history too. The bottom line is, the best brains win – whatever packaging those brains come in.

Hire people who complement you – not (necessarily) people who are like you

If, at the beginning of Apple, Steve Jobs had partnered with *another* Steve Jobs, and not a technical genius like Steve Wozniak, you could argue that Apple wouldn't have ever gained traction. You see, Steve and Woz were a great combination because they complemented each other. Where Steve was weak, Woz had genius and where Woz was weak, Steve had genius.

In the same way, when it comes to your team, always hire people who complement you (counter your weaknesses – or maximise your team's strengths) and not necessarily people who are exactly like you. Very often, however, it takes a Jobs to be smart enough to realise the danger . . . You see, deep down, we all quite like ourselves. As such, we love it when we meet somebody who resembles us – who enjoys the same things we enjoy, has the same skills we have, believes the same things we believe – and yet they might not make the best addition to your team. Do you really need two of you, with the same skills, talents and beliefs?

So, if you find yourself gazing at the candidate across the table all dreamy-eyed thinking, *Aww they're just like me. Aren't they great?*, then make sure alarm bells are triggered *immediately*. They may be great, and they may be your organisational soul mate, but a) if you continue to drool you might freak them out, and b) just check that they're what the team *really* needs in terms of skill set and personality.

Be on the lookout for talent even when you don't have a gap to fill

Because talent is so vital to any team, great leaders (or organisations) don't wait to have a gap to fill before they start looking to fill it.

Let's imagine you've got a lady called Sally working for you. Sally, like the other sales folk, brings in about £50k per month in sales. One day Sally quits and gives you her four-week notice period. Despite being insanely busy, you then start looking for somebody else to fill the gap. You're fully aware that the chances are that Sally's sales for that month will go off a big white cliff, so it's panic stations to fill the gap quickly so as to not hurt revenues.

Within three or four weeks you've been through a billion CVs, you've had some telephone interviews, you've done first-, second- and maybe third-round interviews. Then, at the end of this hurried activity, you sit down, breathe, and reflect on your shortlist and think, *Bugger, they're all pretty 'blah'*. It happens. While you *can* go from zero to hero in four weeks flat, it doesn't happen often and is more dependent on the moons, stars and Lady Luck than your hiring skills.

So what do you do? Well, at this point, faced with a list of 'blah' candidates, one of two things happens out there in the world of business:

1) You decide *not* to hire Mr or Mrs Blah and extend the search to find somebody great (but bear in mind it will often take about four months to find a really good candidate to replace our Sally, in which case the actual cost to the business is £175,000, i.e. three times the £50,000 revenue that they'd have brought in if you had the seat filled and an assumed 50 per cent drop in Sally's performance during her last month).

2) Even worse, because of the time pressure to fill the gap, you end up hiring a total pinhead to join your (previously) grade-A team.

> The average of the team drops and members of your current
> team look at you, shrug their shoulders and say, 'Really?'

Trust me, if you're in this predicament it's better to have a gap than have somebody who's mentally out to lunch. Not having a pinhead join your team and not losing the respect of your other team members is far better, despite short-term cost. This gap-filling happens in all positions from the CEO downwards – and results in about 60 per cent of all bad hires being made.

The gold standard is to not get into this predicament in the first place. The antidote? *Always* be looking for talent, even when you're not hiring. Then, armed with a pipeline of potential grade-A hires, when you come to filling the gap, you'll be 70 per cent there already. (Just one of many tactics great leaders use here is to stay in touch with their previous star performers … You never know when they'll want to come back. It's a great habit).

Hire with your culture in mind

Richard Reed, cofounder of Innocent Drinks told me: '*You* don't create a culture; it's the people that you recruit. I personally believe the most important business decision one ever makes is who you get to join your business.' Jacqueline Gold's strategy, as she explained in our interview, is to 'employ smart, passionate people that I like – and people that I think will work together in our business culture'.

Richard and Jacqueline are absolutely right: you have to consider 'culture' as a factor when hiring. After all, the people you hire define your company's culture more than any other factor. To make sure there's a congruency, just a) know what your organisational values are in the first place (if you think values are something to do with economic value, then it's time to head to chapter 35), and b) make sure that your candidates have a similar set of values. This congruency is vital to keep and reinforce organisational and team values.

The interview process – how to get the most out of it

The most important decision that you can make is who joins your team – and in which theatre does this decision usually take place? Yes, the interview room. The reason that I mention 'theatre' is because some-times, some of the best acting in the world takes place in a job interview. (I've interviewed some people who could claim Oscars for their per-formances.) Far too many candidates either get hired when they shouldn't, or they don't get hired when they should. Yet great leaders are able to see beyond the act, to the real person – easily and mercilessly.

Let's look at some of the key criteria that will ensure you hire the best people whilst dramatically reducing (nobody can eliminate these alto-gether) hiring blunders.

Have checklists (at least for the essential attributes)

All the leaders we interviewed march in unison on one thing: people working for them must tick the essential, must-have checklists. If can-didates don't meet these key requirements then they won't get anywhere near the payroll.

What's on the must-have list? Top leaders usually cite three essen-tial attributes (the common denominators, if you will), which are: intelligence, enthusiasm and integrity. If you just hire on those three, then you can't go far wrong – in fact your candidate(s) will probably fly.

Jacquelyn Smith of *Forbes* magazine wrote about Jack Welch and *his* list of requirements:

> [The list] contains two flat-out must-haves, five qualities that are definitely-should-haves, and one very special quality that, while not exactly commonplace, is a total game-changer. The must-haves are high integrity and high IQ. The definitely-should-haves include: energy, the ability to energise others, edge, execution (the ability to get things done) and passion for both work and life. And finally, the 'game-changer' quality is what Welch calls the 'generosity gene'.

The 'generosity gene' goes back to what Ken Blanchard, author of *The One Minute Manager*, was talking about with the concept of 'Servant Leadership' (see chapter 2), i.e. a willingness to help others, not them-selves. This really is the foundation of exemplary leadership.

Reinforcing a lot of the above, Tom Peters puts enthusiasm above all.

Tom told me in our interview: 'There's nothing as contagious as enthusiasm – no enthusiasm equals no hire. You can help people develop anything, but you can't train enthusiasm; you've got to find it.' It's number one.

In a similar vein, as Southwest Airlines are famous for saying, they, 'hire for will, train for skill'. After all, you can acquire skills and new hires can gain experience, but it's much tougher to train attitude or character. Best to hire that first ...

Here is another interesting perspective from Randi Zuckerberg (Mark Zuckerberg's sis and successful businesswoman in her own right). She wrote an article for LinkedIn, adding another key box to tick: 'Could I see myself ever happily working for them? This means I want anyone I bring onto my team to be someone I can learn from, someone who inspires me, someone I can see taking the company to the next level. Someone I can trust.' What an awesome filter; if you can't see yourself working for your candidate, then, frankly, why would others in the future?

So make sure you have a 'must-have' checklist. It's an essential filter between the outside world and the beauty of that which lies within your organisation. Whatever other gorgeous human qualities you decide to look for, the three qualities that should definitely be on your list are: intelligence, integrity and enthusiasm.

Don't just listen to the candidate (or just trust your gut), seek evidence for the attributes that you need

People who present themselves well often get hired, but an ability to present well is sometimes confused with the ability to perform well. As Jon Moulton, Chairman of Better Capital, told me: 'One of the easiest things to do is to believe that a good presenter equals a good manager, and it doesn't.' He went on to say, 'Good leaders are nearly always good presenters, however, it doesn't always work the other way around, good presenters are not always good leaders.'

Often, the decision to hire somebody because of the way they present themselves at interview rests heavily on the leader's gut instincts. Even Jack Welch, who wrote a book called *Straight from the Gut*, warns of the dangers of using your gut when hiring. In an article for LinkedIn he said, 'When it comes to hiring decisions, doubt and double-check your gut. Go beyond the resumé. Dig for extra data. And don't just make reference calls; force yourself to listen, especially to mixed messages and unpleasant insights.' A sparkling interview technique doesn't always mean a candidate has the right attitude or the right results.

So how can you spot the phony? You have to a) look for *evidence* of previous results, b) look for *evidence* of attributes, and c) *test* for attributes.

Evidence of previous results

As we discussed previously, results don't lie and the great thing about historical results is that, unlike share prices or some other investments, they are a good predictor of the future. Results don't discriminate on anything other than incompetence. As such you have to really search out whether a candidate has a golden track record of delivering results. As Simon Calver told me: 'Why would somebody who hasn't had a history of overachieving suddenly overachieve with you?' Conversely, if somebody has had a habit of achieving great results then, as Simon points out: 'the chances are they'll do it again'.

As I mentioned earlier, it goes without saying that great leaders *never* discriminate on colour, age, sexual orientation, religion, appearance, choice of shoe colour on the day of the interview or *anything* else, except a historical tendency to achieve results. Why? Because this is an indicator of what a candidate is likely to do under their watch.

Evidence of attributes/characteristics/behaviour

If you have on your list 'creative thinking', 'ability to go above and beyond' or 'ability to lead a team' – then look for those qualities and seek evidence of the applicant having these attributes. You can ask them behavioural interview questions (where you ask them to recall an example of where they actually did what it is that you're looking for, e.g. tell me about a time that you had to stay calm under enormous pressure etc.) or you can actually test them (why not? It's always fun too).

So, if you're hiring for somebody who needs to be great on the phone – test them on the phone (interview them on the phone, or do role play with them). If you want them to be able to negotiate, the final interview phase should be how they negotiate with you on salary (and

don't get upset if they do a great job – hire them!). If you want the interviewee to be able to think on their feet and communicate well under
pressure, test them on that.

For example, if you're seeking strong communication skills and the
ability to cope with pressure and think on their feet, you could try this:

> Gemma, you've done really well up to now. If it's okay with you, I'd
> like you to choose a business skill that you're passionate about, so
> that could be time management, or project management, the
> essence of leadership, or something like that – and then I'll call
> another two or three colleagues into the room, and I'll invite you to
> stand up and give us a five- to 10-minute training session on that
> subject. Don't worry, we'll leave you alone in the room for 10
> minutes first with a pen and paper to prepare, and then we'll come
> back in for your presentation. Is that okay?

If your candidate bolts for the nearest exit still carrying the *Hello!*
magazine they picked up at reception, that will tell you all you need to
know.

Whatever the skill is, there's nothing like testing for it in a real-life
environment; it's a great insight as to what you're going to get. Great
companies like Facebook are actually hiring people on short-term con-
tracts before a big hire (this is like living with somebody first before
asking them to marry you – not traditional, but there might be some
merit to it).

Here is an example from my own career of a candidate demonstrat-
ing vital qualities during the hiring process:

> *A few years ago I went to a Chinese Graduate Recruitment fair in
> London with two of my colleagues. We wanted to hire smart Chinese
> nationals with excellent English and a passion for business.*
>
> *That day we met with over 700 students and conducted three-minute
> interviews with them all. By sunset a) we were so tired and looked so
> rough that we could have been on an episode of* The Addams Family
> *(even the Chinese graduates we were interviewing asked if we were
> okay), and b) we had a stack, and I mean stack, of resumés.*

Five days later, still in a state of shock, we started to decipher our notes to hunt for the potential stars. Finding the winners in that pile was literally like looking for a needle in a haystack (a cliché – but very true).

Later that week I was at my desk, focused on something totally unrelated, when I got a call from reception and Helen said, 'A Jenny Zhang is at reception to meet with you'. I said, 'Thanks, but Jenny, Jenny Who?' Helen said, 'Jenny Zhang – supposedly you met her at a recruitment fair and she's turned up to make sure you don't miss out on a big opportunity'. I was about to be all prim and proper and say: 'Sorry, but I won't entertain unannounced visits', when I suddenly thought, Hold on, this is a seriously 'out-of-the-box-do-whatever-it-takes' action. I mean, this was courage – on the verge of audacious. How insanely awesome. So I agreed to meet with her.

When I met her, she said: 'I know that you were not expecting me, and you probably can't remember meeting me at the fair, but I wanted to come and help you … I wanted to make sure you don't miss the opportunity of hiring me. You could easily miss me in all the CVs you have.'

I was wowed. Utterly wowed. I hired her on the spot – she turned out to be one of the group's best hires. In that single courageous act, Jenny showed she a) would do whatever it took to get results, b) was an original thinker, c) could empathise with my unspoken problem of having so many resumés, d) had heroic amounts of nerve, and e) knew what it takes to be remarkable and stand out from the crowd … all of which we could use when we launched in China.

So whatever it is you're looking for, really check to see if your candidate lives and breathes the attributes you seek.

Conduct 360-degree interviews – i.e. get your team's opinion

When you're hiring, it's always essential to have a second interview and a second opinion (just in case they're having a *really* good day and you're having a *really* bad day!). A lot of companies (such as Google) are going further and conducting '360-degree' interviews. These interviews are essentially where a candidate is interviewed by their prospective boss, peers and anybody who will work for them if they are hired. Getting the opinion of one or two of your current team is very smart, but getting perspectives from all angles is even smarter – it's great to involve the people who will actually report to the candidate in the hiring process so they can ask, 'So why would I want to work for you?' and hear the answer straight from the horse's mouth.

To find the truth, go deeper

I was once asked to sit in on an interview to give a second opinion on a possible sales director hire. During the interview I asked the candidate: 'Are you into self-development and continuous learning?'To which he replied, 'Sure, absolutely. I love reading. I love learning. I'm obsessed with business books and sales books. I *breathe* the wisdom from those books – that's pretty much all I do in my spare time.'

Knowing that follow-up, probing questions reveal the truth, I said: 'That's so cool – we love that here. Can you please tell me the name of the last sales or business book that you read, tell me who wrote it, what was one or two of the key lessons that you learnt from it – and whether or not you've been able to adopt those lessons in real life yet?'

He turned a pale grey and, after a minute of staring at the ceiling for divine help, said unconfidently, 'The great habits of seven people?' (I believe he was referring to *The 7 Habits of Highly Effective People* by Stephen Covey). When I asked him to tell me about one of the habits of these seven people, he couldn't name one. It turned out that he hadn't read it, but claimed to want to read it in the future. This guy lacked integrity and was out.

As Jon Moulton says, always 'go one layer deeper than their presentation and probe to find the truth'.

Great leaders hunt for a candidate's intrinsic motivation

The best people to hire, and the best people in your team, are people that have massive intrinsic motivation, i.e. they know exactly where they want to go in life and they (and you) can see how the job you're offering is going to enable them to get there. Randi Zuckerberg wrote on

LinkedIn: 'Obviously, I'm looking for a great, well-qualified candidate, but just as important is their desire to work for my company specifically.'

So, for example, if you're hiring a marketing manager for a publishing company and in the interview you ask them where they want to end up in five years (a personal vision, if you like), and they say, 'I want be a yoga instructor', then you should applaud their honesty but realise it's a safe bet to assume they're going to be taking the job to pay for their advanced yoga courses. Far better to find somebody that either loves marketing or publishing and has decided to climb up in one or both of those fields.

The bottom line is – if you can't figure out how your job is going to help them get to where they want to go, don't hire them. They'll take on the job to fund their other passions, but you're certainly *not* their passion, and they won't go the extra mile for you. So don't hire them – allow them to go off and get a job that they *will* be passionate about. Not hiring them is a win-win for you both.

Conversely, if you can see why what you're offering them can get them to where they want to be in five years, then that's very powerful, especially when it comes to actually getting them to join the team.

Don't forget: sometimes misfits are worth their weight in gold

As a leader, you'll know the power intuition has to play, so on the occasions where you find evidence of the attributes you seek in a candidate who doesn't quite fit with what you initially had in mind, be ready to throw out everything, including checklists (except the integrity one), and make crazy appointments if you really feel it ...

On this, Jon Moulton said to me: 'How do I select the very best? The very best are when I've made wild hiring decisions ... I've worked with some excellent people over the years, and some of those would never have fitted any reasonable HR department's view of what I should have hired – most really good people are actually quite unbalanced.' And you can't put 'must be unbalanced' on any candidate requirements!

I know this has been a long chapter, but if you only have one take-away from this book, it should be to simply remind yourself every day that the quality of the individuals on your team determines your success as the leader more than any other factor.

The idea in brief:

- *You're only as good as your team has the potential to be, so be obsessed with talent – spotting it, hiring it, keeping it*
- *Sports managers know it's all about talent; sometimes this truism eludes the business sector – don't let it miss you*
- *Hire the best people possible; if they're way smarter than you, that's a great thing*
- *Never hire grade-B or -C people to your management team*
- *Build a well-rounded team that's not just made up of folk that are like you*
- *Keep an eye out for talent, even when you're not hiring*
- *Arm yourself with checklists of essential, must-haves and nice-to-haves (don't forget the big three: intelligence, integrity and enthusiasm)*
- *Don't just go with your gut: look for evidence of what you seek – both results and attributes*
- *Test for what you seek*
- *Check for a candidate's intrinsic motivation, i.e. how your job will help them achieve their goals*

22

Get the best talent available to join your party

So now you've found some grade-A talent, how do you make sure you actually get them to join your organisation? After all, for the very best people in the market, you are, as Tom Peters says, in a 'Talent War'.

Once you've got a great person in an interview, your job as the leader is to then sell your company – the vision, the purpose, the team, the leadership development, the role – in fact, sell anything to get a bite. Hear ye, hear ye, if the interviewee is great they will have other options, so you have to act fast and decisively.

To prepare yourself for the day that Mr or Mrs Legendary Oh My, They're Just Perfect walks in, you'll need to make sure you can answer the following two questions – and be able to answer them for 'one minute without hesitation, deviation or repetition' (like the Radio 4 game, for any British readers).

Question 1: 'So why is your company a great place to work?'

Try it now ... can you answer this question for one minute without hesitation, deviation or repetition? (Talking about deviation, I'm deviating for a second: if you struggle with answering this right now or find yourself being able to answer *this* question more easily: 'So why is your company a rubbish place to work?', then you've got some career decisions of your own to make.

So, back to the original question. Here the talent is trying to find out the answers to questions that are really important to him or her, notably (these are just a few ideas – you have to find out what's specifically important to them):

- What's the vision and mission of your company? (If you're unclear, go back to chapter 16)
- What's the purpose beyond making money, i.e. what good do you do in the world?
- What's the actual job like, will it be challenging/rewarding?
- What's the workplace like – is it fun, boring, creative, cool?
- What's the rest of the team like – are they like the candidate?
- What's the training and development like?
- Do you/the organisation really care about staff?

Genuine enthusiasm sells

This is your opportunity to sell your company and inspire and excite a potential employee about the prospect of working with you. They're also looking to gauge your enthusiasm – if you don't care, why would they?

If you can't present your company with enthusiasm, chances are that after offering them the job, you'll get a response like, 'I've been offered something else, but thanks for the opportunity of meeting you.' What they're actually saying is, 'Good luck, thanks for the free coffee, but no way am I joining Loserville.'

However, the key, as with everything, is finding out what motivates *them*, and matching what they're looking for to what you have.

Just don't oversell and do remain candid

Simon Calver said to me: 'You've got to be incredibly careful when you're recruiting talent that you're not overselling; this provides a disconnect in the early days.'

Although you need to present your company in the best possible light, it's also important to be honest in a hiring situation. No department or organisation or team has 'reached perfection' so it's fine to say, 'These are some great things about us, these are some of the things that we're trying to improve.' The interviewee will applaud you for your honesty; as you know, it's the sign of a great leader to have the confidence to say it as it is – it builds trust, and so, rather than repelling the candidate, you'll attract them.

It goes without saying, but don't make stuff up (exaggeration, denial). If you say, 'We all have one day a week for creative thinking and there's a free buffet bar that you can help yourself to – it's easy to get fat here, though, ha ha ha ha', and the reality is that nobody has a single second to spend on thinking, and that the free buffet bar is, in fact, buy-your-own-flipping-food-there's-a-supermarket-down-the-road, then by lunchtime on Day One they'll know you're a lying son of a gun. Not the best start then.

Your organisation's previous success is an indicator of its future success

The best way to attract great talent is to be a great company with a great reputation – and the best way of doing this is to get amazing results (which is what Part Three is really all about). If your company is known for doing great and innovative things, then because of the social world in which we live, your grade-A-er will know this and your reputation will be on your side. If your company is growing at rocket-speed, then you'll also attract a heroic amount of talent. Talking to Harvard Business School graduates in 2012, Sheryl Sandberg (the legendary COO of Facebook) said, 'If you're offered a seat on a rocket ship, don't ask what seat! Just get on.'

Social proof works

In my interview with Ronan Dunne, he told me about his employees at O2:

> They admire who we are and what we stand for as a brand. They admire our corporate and social responsibility ... We have within our company people who are in love with the brand, and I mean that – who absolutely love the brand ... I would say with confidence that if asked at a dinner party, 'Who do you work for?' [out of the 11,000 that work for us] 11,000 people would be proud to say O2.

Giving potential candidates the opportunity to meet other members of your team is a great way to sell your company. Even if they don't ask you to meet their future colleagues, they will be thinking, What are the other folk on the team like? Are they fun to hang out with? Are they my kind of people? So if you haven't got anything to hide (like a vicious team gnashing their teeth at each other) then do roll in the troops. It shows confidence and transparency.

With this in mind, can you imagine how easy it is to get talent to join O2? A candidate would be able to speak to any of 11,000 people and have them say, 'Yes, join up; it's a great career move – you'll love it here'.

Question 2: 'So why are you a good guy/gal to work for?'

This question is sometimes asked, but even if it's not asked, it's *always* thought. So you should answer it anyway. When it is asked, the question has flummoxed, embarrassed and even caused offence to hiring managers around the world. Yet it shouldn't. It's a *great* question that's on the mind of all great hires. Never forget the truism, 'Great people want to work for great people.'

Smart talent knows that there are a lot of rubbish managers/leaders around. A Gallup poll of more than one million employed US workers concluded that the number-one reason people quit their jobs is a 'bad boss or immediate supervisor'.

You as the candidate's boss will play a massive role in their new life, so why wouldn't they want to know why working for you will be so great? Bottom line is, you need to be able to fluently answer this question. Being able to do so is not a sign that you're an egomaniac; it's a sign of a confident leader – somebody who is aware of their strengths *and* weaknesses and can even articulate them to their team (in fact, mention your weaknesses – people love honesty and 'humanness' in their leaders).

Final points on attracting your A++ candidate

The two questions just covered are pretty much all you need to get the best, but it's worth pointing out three final points:

1. Make sure you know your candidate's aspirations

If you ask the talent where they want to be in five years' time and you get the real answer, then you can a) show how you can bridge the gap, and b) impress them with the question and the concern. This is showing a concern and a care for them and their future (we've discussed this at length as it's a powerful retention tool).

2. Emphasise how you're going to make them a rock star

Great people always want to learn and acquire new skills – they're hungry, hungry, hungry. So show them your training programme (if you have one) and show them how what you're offering them will be able to help them get to their ultimate destination. Not only will you show you care about this person's future (and have actively listened), but you've also shown how they can reach their goals. The promise of learning and development opportunities is like mind-candy for an ambitious person.

3. Care about first impressions – or any impressions for that matter

Great leaders will court great people. Yes, hiring the best of the best *does* have similarities to dating. When I was the Regional CEO in my former company, I remember visiting one of the international offices I was responsible for. During the trip, I heard about a legendary product person called Susan (names in this story are fictional, but everything else is true) who was working for a competitor. Susan's reputation was what business fairy tales are made of. We'd been talking about her for months and we knew she was doing amazing things at our competitor. Despite all this, she had a great reputation for being humble, innovative and loaded with leadership potential.

One day I was visiting the office and I spotted Susan in our reception area; it looked like she'd been waiting there for a long time, so I went up to her and asked if I could help. She replied with, 'Don't worry, they know I'm here – I have a 6.00 p.m. meeting with Tom.' I looked at my watch. It was … 6.42 p.m. I smiled, showed her to the boardroom, got her a coffee and asked her to just wait a moment longer. Underneath my calm exterior I was going ballistic, so much so that when I saw Tom I had to use everything I'd learnt about emotional intelligence to stop myself from losing the plot (thank God for Daniel Goleman!). What message was Tom sending to Susan keeping her waiting 42 flipping minutes? It was disrespectful, unintelligent and downright unacceptable (I pointed this out to Tom and he agreed in full – Tom was a great leader and took the reprimand well, and I'm sure (hope) never did it again). Eventually we got Susan to join the team, but we had a lot of work to do to undo the damage caused by her first impression. First impressions matter.

So yes, attracting talent is one of the most important skills that great leaders need to acquire. This is why I have devoted not one, but two chapters to it. The only thing I'd say to conclude is put talent at the top of your agenda; if you hire grade-A talent, 60 per cent of your leadership job is done.

The idea in brief:

- *There's a talent war going on, so when you see grade-A, act fast*
- *Make sure you can answer the questions 'Why would I want to work at this company, or for you?'*
- *Don't oversell for talent to join you – authenticity and integrity are attributes of leaders, and that's you*
- *Remember, first impressions matter*

23

Motivating and retaining talent – love your stars (but inspire 'em all)

'Great leaders are berserk about talent.'

Tom Peters

There's a term that's thrown around like a rag doll in business: 'Our people are our greatest asset.' What? ... *all* of your people are your greatest asset? I don't know about you, but I, like most, have made some great hires, some average hires and some remarkably rubbish hires. I'd never call the folk that came from my rubbish hires 'our greatest asset'. In fact, visualising a few of them now, I'd say a few sat in our greatest liability camp!

On the flip side, the great hires who result in your good, great and rock-star performers really *are* your greatest asset. So let's dedicate this chapter to these beautiful men and women (well, they may not be beautiful, but you know what I mean).

Before we talk specifically about your stars (or the Vital Few in the 80/20 world), it's worth spending a moment on general team motivation. After all, your stars are part of your team and motivating the team as a whole will also retain your top percentile.

To build a motivational workplace and be a motivational leader: view your staff as volunteers

Rather than listing everything that a leader needs to do to motivate, I'm going to ask you to reflect on this quote from influential management consultant Peter Drucker: 'Accept the fact that we have to treat almost anybody as a volunteer ...'

Huh? Well, to find out what motivates people, consider this question: 'If you had to motivate people to turn up to work, but you couldn't pay them a dime, a pence, a cent, a peso, a rouble, a yuan, a rupee, a rand or anything else – then what would you need to provide them with in order for them to still come to work?' (You can ask this question from both an organisational perspective, i.e. what the organisation would need to provide, and from an individual leadership perspective, i.e. what you would need to provide as a leader.)

You see, as Peter Drucker reminds us, money alone cannot be relied upon to be the differentiator that keeps your talent. Why? Because *any* employer can pay your staff money. So it can never be *the* thing (*a* thing, yes, but not *the* thing) that retains your talent. If you rely on money as your only, or primary, retention device, then not only is that an expensive game but you will find your best talent *will* walk. Yet so many poor leaders and organisations rely on cash to keep their folk. It's weak and ineffective.

Having done this before with many teams around the world, some of the top answers you're likely to arrive at are:

- *The mission* – I'd only want to work for you if we are really doing something great in the world and changing people's lives, I'm proud of what we do and the difference we make
- *The vision* – I love where the organisation is going, and would love to see us get there
- *The competition* – I know we're the underdog, but I really believe that we can become number one by really pushing our USPs and our strategy
- *The learning* – my skills and talents are being developed, I get honest and fair feedback and I often get called upon to try new things that are in line with my aspirations

- *The team* – we have a great community spirit in the team and we have great fun
- *The leader* – our leader is smart, authentic, honest and has made the effort to really get to know me. I feel like my leader and my organisation care about me
- *The praise* – we've got a culture of 'catching people doing things right' and my boss is very generous with verbal and written praise. He/she gives us credit when things go well and isn't so quick to blame when things go wrong
- *The innovation* – we're always trying new things and it's a dynamic and vibrant place to work
- *The challenge* – we have goals that are a stretch and it's great trying to achieve them. I'm encouraged to leave my comfort zone and challenged to do new things
- *The freedom* – I'm allowed to get on with things and use my own mind about how to get to places
- *The job* – my role is aligned with my strengths and I'm proud of the contribution I bring
- *The culture* – it's a buzzing place to be and the organisation really lives their values internally as well as externally
- *The communications* – I am kept abreast of where the organisation is going and I know how my role fits within the bigger picture. If there's bad news, I know we'll hear it straight

But don't take my word for it, do it for yourself and see. If, after you've done this exercise, you stand back and look at the list, you'll see it contains all the attributes that make for great leadership, and all the attributes you'll need to create a motivational environment. The key is then to take a few of the most important and make them a reality for your team. Now, back to your stars …

Stars are often ignored and left alone in the corner!

Believe it or not, very often the stars get ignored. How could that possibly be? Well, here are two reasons why they don't get talked to much:

1) The leader says, 'They're doing just fine, so leave them to get on with it ...' What the star hears is, 'You don't value me or invest in me – I'm gone.'

2) The leader says, 'I'm too busy fixing the problem people, and the stars don't need fixing ...' Again, all the star hears is: 'You don't value me or invest in me – I'm gone.'

As leaders, we all get swamped by 'noise' or business administration. (Don't be a Master of Business *Administration*.) It's easy to chase problems as opposed to maximising strengths and augmenting opportunities. However, if you ignore these valuable folk, there's lots of competitors that will show 'em the love.

Here are some other important tactics pertinent to your high flyers:

Get to know your stars personally

Great leaders understand how valuable it is to get to know their stars (and all their team) personally. They'll remember their birthdays (or they'll try to, at least); they might even know the name of their partners (or will try); they'll encourage them to quit bad habits (if they have any); they'll remember the name of their kid or kids (or will at least try).

Get to know what really motivates your stars

Everybody has different motivations and different goals in life, so you *have* to spend time with these folk to get to know them personally, deepen your relationship and get to know their key objectives. When you meet with them, genuinely listen. There's no point in paying your star performer, Susan, another £10,000 a year if actually all she wanted was to find a mentor internally.

Business health warning: don't automatically turn your star performers into leaders/managers

Following on from the point above, one of the saddest events in business today is when an individual star performer gets lifted up from their lovely hands-on job and is promoted to a management job they don't want. Very often, the star performer wonders what they did wrong to deserve this 'people-related-nightmare-role'.

If a star performer isn't suited to management, or it doesn't play to their strengths or passions, don't force it down their throats. By doing so you'll have done two *very* costly things, 1) you've effectively lost a great star performer from your team, and 2) you'll have created an uninspired, demotivated and probably lousy manager!

This reminds me of something one of my whip-smart friends Christian Cormack, a senior guy over at one of those FTSE 10 companies, told me last week: when it comes to motivation, the phrase 'treat others as *you* wish to be treated' should be changed to 'treat others as *they* wish to be treated'. Quite an enlightened thought, methinks.

So instead of sending your stars down the management track, promote them in ways that suit their strengths and meet their personal goals. You could make them into thought leaders, area experts or mentors (and give this career track equal weighting to management positions) but, whatever you do, don't force people into leadership positions if it's not what they want for themselves.

Be aware of their goals and how you can help them reach them

If you know where your stars want to get to (their own ambitions and aspirations) and you can help them get there (perhaps by putting them up for projects, exposing them to new experiences, making introductions etc.) they'll love you dearly and will be massively motivated. Also, if you can align their passions and aspirations with their day jobs, then that is one of the most motivational things that you can do for any follower.

When I asked Daniel Goleman about this, he said: 'I think motivation has to be true – that you need to align the desire to improve with your own sense of values, of purpose; what you really feel is important. What are your dreams? Where do you want to go in life?'

Make sure the mission and vision is alive and kicking, i.e. the value the company brings the world

We talked about this in the chapter on vision and mission, but sometimes the difference between whether your stars stay or go is whether they feel they're providing some value to the world. It really is a powerful retention factor. So make sure that your vision and mission (beyond making money) is clear and carried through in everything your team does.

Higher meaning = higher retention.

Give continued recognition – and praise

I once heard a woman say to her husband: 'You never tell me you love me any more', to which he replied, 'I don't need to tell you – you know I love you'. This not-such-a-Romeo fellow is missing the point.

This communication trap of 'assumed' knowledge, is one that leaders can often fall into. As a leader, it's incredibly important to give positive feedback to your team; don't take them for granted. For some of your stars, it's the feedback in the early months and years that has actually put them in that box in the first place. No matter how many times you say it, keep saying it. Recognition is like vitamin C – *you need to give it out every day*.

Make sure they're being developed

Speak to any smart, high-performing person and they'll pretty much all say, 'I love being challenged'. Yet for leaders, if a star is performing well, it's tempting to keep them sitting doing what they're doing *for ever*. But stars often don't enjoy sitting in their comfort zone too long – getting them out of that will give them a rush again.

As a leader, it's your job to set challenging goals and provide challenging experiences for them. They'll love you for it.

Make sure the cash is appropriate

Although money probably isn't the core reason why these folk work for you (see the volunteer exercise at the beginning of this chapter), money *is* important to them. People who say that money isn't a motivator are living in Cloud Freako Land. (If you don't believe me, try telling them you're not paying them for the next few months and watch the fireworks!)

This is obvious, but the point is, it doesn't matter what your finance department says, your top performers should *always* be earning a lot more money than your average performers. In fact, all great leaders are willing to overpay for their great staff (they are the Vital Few who will make all the difference).

To give you an example of this, Matt Lauer, the famous NBC anchor guy, once told CNBC about a time he met Jack Welch in New York for lunch:

> I'll never forget a lunch one time with Jack Welch in the General Electric dining room upstairs here in Rockefeller Center – and in the middle of the lunch he took out an envelope from under his placemat and he slid it over and he said, 'Congratulations'. I'd only been at the company for about two or three years at that point, and I opened the envelope right in front of him; it was a lot of restricted shares of GE stock and it was enough shares where it changed my life. Instantly. I didn't know what to say. So he just smiled and said, 'Thanks – thanks for everything that you've done.'

Paying for stars is both a good investment *and* a good defence. It doesn't have to be salary or stock – you should use performance-related pay well. The problem with whacking up salary is that some folk are tigers for a few months and then turn back into turtles. Obviously, base pay should be considered for your stars (and it should be higher) but there is beauty in performance-related pay (to get paid as a tiger you have to continue being a tiger). Paying a tiger salary, or say a bonus of 150 per cent to your high performers, should be pure joy.

What to do when you watch a shooting star ...

Sometimes your stars will shoot off. When a star tells you they're leaving, try to correct it, but if they still decide to go despite your wonderful sermon, then don't sulk (you'll be amazed how many do!), but agree to stay in touch. As Sir Stuart Rose used to tell great people leaving Marks & Spencer: 'If you want to go out and get some other experience, we'll keep tabs on you; you keep tabs on us and you can always come back.'

So, ladies and gentlemen, people say staff turnover is always bad. However, high turnover of the duds (or bottom 10 per cent) is a sign of a great leader (and we all hire duds). But high turnover of your stars is a disaster. Focus on them, retain them, and if they do leave, don't forget to send them a lovely handwritten birthday card.

Yes, love your stars – but don't ignore everyone else

Having said all this, some leaders have a tendency to overcorrect and *just* focus on their stars while ignoring all the other ability camps. This too causes problems – not to mention jealousy and clique-creation. However, the biggest problem is that by ignoring the other camps, leaders don't ever improve the average. Nor do they develop future stars.

If, for example, you can improve the performance of the average members of your team by 20 per cent, then you have made a massive volume improvement across the whole group – it's often the new hires, or the rising stars (currently in your 'average' group) who need to be spotted early, loved and developed to raise the performance of your team.

So yes, motivating the whole team is absolutely essential too.

The idea in brief:

- *Ask your team what their motivations for coming to work would be even if you couldn't pay them and make sure you score highly on the things they identify in their answers*
- *Don't neglect your stars and high performers – if you do you might lose them to a competitor*
- *Spend time getting to know your stars, developing and challenging them and rewarding their contribution*
- *If a star leaves, always stay in touch wherever they go; if you do, they may come back – and shine even brighter when they do*
- *Make sure you don't neglect the rest of your team in favour of your stars*

24

Leaders create more leaders

'Before you are a leader, success is about growing
yourself. When you become a leader, success is all
about growing others.'

Jack Welch

Why has John Chambers, the CEO of Cisco, been so successful? This
quote sums up the reason for his success: 'We are growing ideas, but we
are growing people as well. Where I might have had two potential suc-
cessors, I now have 500.'

To be a great leader you have to develop other great leaders.
Leaders grow leaders. You see, if the members of your team are highly
ambitious (and I hope for your sake as a leader that they are), then
what will they value the most? Yes ... development. So one of the
best habits you can acquire is to really work with your team to maximise their strengths and give them the confidence to not just stand
on their own two feet but make them realise they too are capable of
great things. As Sam Walton, the founder of Walmart, said,
'Outstanding leaders go out of their way to boost the self-esteem of

their personnel. If people believe in themselves, it's amazing what they can accomplish.'

However you decide to develop your team, keep in mind the words of the Rhodes Scholar and former three-term Democratic United States Senator Bill Bradley, who said: 'Leadership is unlocking people's potential to become better.'

Organisations that develop talent attract the best talent

By the way, if you're the only leader in the company who believes in developing other leaders – then you have a significant battle on your hands. Companies that invest in their people are the companies that win the long race – and leaders who consciously invest in developing their team will always outperform those who don't. As we've discussed (in chapters 21–23), it's all about talent. Talent always wins, so if you have it, you have to nurture it – otherwise talent will leave. Besides, if you get a reputation for developing great leaders, then you'll have great people wanting to come and work for you! Andy Cosslett points this out: 'Being a great company helps us attract the best out there … so we spend longer on talent and leadership development than anything else.'

As a leader, echo this sentiment – if you can help others shine, learn and improve, then they will be motivated and energised, which is a big part of your day job. Here are a few key ways you can develop the leaders of the future:

Encourage people to come to you with a problem and a solution, not just a problem

In my interview with success guru Brian Tracy, he said, 'Leaders think and talk about the solutions; followers think and talk about the problems.' This is some of the best on-the-job training you can do to develop strategic thinking and leadership, so you should encourage all your team members to come to you with both the problem and a possible solution.

At the same time, you shouldn't be annoyed when your people come to you with problems – that's what you get paid the big bucks for!

Inclusion and shadowing

Start including your star performers in everything you do. Become their unofficial mentor and watch them grow or find other suitable mentors for them to shadow.

Whether you formally mentor members of your team or not, as the leader you will naturally fall in to a mentor position. As such, as discussed in chapter 11, you should never stop your own learning. Not only does it set the example for your team but, if you're learning, then you can also share that wisdom with your team. By believing in and polishing the individuals in your team into diamonds, you'll make them fiercely loyal to you and massively motivated by you.

Challenge your team to think and grow

Leaders believe in their team's abilities and are always pushing them to stretch themselves and move out of their comfort zones. By doing so, you'll ensure they won't get bored – and getting bored is a big reason why smart people leave your offices and disappear over the hills and into the sunset. So look for any opportunity you can to challenge them. It might be anything from asking them to go on a conference and then present to their industry peers, or to be project leader on a vital new initiative.

Feedback is a beautiful thing

Leaders recognise that feedback is a crucial way of developing individuals in their team. Equally, great talent recognises that without feedback there is little chance of transformational improvement or self-development. Without feedback nothing can improve, so let's explore the various forms feedback can take:

360-degree feedback

John Studzinski defined the 360-degree feedback process as one in which people are 'evaluated by people who they work with; who work above them, who work below them and their peer group; it's aimed at finding people's strengths, as well as the areas in which they need further development'.

The 360-degree feedback process is a way for your team to get to know their strengths and weaknesses. It's a potent tool for junior employees all the way to the CEO. In fact, one of the best CEOs in India today, Vincent Nayar (who is the top chap at HCL Technologies), is famous for not only insisting a 360-degree assessment is done on him, but also posts the feedback he receives for all to see. Ultimately, for people to get the best results, they do need to focus on their strengths, but if there's a major roadblock (a key, defined weakness) that's really impacting performance, then you, as the leader, need to coach and develop this to minimise its current and future impact.

Direct from you (the boss) – catching people doing things right

As a leader, you have two ways of using direct feedback at your disposal: positive (carrot) and coercive (stick). Both can be used, but the carrot is far better than the stick, especially in the long term. People love recognition and being rewarded for doing well, so get into the habit of being very generous in your praise. It costs nothing, but the value is exceptionally high, so why not?

There's a commonly used line that says 'praise loudly, blame softly'. It's true, yet so many leaders don't even see things to praise. The exercise we did back in chapter 19 showing that you find only what you look for (if you're looking for red, it's hard to see green) applies very well to giving feedback too. Many leaders limit their impact because they've got into the ugly habit of just looking for the red (the bad) and not the green (the good). The most influential leaders have a habit of seeing the good or, as Ken Blanchard put it, 'Catching people doing things right.' In my interview with Ken, he suggested the following:

> Once people are clear on goals, you've got to wander around and see if you can catch people doing things right. Of all the things that I've ever taught over the years, that's the one thing that I would hold onto, because I think that the key to developing good relationships and great organisations is to accentuate the positives and celebrate people's success.

The idea of positive reinforcement and catching people doing things right and not wrong is one of the most powerful leadership concepts in this book. So be very generous in your praise – in fact, hunt down opportunities to thank people and show appreciation. Jon Studzinksi advises being specific in your praise. He said: 'You have to encourage – you get so much more from talented people if you sit down with them and say, "You know you did five great things over the last month – let me tell you why they're great."' Specificity always wins when it comes to giving feedback.

Delivering negative feedback

Of course, not all feedback can be positive, but when giving negative feedback, always deliver it in private (never slam your laptop shut and shout it across an open plan office), in person (never by email where what you say might not come across to the recipient in the way you intended) and in a constructive way. You should also deliver negative feedback swiftly, so that the issue doesn't fester. Despite the fact that all leaders find tough conversations uncomfortable, it's what leaders do so they just get on with it.

They also ensure that the feedback isn't personal, by keeping it focused on the behaviour or result that needs to change. A powerful technique to use in those situations is to use a reaffirmation. As Ken Blanchard says, 'always end a reprimand with a reaffirmation; saying, "You know, you're better than that."' Make it about the task and not the person.

To turn a situation in which you are delivering negative feedback into an opportunity for learning and growth, make sure you ask questions to find out why and where the person involved thinks things went wrong and why it wasn't up to their normal high standards (a reinforcing almost consultative approach that depersonalises the situation or short-coming). Listen, empathise and ask what their solution would be. Have your say, then agree to go forth and conquer.

Get team members to improve their strengths, not work too long on (or beat themselves up with) their weaknesses

Nothing demotivates somebody more than working on the things that they hate, or which they've struggled to master (they usually go hand in hand) over a prolonged period. Focusing on strengths is a success mantra for all great leaders (as discussed in chapter 3) and this thinking applies to their teams too.

John Studzinski said:

> You need to find out what people's strengths and weaknesses are –
> no two people are alike, and if you're a good manager you'll spend
> most of your time understanding someone's strengths – and you'll
> manage around their weaknesses. It's very important that you do
> that – successful organisations have strong people who are
> surrounded by people who supplement their weaknesses. If you
> think that you have very strong people who are perfect, you are not
> living in the real world; very strong people have support systems
> that compensate, cover up or modify their weaknesses.

Philippa Snare echoed this:

> When I've been building teams, and working with individuals, it's
> always [a case of asking] 'What are you good at?' – and saying to
> them, 'Putting your job description aside for a minute, what are the
> things that you're just naturally good at?' You see, if you put yourself
> in those positions, you tend to be brilliant at [the job], and
> everybody else can feel that – and you get more and more
> opportunities. I think about how I can put people in positions where
> they use their strengths naturally.

If you can structure your team so that the vast majority of the time they're working on things that they're good at and enjoy, not only will they be happier, but your team will have a remarkable improvement in results.

People learn by doing – so delegate

There is no better way of learning than by 'doing' under the guidance of somebody like you. So think about what you can delegate to members of your team that might be outside their remit, but which they might relish the opportunity to take on. Just remember: your job as a leader and a developer is to delegate (not just the boring stuff, please), and that's good and smart, but just make sure that, when you do, you strike a balance between not abdicating (i.e. giving them the task and then running away) and trusting them to find the best route to the result. Sure, you might want to give them flexibility to figure out the best methodology but make sure you check in with them before the work is due!

Leadership training/development

For both high achievers and potential high achievers, having a forward schedule of learning and development is more motivational than looking at a blank cheque. (Maybe not quite, but almost.) So even if you can't afford to bring in the greatest professors from around the world to deliver leadership development programmes, make sure that you've got some of the internal folk up to speed on how to run skill-based workshops. Whether it's internal or external doesn't matter, but good people want formal training, so as a leader you have to provide it.

To conclude this chapter I'm going to use a quote from Jack Welch's book *Winning*: 'Remember, when you were made a leader, you weren't given a crown; you were given a responsibility to bring out the best in others.'

The idea in brief:

- *A leader's job is to develop and grow others*
- *If you develop a reputation for growing great leaders, people will want to come and work for you*
- *Delegate new areas for your team; there's nothing like learning from doing*
- *Challenge your team in their thinking*
- *Feedback is one of the most powerful leadership concepts — make sure you're delivering it often and in the right way*
- *Good is better than bad in encouraging future behaviour — catch people doing things right!*
- *Get people to work on their strengths — remind them that this is the best path for them to get to greatness*

25

The bottom 10 per cent (or so) – letting them go

'For people that you think are not going to be able to make it in an organisation, the worst thing you can do to them is to keep them – let them go to somewhere where they can.'

Allan Leighton

We all make hiring mistakes – we're all human. So don't beat yourself up about it. But great leaders always remember the mantra 'hire slow, fire fast'. Once you've identified a hiring mistake, then you have to deal with that professionally, by acting with good values, courage, integrity and, crucially, with speed.

Why this chapter is called 'letting them go'

Inspired by Allan Leighton's quote (above), the full title should probably have been: 'Letting them go to find something they are good at.' You see, *nobody* wakes up in the morning and thinks, 'Yes, I'm going to be a great failure today, so let's go and see how many leaders I can disappoint', and nobody likes feeling like they're not adding value or contributing. As such, if somebody is continually not performing in the role with you, and you've tried to correct it, then at some point you need to explain it's not their strength area and let them go. By doing so, you are liberating them to go and find something they *are* good at.

This is a very powerful way of looking at it. Remember that we discussed in chapter 3 that a leader's job is to get people focused on their strengths; equally, if the role isn't suited to their strengths, leaders need to take the action to address it. Peter Drucker encapsulated this message well when he said, 'A manager who hires and keeps an incompetent employee is incompetent himself.'

When you let people go, the 'no surprises' route is the best

Jack Welch, former CEO of General Electric, maintains that there shouldn't be any surprises when firing people. What he means by this is, if you've done your job as leader, then you'll have given the individual in question clear targets and reviewed them frequently to discuss any shortcomings and problems in a proactive and transparent way. As such, if there's continued and sustained inability to improve results, they should not be surprised the day they're fired. In fact, many will graciously resign before D-day.

Jack Welch also used to say that the bottom 10 per cent of performers each year had to go. If you were in the bottom 10 per cent you were out. This methodology has its pros and cons, so it's up to you if you want to deploy that initiative, but it's certainly transparent, open, and avoids doubt.

All the great leaders have a *lot* of patience and time for smart and motivated people but very little time for the lazy and incompetent. However, this doesn't mean that they don't treat them with respect and integrity.

If you dither and delay on letting people go – you'll do significant damage

Dealing with a hiring mistake quickly and decisively is the best way to make sure a situation doesn't get out of hand. Once you've decided it's not right, act swiftly. Cut your losses – every day of inaction costs you and the company money.

Take this scenario: David is supposed to be bringing in £50,000 sales per month, but for the last nine months he's only brought in £15,000 in sales per month (on average). Let's also say that you're paying David £5,000 a month in salary. The decision not to fire David is costing you £35,000 in lost sales per month, plus £5,000 in salary (not to mention overhead costs). This David chap is costing you a rather sizeable £480,000 per year!

Now imagine that rather than the company paying him through the payroll, you have to pay him that money using £20 notes from your own pocket. How long would he be around for if that was the case? (By the way, great leaders reach great heights because they treat company money as though it was their own.)

Going further still, what happens if you have four Davids hanging around? That's a loss of almost £2 million each financial year. Plus, the indirect cost of keeping David is that you're sending out a very loud message to the rest of the team: 'Guys 'n' gals, chill out! You don't need to perform here – it's a nice day. Why don't you all go bird watching or on a treasure hunt?'

I'm not advocating a hire and fire culture – that's not a good culture. Indeed, the best way to reduce firings is to hire better in the first place. It's just that we all make bad hiring decisions – and when we do, it's about dealing with them swiftly and with grace. The cost of inaction can be really impactful.

When it comes to chronic underperforming employees, doing the right thing is always more important than being liked

Some leaders don't want to make hard decisions, like letting go of lovely Lucy in accounts, because they want to be liked – they need affection. However, as a leader it's results that you're after not affection.

Affection is why you marry people, and have friends and pets; it's not why you lead people. I'm not saying that it's good to be despised – quite the contrary, the more love the better, but you never prioritise it over results. With results will follow respect.

Somebody who's focused on being liked (or loved) will sometimes decide on the popular decision, not the *right* decision for the organisation. It's far better to be loved for your results than your niceness – the former is much deeper.

Echoing this idea, Allan Leighton told me about the best CEOs that he knows: 'None of them are in it because it's a popularity contest ... [they] don't do things because they're popular; they do them because they're the right things to do – and by doing that you will make the business a success and you'll win the admiration of those around you, if that's what you're after.'

Make no mistake, firing people and letting people go, especially if they've got great attitudes, is one of the hardest jobs a leader has to do – nobody likes it, but it has to be done. As we discussed at the beginning of this chapter, letting underperformers go will benefit them in the long run and is an economic necessity for you.

The idea in brief:

- *Leaders make no secret of the fact that a percentage of their hires will be bad hires*
- *Once a bad hire has been identified, the leader must act with integrity, respect and speed*
- *The cost of having somebody that doesn't have the skill, the will, the values or even the integrity is very high to you and the business – it's far better to have a gap to fill than the wrong person in the gap*
- *It's the kindest thing in the world to let somebody go if they're not naturally suited to the job (i.e. allow them to find what it is that they are good at)*
- *Do the right thing, not the popular thing*

26

Set goals and reward results

'We set everybody quarterly goals ... and pay bonuses accordingly ... Success in any business is about focus and clarity.'

Simon Calver

Goals help you to achieve clarity (which equals leadership bliss)

One of the most beautiful things about goals is the clarity that they bring leaders and teams. Clarity, especially in the complex and noisy world of managing others, is vital, so written goals are worth their weight in gold.

In my interview with Brian Tracy, he told me:

My favourite word in management is 'clarity'. In fact, my favourite word in life is 'clarity'. The greater clarity you have in what you're trying to accomplish, the faster you'll achieve it. So make sure that everybody who works for you is crystal clear about what job they're supposed to do. After all, the job of a leader is to set and achieve business goals.

Goals give your team something to aim for

According to Brian Tracy, 'People with clear written goals, plans and priorities, accomplish 10 times as much in life as people without'. Goals give people targets to hit – something to strive for. Some cynics may argue the reason there's an uplift in results is because staff are scared to death what management will do if they don't achieve them. Perhaps there's a slight truth to that.

But the core reason for the success of goal-setting is more simple: goals give people something to aim for – without goalposts, nobody can score. (This is why goal-setting is such a critical part of creating an execution culture in an organisation – more on this in Part 3.) If somebody doesn't know what success looks like, then how can they achieve it? How frustrating if you're playing a game of hockey with no goalposts. – where are you going to run, where will you aim, and how will you know if you're winning? It's the same in business. Furthermore, goal achievement releases endorphins, nature's wonder drug, and this is why Brian Tracy told me, 'We're goal-seeking organisms.' Goal attainment is in our nature, so give your team the opportunity to follow those natural instincts.

Goals create urgency – make no mistake, urgency is good

A goal with a deadline is a lovely source of pure unadulterated urgency. Urgency is a powerful leadership and productivity weapon.

Sir Stuart Rose told me: 'Many of us do our best work when under pressure ... you can surprise yourself when you're under a hell of a lot of pressure and you've got a deadline ... your work quality and your work capacity goes up.'

In fact, some people in your team might categorically need deadlines to get anything done! They positively thrive on the adrenalin associated with: 'I've only got two nanoseconds to write and submit my 90,000-word report'. (Actually this sounds remarkably like me with this book!) They love this rush – in fact, it's cruel not to give them deadlines.

In his book *Urgency*, Harvard Business School Professor John Kotter points out how critical it is for you as leader to convey urgency to your team in the pursuit of important goals all the time – verbally, but non-verbally too: keep meetings tight (no glazed buns, comfy seats and late starts, as we discussed in the time management chapter), conversations tight, and bring *everything* back to results and important goals. (But be careful not to promote *false urgency*, which is when you whip up a storm about unimportant, low-value stuff – delegate that job to a drama queen.)

To create a sense of urgency you also need to keep your goals flexible and relatively short term. If you say, 'Bob, I want this Competitive Intelligence report by 1 p.m. on 2nd October, 10 years from now', then that's not going to generate much energy or immediacy. Simon Calver advocates setting goals on a quarterly basis: 'With quarterly goals you have immediacy; you have clarity; you have the ability to cascade objectives through the organisation; and you also have the ability to move the ship on a quarterly basis … What you can't afford to have as an organisation, and as a performance-driven organisation, is no immediacy in your goal-setting.'

Some hyper-agile companies even set weekly important targets (discussed below), though that's not for everyone (at least not on a mass scale).

Goals enable you to keep your team focused on the important

I know you know that success comes more from focusing on what's important, rather than focusing on everything. However, we all (you, probably, and I, *definitely*) get sucked back into the '*stuff*'. The key is to be able to bring your team back to what's important. Goals do that – particularly if they're stuck in front of your team's faces on their cubicles or computers or somewhere else hyper-visible (on the inside of their glasses if you can).

What will happen to your team without goals? They drift like a rudderless boat. They'll just react to what's happening rather than making things happen. Teams and organisations that are merely reactive will be unknown. No great individuals, teams or companies have ever reacted their way to success.

Goals create transparency on who your high and low performers are

Again, Simon Calver (who, as you can see, is one of Britain's best at organisational performance and goal-setting) said:

> At the end of every quarter I sit down with my team and I have everybody's performance-related pay in the organisation ...We then pick out high performers, which I take out and recognise. Next we identify the people that are underperforming. If people are below 100 per cent two quarters in a row, we begin to have conversations.

Goal-setting and linking to PRP (performance-related pay) creates the ultimate meritocracy and transforms your goals into live ammunition rather than blanks. Wherever possible, link pay to performance. It's a great way for you to over-reward great talent – and ensure that your stars are always getting paid more than your average.

The case for going public with goals

Some organisations feel it's advantageous to publish the quarterly goals of individuals in their team for everyone to see. Philip Rosedale, the founder of Second Life (the virtual world based in California), who built a hyper-agile company culture, gets people working to *weekly* goals. Here's what he does:

> Each week we get people to write in an email three or four things they're going to achieve for the week – not everything, just the top things that they think are important. Then the next week, when they send the next email, they cut and paste from the email from the week before, and they simply write: done, or not done, next to each point. This email list goes to the whole company, so anybody in the company can see everyone else's work list. This idea is very powerful.

When making goals, make them SMART or SMARTER

Setting goals is crucial when it comes to leading a team, but you also need to make sure you're setting the *right* goals.

For a while now people have been talking about SMART goals, an acronym for: Specific, Measurable, Attainable, Realistic and Time-framed. In an attempt to be a SMARTASS (we all have to at least attempt it once in a while), when setting goals for my team, I have added two letters to the acronym, which stand for Exciting and Relevant.

Specific – make the goalposts clear not vague

Measurable – they have measurability and you can see if somebody has crossed the goal line

Attainable – make sure they're stretch goals, but not impossible – otherwise people will simply give up

Realistic – make sure that it's realistic considering other deadlines, resources etc.

Time-framed – all goals need a deadline, period

Exciting – people need to be excited about their projects – you too

Relevant – they all cascade up to a greater strategy, vision and purpose

The SMART acronym is a good starting point and it represents the best school of thought out there pertaining to goals. Indeed, by making your and your team's goals SMART (or now SMARTER) you will successfully plant these goalposts into the ground. However, like all tools, there can be unintended consequences to be aware of. A side effect of using the SMART framework is that your team can be tempted to dump other important areas that have not been specifically set as goals.

For example, when Starbucks founder Howard Schultz returned as the CEO, he found that the company had lost ground because it had put all its energy behind a specific goal, at the expense of its other objectives. It had set most of it targets around reducing the amount of time it takes to serve a customer. As a result, everybody was served faster – much, much faster. But the unintended consequence of this was that it left less time for interaction with customers and consequently, the overall customer experience was diminished. In fact, it was diminished so much that coffee lovers – or more like frappucino, caramel macchiatto (with extra caramel and whipped cream) and chai tea latte lovers – all around the world were left scratching their heads, thinking, What have we done to deserve this? Where has the love gone?

Luckily for Starbucks' customers, when Howard Schultz returned to the captain's deck, he made sure the company started serving love again.

So if you're using the SMART (or SMARTER) framework, you need to make sure that the five or six goals you set, if achieved, really will be what you want and won't have unintended consequences that might be detrimental to the customer or your values.

Allow creativity on the way your team achieve their set goals

Great leaders are those who are firm on the 'what', but flexible on the 'how' – the method used to achieve the goals they set. By delegating the 'how', the leader fosters a culture of entrepreneurship and creative thinking which can be incredibly rewarding for the individuals in the team.

Moreover, if you allow people to have input on the 'how', then you will never know when the next brilliant departmental innovation is heading your way. As General George Patton, America's greatest combat general of World War II, said, 'Never tell people how to do things. Tell them what to do and they will surprise you with their ingenuity.'

Similarly, Bill Clinton told *Fortune* magazine that leaders need 'steadfastness in the pursuit of a goal, flexibility in determining how best to achieve it'. This couldn't be more true – market, economic and technological circumstances change at lightning speed these day so you need your team to be able to adapt and think fast.

Celebrate achievement – loudly

If your team has done exceptionally well on their quarterly goals, or has reached a major team target … then celebrate! *All* great leaders, from victorious battleground leaders with their surviving armies, to the tech teams of software giants today, celebrate victory.

Why? There are two fundamental reasons, both equally important:

1) It enables you to deeply reinforce the message that everybody is part of a winning team (which will increase chances of the team scoring bigger goals in the future).
2) It enables you, and the team, to significantly overeat and overdrink once in a while – which is, well, just great fun.

The idea in brief:

- *Goals bring clarity, which is, arguably, one of the most important words in business (and life)*
- *Goals drive results northwards and provide a much-needed source of urgency*
- *Urgency is one of the most important things a leader can cultivate*
- *Use short-term goals to make sure you've got agility hard-wired into the organisation so if the strategy changes then your goals can too*
- *Goals ensure your people are focused on grade-A activity – not 'stuff'*
- *Use goals to identify low and high performers and reward accordingly*
- *Allow your team to do some thinking on the 'how' – you might be surprised by their ingenuity*
- *Celebrate success!*

27

Communicate, communicate, communicate

'Be clear on your purpose and then communicate, communicate, communicate.'

Ronan Dunne

In my interview with Ronan Dunne, I asked him for his top piece of leadership advice, and his answer was the quote above. Whether that's at the podium, at the water cooler, emailing from your computer, or even in a crowded lift pinned with your back against the wall on the way to the 18th floor, you have to be a master communicator.

Here are a few Golden Rules for communication from the leaders I've interviewed:

Learn public speaking skills (even if you'd far prefer to lick a stray cat)

Ahem, excuse the slightly strange comparison – but you see, so, so, so, so many people hate public speaking. Indeed, this is the part of the book that might make you slam it shut, throw it across the room and forget this leadership malarkey.

But when Warren Buffett was asked the 'one piece of advice for leaders' question by a student at the University of Nebraska, he said: 'Whether you like it or not, get very comfortable with (though it may take a while) public speaking. It's an asset that will last you 50 or 60 years. Yet it's a liability, if you don't like doing it, that will also last you 50 or 60 years. It's a necessary skill.'

Why is it such a necessary skill (even if it scares the living wits out of you)? It comes back to leverage. Let's say you have come off the stage having spoken to 500 delegates for an hour. How long would it have taken you to get your message to those folk if you had had to meet with those 500 people one on one? Yes, 500 hours. Do you have that time? Nope. This is why all leaders do public speaking (the vast majority don't like it, but they still do it – it's part of the job of the leader).

If you hate public speaking, you are not alone, but you have to do it. As Sir Terry Leahy said, 'take a deep breath and get on with it'.

So what is the key to mastering the stage? Just get up there as much and as often as you can and get honest and insightful feedback on how you performed. The next time an opportunity arises, raise your hand and volunteer. After all, if you can crack public speaking then, because so many people hate it, you'll have a great USP.

Be candid and honest (with good or bad news)

'I think you've got to be completely open with everything you tell everybody, your staff, your shareholders; when you start to hide truth, when you start to conceal things, it always ends in disaster – just be open.'

Tim Waterstone

If you're known for saying it how it is, then your team will know that you don't hold things back (akin with chapter 18 on authenticity). If your followers don't trust you, or they think that you withhold information, that's when paranoia can kick in. It's far better to tell them the bad news up front, exactly as it is, rather than leave it to speculation, suspicion and fantasy.

Being honest builds trust and means your followers won't go around thinking, What is it that we're not being told? As such, they'll spend their energy on more profitable activity.

Jacqueline Gold is also hugely in favour of keeping channels of communication open in the workplace:

> Years ago, when I first started, there was a different culture – the feelings then were that you keep things close to your chest, and you don't share. But I totally buy into transparency; I think it's absolutely vital – it stops people speculating and staff feel that they can trust you; everybody feels part of the family and they feel as one.

As Twitter CEO Dick Costolo told the Disrupt TechCrunch Conference:

> The way you build trust with your team is by being forthright and clear with them from day one ... You may think people are fooled when you tell them what they want to hear. They are not fooled. As a leader you are totally transparent, people are looking at you all the time ... If you try to lead in a way that isn't true to who you are, they will see through it and you will lose the trust of your team.

Allan Leighton echoes Costello's thoughts. Referring to his experience in becoming Chairman of Royal Mail, he said, 'You can give people bad news, but you just have to be honest with them ... I had to give lots of people good news and lots of people bad news, and I always try and do it the same way – I just tell people how it is ... even if they disagree, they'll respect you for it.'

The most important thing to remember is that honest communication is vital in winning the trust of your team. As Andy Cosslett told me, 'People can take bad news. What they can't take is no news.'

Communicate, don't broadcast

Effective communication with your team doesn't just mean providing them with information; it also involves what Tom Peters told me was the 'most underutilised tool in leadership' – listening. So get into the habit (and it is a habit) of asking for thoughts, opinions, feedback, ideas, anything and listening intently to the answer. By doing so you'll find out everything that you need to know while tapping in to the collective wisdom of your team.

It's a cliché that we all have two ears and one mouth, so we should use them with the same ratios – but it is true. One of the most under-utilised and underestimated physical communication assets we have is our ears. Rather than explaining why, I'm going to hand over to John Studzinski. This is what he said during our interview:

> I can always tell this when I meet a brand new CEO: I always know if they're going to succeed or fail, based on one thing, and it's whether they're good at the art of listening ... The ones that succeed are the ones that go in there with an open mind, a clean sheet of paper and they're there to listen; they listen to all the stakeholders, their employees, their predecessors, the old board members, the new board members – and they make sure that they continue to listen once their honeymoon is over. As a good CEO, 80 to 90 per cent of what you need to know, to do your job well, you'll get if you take the time and listen.

Consequently, one of the most powerful techniques that a leader has at their disposal is the ability to ask questions. The greatest leaders on the planet today ask heroic amounts of questions, and then listen intently to the answers (they don't just think about the next smartass question in their head).

Encourage debate throughout the team

All the best leaders are confident enough to allow their people to debate – amongst themselves and with them, the leader, too. Debate is a powerful tool for leaders as a) it gets people to have their say about a course or a strategy, and b) because people can get emotional in debates, they forget their inhibitions and blurt out what they really think, which always reveals powerful insights that can help your decision making. Confident leaders don't care if their premise is proved wrong, indeed many of them go around preaching, 'it's not who's right, it's what's right' – a powerful truism in business that many leaders brush under the boardroom carpets because they feel that as leaders, they must be right and they don't have the confidence to lead a robust debate. Yet, without debate, the greatest thinking is never heard. Do you agree? If not, why not debate it?

When people become impassioned during a debate, conflict can ensue, so if you encourage debate in your team, remember these three things:

1) Conflict is a healthy sign – if your team didn't care they wouldn't argue and apathy is a much bigger and graver problem.
2) Very often conflict arises out of miscommunication or misunderstanding, so as a leader it's your job to step in and clear up any confusion.
3) Don't get upset or sulk if people disagree with you, which wouldn't be setting a good example to your team (remember the phrase 'It's what's right not who's right').

After a healthy debate, remember that no matter what the difference of opinion was during the discussion, the whole team must support the outcome and be 100 per cent committed to making it work. When I interviewed Matthew Key he said:

It's a sign of a great team – that you can have tensions in the boardroom, but as soon as you walk out of the boardroom you're all absolutely aligned behind the decision. I call it constructive tension: constructive tension is very good, destructive tension is not good. Have the debate, decide what you're going to do, but when you walk out that boardroom you have to be 100 per cent aligned – as a team.

Even if the team's decision hasn't gone your way, you need to swallow your pride and get behind it. After all, great leaders sometimes need to be great followers. As Aristotle once said, 'He who has not learned to obey cannot be a good commander.'

Be a cheerleader and storyteller!

In my interview with Ronan Dunne he said: 'The key, once you understand your purpose, is to inspire and enable in equal measure. When I was appointed the CEO of O2, I stood in the atrium in front of our colleagues and explained to everybody that my job is chief cheerleader and storyteller.'

Repeat – *'my job is chief cheerleader and storyteller'*.

Similarly, the legendary Tom Peters told me: 'There is no question in my mind that this [to be able to tell stories] is certainly number one or number two on the list of political leadership skills; everyone from Prime Ministers to Presidents induce people to change things by telling stories.'

There's magic in stories. In fact, if you listen to great leaders and CEOs they'll always elaborate on their points with a whole host of communication devices and stories are right at the top of the list. If you've ever been on a public speaking course, you'll have been advised to, 'illustrate each point, with either a case study, an anecdote, a metaphor or perhaps a well-chosen quotation'. This is exactly what great leaders do, not just when they're on stage, but whenever they're communicating. Why? Because it grabs the imagination of the listener and makes their message far easier to remember and understand.

To practise what I preach, I'm going to illustrate this point with an anecdote about the legendary Warren Buffett. As mentioned in chapter 17, Warren Buffett peppers his annual reports with jokes of all varieties. Carol Loomis, editor of *Fortune* magazine and friend of Warren Buffett, said of his jokes: 'I think he saves them up, he must have a file back in Omaha'. Nothing wrong with that, in fact, there's nothing wrong with having an electronic file for jokes, metaphors, quotes, sayings, anecdotes or anything else. It's great for your communication and a relief for the memory recall unit in your head.

Connect with the heart, not just the head

You may have heard of the military term 'hearts and minds'. Let's look at the order of that for a moment: yes – it's hearts first, and then minds. As Robert Senior told me: 'Emotion leads to action . . . let's dare to move people.'

If you use emotion when communicating, people will relate to you – as their leader but also more deeply as a real human being (that authenticity thing again). I'm not suggesting that you cry uncontrollably at each weekly meeting, but if you are passionate about what you do, it's important to convey this to your team at all times. However, this passion has to be genuine and not misplaced – there's no point in trying to give a spine-tingling speech with a standing ovation if all you are doing is making an announcement that all the loos in your building are getting refurbished.

But if you do genuinely care about something, then show that you care – be enthused, sound excited. Passion is infectious – it will spread to your team if you communicate it to them.

Communicate by walking about – the power of the Visible Leader

Top leaders rely as much on informal communication as they do on formal interactions, and they're always approachable. There have been several cases (not just in films) where new CEOs are shown to their corner office with the mahogany door, at which point they put down their briefcase, produce a screwdriver and remove the door. It sends a message to the entire team and staff: 'Talk to me – there are no barriers between us.'

Then they go and walk about: they're out with the staff having lunch, they sit on people's desks to have a chat – in essence, they're *visible*.

As Ronan Dunne said, 'Inspiring people in 30 seconds at the water cooler is probably about the most powerful thing a business leader can do.' So get up and start walking around and connecting with your team.

Check that what you've communicated has been received

Let's look at you for a minute: think about the absolutely critical messages that you need to convey to your team. What are the key things that they should know? You need to be sure that this crucial information has been communicated clearly to your team – and the only way to do this is to check.

One of the best ways to test the effectiveness of your communication is to go up to anyone in your team and ask them four questions that relate to the key information you want your team to know and understand. For example, if you're the CEO, these could be:

1) What value do we bring to customers?
2) What's our vision?
3) What are our values?
4) How do we make money here?

And, while you have a captive audience, why not ask:

5) What do you think we should be doing better around here?
6) How can I help?

If you find that people have difficulty answering the first four, then the way you communicate on those points could probably use a bit of improvement.

World-class leaders love simplicity

In a very powerful message, Tim Waterstone said to me '[Simplicity] is the secret of great politicians – that they have a very simple tune to whistle. The message has got to be simple and clear.'

Great leaders speak in simple language that *everybody* can understand. Insecure and bad managers hide behind many convoluted words. Leaders go out of their way to translate complexity into simplicity. This is why they're great communicators. As General Colin Powell said: 'Great leaders are almost always great simplifiers who can cut through argument, debate, and no doubt offer a solution that everybody can understand.' Always look for simplification ... simple.

Communicating to the masses

All of the leaders that I interviewed agreed on one thing – that once in a while they have to communicate to *everybody* in the organisation. It's good for them delivering their message (so that it's not lost in translation down the ranks), and it's good for all people to know what's going on, straight from the top. Let's look at two key mediums for mass communication:

Company-wide meetings

Jacqueline Gold told me, 'Every month we have an "all-comers" meeting in our reception, where we invite all of the staff from all of the departments and they hear about what the figures have been doing, what our new initiatives are (so they don't feel that we're keeping anything from them), they hear about the fun stuff and the exciting opportunities; it has worked very well.'

If you can get your whole company (and/or team) together once a week, or once a month, or once a quarter, then definitely do it. Company meetings are a great way to celebrate successes, mention notable things, announce strategy, reinforce your organisation's values and, very importantly, to have some fun.

By email

Email is a great way to regularly communicate interesting and relevant information to an organisation. Ideally the CEO should send out an email to *all* employees, with updates for the month or the quarter (at the very least) but it can be done more frequently if there is something important to share. The emails should be written in the normal, everyday language used by employees, rather than highly convoluted MBA speak. Keep it human.

Greg Dyke told me that when he was at the BBC, 'We did loads of emails to everybody. They came from me – only I (as Director General) could write them; they could never be more than a page; they were always just signed "Greg", and they'd always be trying to tell you something that mattered – so sometimes you'd go weeks without sending one, and other times you send two in one week.'

As you can see, there are many guidelines for great leadership communication and many ways to deliver your message. Whatever communication device you choose to use, remember what Dianne Feinstein, the Mayor of San Francisco, once said, '90 per cent of leadership is the ability to communicate something people want.' So never forget the acronym WIIFM – which stands for 'What's In It For Me?' – when it comes to communicating with your team and wider organisation.

The idea in brief:

- *Develop a love of public speaking (even if it scares the wits out of you)*
- *Become known for being candid in your communications – it's a great leadership asset*
- *Know when to keep your mouth shut and listen*
- *If you're the CEO, your job is chief cheerleader and storyteller so don't become stuffy when communicating*
- *Use colour in your communications, including, but not limited to: metaphors, anecdotes, similes, wit*
- *Encourage debate – just have a thick skin and don't sulk (it was your idea!)*
- *Walk about – the role of the visible leader*
- *Two effective ways to communicate on a large scale are: company-wide meetings and email*

28

Win through better thinking – the foundation of strategy

'People do not spend enough time on thinking.'

Edward de Bono

Not enough leaders bother with thinking

I was fortunate enough to interview the world authority on thinking – Edward de Bono, who came up with the term 'lateral thinking' and is the author of books such as the world-famous *Six Thinking Hats*.

One of the key things he was adamant about putting across in the interview was that leaders of organisations are *not* investing enough time in encouraging their teams to simply think. It sounds crazy, but it is, in fact, a very powerful, cheap and potent differentiation opportunity: to win through better thinking. As leaders we normally deploy creative thinking the most when solving a problem; however, the greatest leaders also use creative thinking when trying to work out how to achieve a lofty goal or vision, how to augment existing strengths or find the next big breakthrough that could transform the organisation. After all, having just one insight, one powerful thought or idea that you act on can be the thing that differentiates you from the competition for the next 10 years.

Military leader Sun Tzu said, 'It is more important to outthink your enemy than outfight him.' This advice is as true for businesses strategy today as it was for military strategy back in ancient China.

If thinking is free and could transform you, your team and your company (and possibly your industry), why wouldn't you spend more time thinking?

How much does it cost you, or you and your team, to get into a room and think about how to achieve your goals or exploit opportunity? The answer is 'nothing' – it's free. (Okay, for the real finance folk reading this, you could argue that it costs you the salary of the person, the cost of the meeting space etc., but apart from these overheads, it's free.)

Applied to your most important goals and Vital Few activities, thinking is one of the cheapest, most underutilised, yet most powerful assets in business (as well as personally). Thinking can transform results; it can offer a paradigm shift that changes everything. Apple even used 'Think Different' as an advertising campaign and they've done okay! Thinking is beginning to come back into fashion. *Harvard Business Review* quotes Avon CEO Andrea Jung as saying: 'Clear thinking in senior leadership is a primary attribute we look for.'

How can you make sure that you incorporate thinking into your strategy? Like all Vital Few activities, you have to block time out for it. As Edward de Bono said in our interview: 'There's a real need to decide to spend one hour a day, or one day a week, or one day a month for thinking and sitting down to generate new ideas.'

Here are two exercises for getting your team to think like da Vinci, Newton or Aristotle – and turning this free resource into significant economic value.

If you *had* to achieve something, how would you do it?

When I was the Regional CEO of my former company, I used to fly out to visit our international offices as often as my diary would permit. After all, turning up and being with your employees and your customers is the most important thing a CEO can do.

Every visit, I used to grab some time with each department and do a thinking exercise with them. For example, I'd take the entire marketing team to a meeting room where the conversation might go something like this:

'If you had to double your marketing revenues this year, but on half the budget, what would you do?' (Note – this can be any goal whatsoever).

Very often they'd then reply with something like: 'Umm that's just not possible. We couldn't double our revenues with half the budget.'

I'd then say something like: 'Oh I see, but what if you had to? What would you do?'

They'd come back with: 'Anthony, it's just not possible. We can't double our results with less spend than we have already. No way.'

I'd then say something like: 'Oh I see, it does sound hard, but what if you had to? What would you do?'

Then they'd say: 'We can't, Anthony – it's just not possible.'

I'd then reply with: 'But what if you had to. what would you do?'

They'd then say: 'We can't.'

I'd then reply with: 'But what if you had to, what would you do?'

They'd say: 'We can't do that.'

I'd say: But what if you had to, what would you do?'

Eventually – and only because they wanted me to shut up so much – somebody would blurt out, 'Okay, well if we had to, I mean if we had to – I don't know if it would work, but I guess we'd try Blah Blah Blah.'

Then I'd say, 'Great! Perfect! Congratulations, Steve. I love Blah Blah Blah … Now I want no less than 25 of these ideas.'

Then, as sure as night follows day, the 'creative thinking' process would kick in and we'd get some wild, but crazy ideas … and we'd reach 25. Sure, some of these 25 ideas were never going to work (although you never say that at the time!), some of those ideas were average, some were inspired and some were game-changing! So at the end, as a group, we'd agree on the five best and put two or three immediately into prototype. Testing is everything.

This exercise can be done for any important business goal – everything from, 'How can we get a partnership with Google?' to 'How can we become number one in our sector?' to 'How can we practically make sure that we put the customer at the heart of everything we do here?' Whatever your most important goals are, it's worth investing thinking time to come up with a list – it's free and it's all-powerful.

I know a business consultant who actually takes this exercise a step further (or maybe too far) and takes entire management teams into the London Eye (for those who haven't been to London, it's essentially an oversized Ferris wheel), equipped with a flipboard and two or three key goals to brainstorm. Everybody then has to come up with at least 20 ideas *each,* before they can get off. It takes 45 minutes to go around the London Eye, so a lot of the crazy ideas come up when a) they get desperate for the loo, or b) just before they're about to go around again *for another 45 minutes.*

This kind of thinking comes up with the next 'remarkable' thing

As you will know, success in this ever-competitive world is about standing out from the crowd. Sometimes it's the 'crazy' ideas that, once implemented, actually work and transform results. Not only will they work, but because they're so new, people are more likely to remark about them – and in today's world that can bring great visibility, simply because the world of social media is made for sharing people's opinions on things.

If you read the chapter about talent (chapter 21), you'll remember a Jenny Zhang from the Chinese Recruitment Fair. It was this kind of thinking that made her conclude, 'If I *had* to get a job there, then I'd go and see Anthony in his office unannounced.'

So always practise this type of thinking with your team – the rewards and laughter from these meetings are invaluable.

The Business Wheel or Leadership Wheel – a tool for reflection and thinking

The Business Wheel is a great tool to use with your team to a) rate themselves on where they believes they are in some of your key defined areas of strategic importance, and b) to create a list of possible actions that would improve your score, and your strength in these areas.

The process is:

1) Get your team together.
2) Choose the key competencies/attributes/strengths that you wish to measure (again you could apply this to yourself, your team, your departments, or even your entire organisation).
3) Plot these attributes on a diagram (see illustration overleaf), 0 being in the centre of the wheel and representing total incompetence, and 10 being on the outside and representing near perfection.
4) Have yourself and your team agree on a current score for the business (this is just an exercise for thinking about strengths – it's not worth getting the CEO to settle the dispute between giving yourself a five or a six in any set area!).
5) Visualise what a 10 would look like, and what it would mean to be 10.
6) Brainstorm (THINK) what you'd need to do in order to get that perfect 10 – and what action steps you can take to get to that level of perfection.
7) Capture all the ideas that come out of that meeting (don't judge them during the meeting).

8) Together choose two or three key ideas to implement and put into practice. These can become your drivers for internal ideation – a key component of innovation.

Doing this exercise with your marketing team might look something like this:

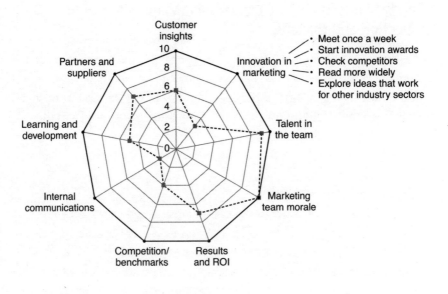

The business wheel example

The beauty of the wheel is that it can be used for any function, any person, or any organisation to provide a great snapshot and idea-generation tool for any business unit. However, just remember to choose what you measure carefully; so, for example, something on which you're scoring a three on currently, you might decide to outsource, rather than spending the next six months trying to make it a nine or a 10. Deciding what you want to become excellent at is part of strategy; it's about identifying what's really important … and that's down to you.

To go from good to great (or poor to great, or great to greater), you can't beat hiring smart people and then using whatever method works for you to spend some time getting them to actually think. Good luck.

The idea in brief:

- *Not enough organisations spend time on proactive thinking: not just solving problems, but enhancing strengths or achieving goals*
- *Getting smart people into a room and thinking about how to achieve something is a great business weapon that costs nothing*
- *Creative thinking puts you ahead of your competitors and creates unique solutions so that differentiation is easy*
- *Let your team know that ideation is part of their job with immediate effect*

29

Leadership styles that get results

'Effective leadership is not about making speeches or
being liked; leadership is defined by results not attributes.'

Peter Drucker

To get the best results, you must select the *best leadership 'hat'*. At the end
of the day, all great leaders know that they've been hired to get results.
Indeed, Brian Tracy told me categorically, 'The responsibility of a leader
is to get results.' As I've said before, nothing is more true.

Brian went on to say:

The measure of leadership is how many results you get, and how
predictably you get results – and there's a wonderful osmotic
process in the free market that if you get results at one level, you'll
be given higher responsibility to get results at a higher level, and then
a higher level. Getting results is learnable; you can learn how to get
lots of results.

Everything else is noise.

So, to get the best results, do leaders need to have the same style in *all* situations? No. They need to adapt their leadership style accordingly, to select a style that will get the best result for the situation at hand.

Let me elaborate: all leaders have a preferred 'style' of command. However, they select an appropriate style for each situation (or the person that they're dealing with) in order to get results; they dance between the styles with ease and fluidity. Although they'll feel most at home in one of the styles, they know that they have to select other styles or perspectives to suit each situation. This is why Ken Blanchard coined the term *'Situational Leadership'* and talked about it in my interview with him.

For example, if your office building is on fire, you don't want to call a meeting, get everybody in the conference room, seek all the options available to you and then vote for consensus to ensure buy-in before you take action. You need a very different style. Nobody will get upset if you bark orders that day! Thomas Jefferson once said, 'In matters of style, swim with the current; in matters of principle, stand like a rock.' (These American Founding Fathers have a way with words.)

With this in mind, this chapter will look at the main styles and perspectives that we as leaders have available to us, and when it might be appropriate to use one vs the other.

Different leadership styles

I remember when I was the Regional CEO of my former company, I took the entire Singapore management team out for dinner, and drinks. During the wine-fuelled, post-dinner chat (always the most lively of any business communication) I was talking (perhaps rather boringly) about that fact that, on a macro level, there are two different 'types' of leader: a visionary type of leader and a detail type of leader. When I'd finished, our whip-smart CFO called out, 'Yo, Anthony, which type are you?' I replied, 'Visionary', to which he asked, 'So what's your vision?' I replied, 'Vision? Oh, that's just a detail.'

On further reflection, I realised that there aren't just two types of leader, there are as many styles of leadership as there are leaders on the planet. Everybody is different, everybody is unique and therefore has a different style. To find some order in the chaos, Daniel Goleman groups the infinite styles of leadership into six macro-style categories in his book *Primal Leadership*. The most effective leaders are those that, although they might have a natural preference towards one, move between the styles, adopting the right style for the situation at hand.

1. Visionary leaders

This leadership style is all about sharing your end goal with the group, and setting people free to innovate, experiment and take calculated risks in order to get there. These leaders are big on innovation, future-thinking and lofty goals. They will often say, 'Come with me.'

2. Coaching leaders

These leaders are focused on the individual members of the team and trying to improve their performance through extensive coaching. These leaders will often say, 'Try this.' They'll make sure that people are getting one-on-one time to be developed.

3. Affiliative leaders

These folk are focused mainly on the team as a whole, getting the team to perform well, and praising the team. They're most focused on making the team and the organisation feel part of a whole – a community if you like, fostering a shared happiness and feel-good factor. These leaders will often say, 'People and team come first.'

4. Democratic leaders

These lovely team players always seek to keep harmony by getting consensus within the group. These leaders will often say, 'So what do you guys all think?', which is great for getting commitment and buy-in from the team, as well as using the input from your supersmart folk to influence the decision. The downside is that committee meetings take a long time. However, for the important decisions it's worth it.

5. Pacesetting leaders

These trendsetters are the leaders that set exceptionally high perform-ance goals ... and then expect them to be hit. They set them for others and they set them for themselves – what's more, they lead by example, are committed to excellence and expect others to be the same. These leaders will often say, 'Do as I do, now.'

6. Commanding/coercive leaders

These hierarchical leaders will command from the top down. They will often say, 'Do what I tell you.' These leaders have the least positive impact on the climate. They demand immediate compliance. Working for one of these coercive leaders full time is as much fun as licking a hedge-hog. It's sometimes good to remind these folk of what Dwight Eisenhower once said: 'You do not lead by hitting people over the head – that's assault, not leadership.' However, don't forget, if the building is burning down, this is about the best style around – so like every type, there's a time and a place for it.

Whatever leadership style you adopt, remember that long term it's better to have people feeling inspired and wanting to follow you, rather than becoming demotivated because you're pushing them around.

Here's a great exercise to do in your next team meeting: get every-body together and then ask them to stand up and raise their right hand. Ask them to turn to the person on their right and place their hands against each other. Then ask them to put pressure on the other person and push. Then push a little harder ... then harder still ... and even harder ...

What does the other person do? Yes, they push back. The harder you push, the harder they push back. It's the same with leadership – far better to take others with you, to lead them and for them to follow you; that's when leaders and their teams dance.

The team, task and individual: three-way focus

Leadership theorist John Adair takes a similar approach to Daniel Goleman, in his case identifying three core areas that great leaders need to look after at any one time:

- TEAM – getting people to reach consensus, making sure there's healthy debate, good synergy and high team morale.
- TASK – making sure that the task gets done no matter what, and keep driving back to the task and results.
- INDIVIDUAL – making sure that you're coaching individuals, giving appraisals, reviews, feedback, goals and so forth.

John goes to great lengths to point out that you need to spread your focus across all three areas, rather than zooming in on one area at the expense of the others:

Leaders with a bias towards Team will always be focused on team morale, team-bonding, team cohesion and community and team belonging, but can sometimes fail to focus on coaching or task-setting and hitting targets. Everybody will feel part of the team, it's just that they feel part of a loser team.

Leaders with a bias towards Task will put all the focus on tasks, task-setting, task-reaching, task analysis – everything is about the task. If taken too far, there's not enough focus on the team as a whole or the individuals within it. As a result, team morale will slip and there could be a lack of one-to-one training, which will lead to lower motivation and retention.

Leaders with a bias towards Individual will take people out to lunch one-on-one, will focus on coaching one-on-one, will meet one-on-one. If taken too far, there's not enough focus on the team or task; this could result in team politics and favouritism, and clique-ville.

The best leaders strike a balance between all three areas and succeed in leading exceptional teams and the diagram overleaf shows John Adair's picture of perfection. It can be useful to put this diagram on the wall in front of you, to remind yourself that every day you should do something on all three areas: individual, team and task.

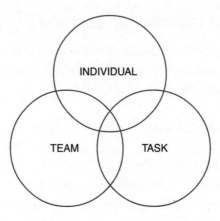

The three core areas of leadership

Like vs respect (respect is essential, both are preferable)

When discussing different leadership styles, there's an important question to be considered, which applies across the board: is it more important to be respected or liked by your team? Well, the simple answer to that is respected, because respect implies results. Never forget that people will respect you for what you have been able to achieve, not for how nice you are.

So is being liked even important? The answer to that is, yes it is – but it's not critical. Results are critical, likeability isn't. However, being liked is very favourable so world-class leaders make the effort to attain *both*.

The necessity for striking this balance for effective leadership is as relevant in business as it is in parenting! As Joseph Folkman wrote in an article for Forbes.com: 'Parents start to choose one side of this equation or the other. They want to be their kid's best friend or they want to be the supreme commander.' For the best results, you need to be *both*.

Great leaders are successful at striking a balance: if you're exceptionally chummy with your team and you're at their houses on weekends and always last to leave a party trying to hunt down the last free drink, then you might be heading down the path of over-familiarity. Yes you need to be social and head out for the drinks, but you probably shouldn't be the last one standing.

Whatever your natural style is, to be a great team leader you need to make all the different leadership styles part of your repertoire so that you can change and adapt based on the situation at hand. It's all about putting on the right hat for the best results.

The idea in brief:

- *Adapt your style to get the best results in any given situation, or meeting – if the building is on fire, you want to wear your 'commanding' hat, not your 'let's have a meeting' hat*
- *Remember, you have three responsibilities as a leader: Team, Task and Individual and you need to strike a balance among those areas*
- *It's far better to take your team with you, than push them to follow you*
- *Choose a style that ideally fosters both like and respect, but, if you have to choose, always remember to choose the style that will get the best results, over being liked. Leadership isn't a popularity contest; it's a game of results*

Congratulations on getting to the end of Part Two. Now that's you and your team sorted, let's move on to your organisation ...

PART THREE

ORGANISATIONAL Leadership –

building and leading world-class *organisations*

If you have mastered self (so you're firing on all cylinders) and team (so you have a whip-smart, complementary and buzzing team around you) but you have no idea what the leaders of great organisations do differently, then, if you ever get to the top echelons of the organisation, in the words of Blackadder, you'll be as effective 'as a cat flap in an elephant house'.

To be a world-class leader you can't just be a master of individual excellence or team leadership excellence; you must also know how to lead *organisations* to excellence. This means understanding what really makes the difference between average, good and excellent organisations: the elements that lift an organisation to greatness and market leadership, as well as the traps to avoid that lead them to mediocrity, or worse.

Obviously if you're the CEO running the company, your ability to understand this difference and to deliver organisational excellence is your day job, but even if you're not the CEO, or have zero intention of being the CEO (yes the job pays rather well, but boy, it can be lonely at the top, so it's not for everyone), you still need to know what great organisations do differently. After all, you're leading a team in the context of its environment and if you're in a healthy organisation, you should be able to shout upwards to get things changed for the better.

So Part Three is about putting the focus not on you, or your team, but on your organisation. Everything in this section is applicable to organisations of all sizes in all industries: essentially, it's what all organisations can do to rise above the rest. It shares lessons from some of the world's most famous leaders who are running some of the world's most successful organisations, or those who have started them from scratch.

Good luck in your quest for organisational excellence.

30

Customers first – love them and put them at the heart of everything

'We're not competitor obsessed, we're customer obsessed. We start with what the customer needs and we work backwards.'

Jeff Bezos

In 2011 a very smart three-and-a-half-year-old called Lily Robinson wrote a letter to Sainsbury's. She wrote a letter because she was concerned that the pattern on their 'Tiger Bread' looked more like the hide of a giraffe. Lily's letter said:

Why is Tiger Bread called Tiger Bread?
It should be called Giraffe Bread.
Love from,
Lily Robinson (age three and a half)

A short while later, Chris King from Sainsbury's customer services team replied with the following:

Dear Lily,

I think renaming Tiger Bread as Giraffe Bread is a brilliant idea – it looks much more like the blotches on a giraffe than the stripes on a tiger, doesn't it?

It is called Tiger Bread because the first baker who made it a long time ago thought it looked stripey like a tiger. Maybe they were a bit silly.

He included a gift card for her, and signed the letter:

Chris King (age twenty seven and a third)

Sainsbury's went on to rename its Tiger Bread as Giraffe Bread across all of its stores. In that brief exchange, Lily Robinson showed what a smart and observant customer she was and Sainsbury's demonstrated how they lived and breathed their customer-orientated values, not just for mums and dads, but for the little ones too.

This chapter is about reaching those lofty heights of customer appreciation and centricity. To create this level of customer love it takes leaders who are clear about what's important for this business and great leadership skills to instil those values throughout the organisations they lead.

If you listen to some modern-day business leaders – legends like Jeff Bezos of Amazon, Marissa Mayer of Yahoo!, Sheryl Sandberg of Facebook, or Tony Hsieh of Zappos, it's not long before they mention the sometimes underused word in business: 'customer'. Why do they keep bringing conversations back to the customer? Because they know that without their customers, they'd be *nothing*.

Yes, this might be unremarkable, in that we all know companies need customers to pay the bills, but the difference is that these world-class leaders translate this awareness into a genuine and heart-felt gratitude, a love (or even an obsession) for their customers and they embed this customer-centricity into the heart of the companies they lead. Indeed, these enlightened leaders get a genuine buzz when they're able to solve a customer problem, or meet an unmet need, or see the delight in a customer's eyes when they're amazed by the quality of a company's product or services. In essence, they love serving their customers in better and better ways. It's what they do – it's an obsession.

As a result of this obsession, these leaders do very well economically – why wouldn't they? After all, as the influential management consultant Peter Drucker once said: 'There is only one valid definition of business purpose: to create a customer.'

Yet, there are a lot of phonies around too. There are leaders who spout out that they're customer obsessed, and customer-centric. But they're not really. For these leaders, their magnificent obsession might manifest itself in the real world by picking up the phone once a week to a customer service rep to ask, 'So how you doin?', not listening to a word, mumbling, 'Oh good, oh good' at the end, hanging up, and then getting back to their day job. Not really world-class stuff, is it?

It's not that these leaders don't care; it's just that they're so busy with other things they haven't got time for their customers. Does that sound right to you? If your boss asked you for a meeting, would you say, 'I'm too busy this year, I might be available on the 3rd of October next year, but as I've got something pencilled in already, we'll have to see closer to the time'? Probably not. So why do so many leaders adopt this attitude towards the people who keep their organisations going?

More often than not, it's because these leaders are so focused on internal issues, so obsessed with their organisation's structure, or so obsessed with their own results, metrics, processes, issues (also known as 'stuff') that they almost forget that there's a big world outside the walls of their organisation. Not only do they become insanely dull to go to lunch with, but they become woefully ineffective too. I once asked a chief marketing officer when he had last spoken to one of his customers, either face to face or on the phone. He replied, 'Oh, I've been trying to keep up with all the marketing technology and things, so it hasn't really been my focus. I don't know – about three years ago?'

Three years! How can you formulate marketing strategy without knowing or speaking to the market directly? I reminded him that the word 'market' was even in his job title. Yet he'd become obsessed, not with customers, but with marketing processes.

In fact, as the best leaders know, the opportunity for big wins lies outside the walls of the organisation – with customers. These leaders don't allow internal stuff to pull them like the tide away from their customers. The magical Sir Terry Leahy was so obsessed with his customers during his time at Tesco that he never had to worry about putting a strategy for growth in place – it happened organically:

> CEOs always worry about where the growth is going to come from. [At Tesco] I never had to worry about where the growth was going to come from. Yet we grew from seven billion to 70 billion, in a slow growth industry. Why? Because I just decided: I'm going to stay as close to customers as I possibly can – where they go, and want to go, I'll be with them. It proved to be a success. I didn't need a strategy beyond that!

During Sir Terry's time at Tesco, this love for customers formed part of the company's core purpose and was encapsulated by the phrase, 'No one tries harder for customers.' Expanding on this, Sir Terry told me: 'The idea of really focussing on what customers wanted proved to be tremendously powerful, as it provided a single purpose that the whole organisation could fall behind.' I repeat: single purpose.

The leaders who really do focus on the customer and those they serve always reach great heights, and so will you. It's all about asking, 'How can I serve my customers better, how can I meet their current needs and future needs?' And for some, like Amazon's Jeff Bezos, becoming quite obsessed with it. After all, it's a high-calibre (and lucrative) obsession.

Great CEOs and leaders schedule time each week to spend with customers

Like all things important, if you don't schedule protected time in your diary, it will get filled with other things like, Does Jimmy deserve a new laptop (or whatever)? In fact, when I asked the legendary and iconic Philip Kotler (Professor at the Kellogg School of Management) for the one piece of advice he would give to CEOs who want to be world class, he replied with the following plea:

> Please, Mr or Mrs CEO, please visit customers. Do you know that Jack Welch, who we admire greatly as the former President of General Electric, when asked the question 'How much of your precious time

do you spend with your customers?', said, 'Fifty per cent of the time.'
Even with a lot of other things to do – he's got to do financial
reports and public relations – he manages to spend 50 per cent.

Jacqueline Gold echoed this idea when she told me, '[As CEO] don't
shut yourself away in an ivory tower – make sure that your directors get
involved at all levels: work in the stores, get out and meet customers!'

By spending time with the customers this a) sends a message to the
entire organisation that customers matter (and your direct reports *will* pick
up on this focus), and b) when you make your big head-honcho strategic
decisions, you'll be able to actually hear the voice of your customer in your
own head, therefore you'll make far, far, far better business decisions
(which will make you a far, far, far better leader). Here are two examples
of how leaders spend time with their customers on the front line:

In my interview with Markus Kramer, Global Marketing Director of
Aston Martin (yes, I think he gets a company car to drive!), he said:
'Building a sustainable competitive advantage is all about understanding your customers – but not just from a figures and data perspective;
you really have to spend time on the front line – at events, in dealerships,
you have to intrinsically feel and understand who these people are and
why people buy your products and your brand.'

Then there was Sir Terry Leahy, who, despite the fact that he was
'hopeless' at scanning Cornflakes and weighing onions on the tills at
Tesco, told me:

I used to work as a general assistant every year – and the deal I did
with the top 3,000 managers is that they'd do a week as well. It's a
very good thing. You get to see the business from a very different
perspective: you're on the receiving end of your own decisions,
which can be very sobering – and it keeps you in touch with what
the business is about and the jobs that most people actually do.

There is nothing like spending time on the front face with front-line staff
and with customers. Whatever business you're in, schedule some time
this week to either meet with your most important customers or head
to the front line where all the action is happening and find out what they
really think.

Great leaders obsess about customer experience

A lot of leaders put their organisational brand values on the wall and say, 'That's us – aren't we clever and quite lovely?' But very often there's a massive disparity between what *you* think your company stands for and the actual experience of the *customer* and the way they perceive you.

Tom Peters defined the concept of brand to me as 'the experience people have with you'. He couldn't be more right. This idea applies to all areas of business (the experience new hires have with you, the experience your suppliers have with you, etc.), but is particularly important when it comes to your customers. So although you think you treat them all like one of the 26 active sovereign monarchs in the world today, *they* might think you treat them like a schmuck – and perception is everything. So how do you find out and put things right?

In my interview with Ken Blanchard (author of *The One Minute Manager*), he explained to me that every time a customer comes in contact with you, it's actually a 'Moment of Truth', i.e. an opportunity for you to reinforce your brand, your values and your exemplary service:

> It's a Jung Carlson concept. He was the president of Scandinavian Airlines and he said, 'We're not going to beat the competition because we have good airplanes; we're not going to beat the competition because we have the lowest price; we're going to beat the competition at the 'moment of truth' – which is any time a customer comes into contact with your organisation.

So how can you find out whether your organisation is living up to its values at these moments of truth, and how can you put things right if it isn't? The only way to do this is to put yourself in your *customers'* shoes and test the key moments of truth yourself. At each moment of truth, you test, make copious notes on things you like as well as the things that you find as irritating as sitting next to somebody on a long-haul flight with loud rap music thumping from their massive earmuffs (sorry, I'm experiencing this as I write, at least it's off my chest now). Then from this list, make sure you keep the things you like, and go about correcting the things that are annoying or irritating.

It's worth the effort. You see, there are probably about 30 key moments of truth that an average organisation should test and improve, and, as the leader, you need to do it yourself once in a while.

Typical moments of truth might be:

- When a customer tries to find your telephone number on your website, are they having to spend 28 minutes trying to find your 0845 number because it's hidden in the smallest font in the furthermost corner of your webpage? If so is that a good customer experience? No siree!
- When a customer emails you about something, do they get a response within an hour, or a month, or never?
- When a customer calls your customer helpline, does it take them five frustrating minutes of optimistically hitting * or 0 to get through to someone?
- When a customer arrives at one of your physical stores, do they get a warm welcoming smile from somebody seeking to help, or are they faced with a cranky, frump of a person who sees the customer as an inconvenience who has just disturbed a very pleasant chat they were having with their colleagues?

Begin with the end in mind

Once you've gone through the process of testing the key moments of truth for your business, you need to be committed to fixing any holes in the experience you're offering your customers. To quote Stephen Covey, the best way to do this is to 'begin with the end in mind'. Put budgets, costs, logistics, reality and every other limiting factor to one side for a second and allow yourself to dream about the ideal customer experience. What would it feel like and be like to experience your product and your organisation in those aforementioned moments of truth?

When you think about this, you need to go through each journey that a customer can take with you and make it ... well, sublime. Think about the values, the fun, the 'wow' factor, the ideal experience your customer would have at all moments of truth.

Once you've got the ideal in your mind, fight tooth and nail to make it a reality – bully, beg, plead, charm – whatever it takes to get the budget. (If you're the CEO you might not have to do that – what a luxury. So now use that!) You can blow people away with an amazing experience – the best leaders *insist* on it.

Consider investment in the customer experience as a long-term play

When you try to implement your 'ideal customer experience' at any moment of truth, you might hear the objections, 'Oh my, this might involve that dirty little word: cash'; 'Oh my God! Are you going to ask for a budget?'

Yes, this *will* require funding and what's more, the financial payback for the organisation might not be in three weeks, three months or even three years. But the best CEOs and companies get that sometimes long-term investments do need to be made – especially if there's an immediate positive impact on the customer experience. As Jeff Bezos of Amazon said:

> Any company that wants to focus on customers … [or] to invent … has to be willing to think long term; it's actually much rarer than you might think … most of the initiatives we make take five to seven years before they pay any dividends for the company. They may start paying dividends for customers right away, but they often take a long time to pan out for shareholders and the company. So that ability to think in five- and seven-year time frames really is very, very useful …

One of the most prolific failings of modern organisations is that they become so focused on pleasing the shareholder in the short term, that they negate the customer in the long term. It takes courage and fortitude for a CEO to take on short-term cost for what might be long-term gain.

Go to battle to defend the user experience

It's inevitable that during downturns things have to go (see chapter 37 for more on this), but just be careful about shredding the customer experience. If you do, many competitors will be salivating at the possibility that they might be able to steal your beloved customers away as you stumble and drop the golden ball.

This advice is applicable even when you aren't operating in a tough economy. If you always err of the side of cost preservation, then, over the process of iteration that too can erode the customer experience. Not many leaders wake up and say, 'Let's make our customer experience worse', but it's a death by a thousand cuts – eventually that's what they get. If for example you're flying a plane from London to New York and you keep banking half a degree to the left you will end up in Ghana (well not necessarily Ghana, but somewhere and definitely not New York). The customer experience your organisation offers is the net result of your small decisions, so make each wisely – if you don't then your customer experience can deteriorate from a great one, to one that *totally* sucks, in just a few weeks or months.

Simon Calver experienced the impact of iterative decisions when he was CEO of LOVEFiLM: 'We were making too many of those marginal decisions *against* the customer, rather than *for* the customer ... so if there is any decision that is going to make the customer experience worse, I want to be involved.'

To avoid this, imagine you have a rather vocal customer in *all* your meetings

As your customer isn't sitting with you in important conversations and meetings (well, usually), their voice can be forgotten. To stop this, many great organisations have adopted tools to remind everybody in every meeting to consider the customer in every decision. To give you a few examples, Amazon has an empty chair at every meeting to remind them of the customer voice; LOVEFiLM has a mascot representing the customer in each major meeting and EE ... well, they've actually got a real, live, warm-blooded, person. In my interview with EE CEO Olaf Swantee, he told me:

> I've got a person in my team who represents those customer issues and the customer experience. She represents those issues at the board level and she has a veto; she is allowed to say: 'You can't do this – this will have too big an impact on our customers in a negative way' – and by bringing customer experience into the board, by somebody who is not in a functional position but in an operational

role, we can work through those issues and make sure the
customer's voice is heard.

Whatever you decide to do, making a particular effort to remember the
voice of your customer at meetings is a powerful way of remembering
that your customers matter.

Great leaders raise the bar from customer 'satisfaction' to customer 'love' (and customer tattoos)

'Satisfied' – huh? That's so last century, darling!

If you're still talking about customer satisfaction, then you might get
eaten whole by a company that talks about customer love, or the ideal customer experience. The latter trumps the former every time. According to
Ken Blanchard, 'Satisfying customers is not enough – you have to create
a situation where they go, "*Wow*, I can't quite believe that happened."'

You have to design these moments – they don't happen by accident.
It all comes back to creating the ideal experience and then working back
from there.

Making customers love your company and brand will pay dividends,
particularly when it comes to marketing. Philip Kotler, in reference to
Aston, Harley Davidson and the other brands with a cult following, said:

> It's interesting because these are companies [Aston, Harley and the
> beloved brands] that spend less on marketing; you might have said,
> 'The reason they're a cult brand is because they've spent so much
> on marketing.' No. The fact is, it's the customer that does the
> marketing; the customers are talking about you all the time and so
> why should you spend that much money on marketing?

That's a nice scenario to have. Richard Reed, cofounder of Innocent
Drinks, told me about one customer who 'loved [Innocent] so much he
had our logo tattooed on his arm'. How can you inspire that type of
loyalty from your customers? While the lion's share of success in business comes down to having the right product, often the game is won the
day a leader in the company asks, 'What would we have to do for our
customers to be wowed by their experience with us?'

Some companies have spent huge sums in wowing their customers – think Matthew Key's development of the O2 arena. But let's say you don't have the opportunity or resources at your disposal to sponsor a huge project like the O2; creating that WOW moment doesn't always have to be expensive. For example, around the release of the much-hyped and coveted Sony PlayStation, Virgin Atlantic installed them in their departure lounge for passengers to use. It was a low-cost 'wow' moment that made their customers feel great about flying with Virgin. As Ken Blanchard told me, it's about: 'doing that little extra that blows people's minds'.

So, what little extra things could you do to blow people's minds along the typical customer journey with you? Are there any high-value, low-cost things you could provide for your customers right now that would WOW them?

Great leaders know happy employees make for happy customers

Who is dealing with your customers the vast majority of your time? Yes, it's Jim and Jane at the front line. If Jim and Jane love working in your organisation, they'll be happy; this happiness comes through to your customers. It's one of the *main* reasons that you need to drive a motivated workforce.

It's an amazing customer experience going somewhere and being greeted by a warm, pleasant and happy person. A warm, loving, caring smile (not a fake smile or a snarl) is the best customer marketing and best customer retention tool there is on the planet.

A perfect example is when you check-in your bags for a flight. When you *eventually* get to the front of the queue with your bags and go up to the counter, clinging on to your passport, how do check-in staff treat you? Do they greet you with a beaming smile and eye-contact, or a dropped chin and apathy? Or even worse, with hostility? You see, something as simple as the way the staff interact with you is a reflection of the airline's attitude towards its customers. A positive experience might encourage you to fly with the airline again, a negative one might put you off for life – business is won and lost on the front line.

Think about your business's equivalent of the check-in desk. Are the people at the front line of your organisation as engaged with the idea of serving the customer as you are? Make sure they're truly motivated by visiting them and telling them you value what they do and ensuring that they feel connected to the importance you've placed on customer experience in the wider business – after all, they've got the most important job around.

So to wrap up this chapter (I hear you, yep, it's been a long one … wrap it up, chap)

The best leaders are not those who are masters of performance reviews, hiring processes and all things *internal,* the best leaders are those who get out of their seats and use their skills, passion and influence *to meet customers and make their entire organisations customer-centric*. It's when leaders recognise that they live to serve and 'wow' their customers that greatness in leadership can and shall prevail.

The idea in not-so-brief:

- *Develop a passion for and obsession with serving your customers – their current needs and unspoken future needs*
- *Customer-centricity must come from the top, but if you're not at the top, do it anyway*
- *As a leader, never drift too far away from your customers: bad leaders fall into the trap of internal fixation*
- *Lead by example on this one – block out time to spend with your customers today*
- *Meeting needs of customers is the job of everybody on the payroll – it's not just marketing*
- *Customer experience is the be-all and end-all of everything so invest in transforming the moments of truth – these are all opportunities*
- *Look for high-value, low-cost ways to improve customer experience*
- *Have your customer attend all meetings, even if it's just in the form of a mascot or an empty chair*
- *Customer satisfaction was a buzzword in the 1970s; it's time to drop it and aim for customer tattoos*
- *Business is won and lost on the front line, so make sure your love for customers is shared by your front-line staff*

31

Tough calls – cutting losses, mistakes and failures swiftly

'As a leader, you need to care deeply, deeply about your people while not worrying or really even caring about what they think about you.'

Dick Costolo

Unfortunately, leadership isn't always about creation and building and doing things, such as catching people doing things right, or giving praise, or setting the vision, or creating new partnerships and launching new teams.

Leadership has another side to it, and it's a contrary and opposing force to the aforementioned, and that's *reduction and cutting* – making hard decisions and having the resolve to follow through on their execution. This can manifest itself in the real world in many ways. Sometimes it's making tough cost reductions that are unpopular; sometimes it's making teams of people redundant because the macro-economic outlook demands prudence; sometimes it's closing the investment behind a 10-person innovation project because the line in the sand has been passed and it's time to call it a day.

Yet these opposite forces of creation and destruction are truly inter-connected within the minds of great leaders. They understand that to be highly successful, they need to be fluent and highly capable at both. It's pure Yin and Yang. Great leaders are able to seamlessly shift from one to the other – and wear different hats as the situation dictates.

Turnaround CEOs vs growth CEOs

For example, many executives and academics believe there are two different types of CEO:

1) *Turnaround CEOs:* these CEOs are known for their ability to be parachuted into a failing company, quickly identify what needs to get done and then sacrifice whatever it takes to turn the business around. Most of these folk have a bias towards being 'thinkers' not 'feelers' and are known for their very calculated 'hard' and 'tough' decisions.
2) *Growth/Building CEOs:* these CEOs are much more focused on brand, product development, long-term customer satisfaction, succession-planning and talent development – more nurturing souls, if you like.

But should they in fact be different people? Or should leaders and CEOs be able to switch mentally from one type to the other as the situation demands? Here's what Allan Leighton told me: 'There is a view that you have to be different types of person to do one and do the other – I don't agree with that. I think if you're a good leader you should be able to do both, because a lot of the time you have to build, rebuild, build, rebuild, build, rebuild.' I totally agree with Allan – the world's best CEOs are those that can do both.

One of the most respected CEOs in the world is Charles Wilson. He's both a master of turnarounds (like the Arcadia Group) but also a master at building companies over the long term (the rise of Booker). Somebody like Charles fits right in to the *Ideal CEO* section.

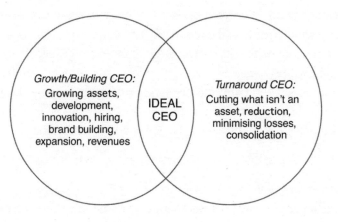

The ideal CEO strengths

Choose what's right for the business *long* term – even if it scares the pants off us short term

The one common denominator in tough calls is usually cash: an individual employee, a team, a division or a branch isn't making money, or there's a new competitor on the scene, tougher market conditions or a merger.

Some people say that business folk are money obsessed, and point out the best things in life are free. That's fine for *individuals* and if they want to take that philosophical approach, then go for it, but it's not the mantra of leaders pertaining to the organisations they run. If leaders have a nonchalant approach to money, they're doing the people a disservice.

As a leader you have to remember that CASH is king. This is true for charities, institutions or the private sector. Money is your organisation's life-blood. If you don't care about money, if you're not commercial, your organisation *will* fail. This is not just a shame, it's an unmitigated disaster for all the employees that rely on you to feed their families. And it's a shame for society – after all the more money you make, the more corporation tax you pay, and the more you can give away through corporate social responsibility or other initiatives.

When turning around General Electric, CEO Jack Welch told CNBC he was 'laying off an army of people, but [he] did what had to be done'. Nothing should come in the way of the economic prosperity of the company. Leaders need to act swiftly if the organisation is being drained of its lifeblood (its money).

So what are the common scenarios that require tough calls to be made?

Economic crisis, joint ventures, mergers, turnarounds

Sometimes external circumstances come in and shake up the playing field. It's not anybody's fault – it just happens. Sometimes the business has fallen off a cliff, for whatever reason, and the company is in a turnaround (perhaps a disruptive competitor with an innovative business model or a new technology). When that happens, how you respond as the leader can make the difference between lights out and market leadership.

When I was Regional Managing Director in the US in 2001, our revenues dropped significantly after the terrorist attacks on the World Trade Center. It was my responsibility to go to our Chicago office, which had about 70 staff, and let everybody go (including some great talent and great friends) as we had four offices in the US and we needed to consolidate. It was, without doubt, one of the toughest weeks of my career so far, but it's what *had* to happen for the US operation to thrive.

Olaf Swantee, talking to me about the merger between T-Mobile and Orange, said: 'I don't like to reduce employment, or to tell people that they have to leave, but I had to do that because we had far too much management in our company – we had 26 people reporting to me.'

Failing business unit

Business is all about risk and all the world's greatest leaders in business are incredibly comfortable with that, because they know that doing anything new involves risk. Hiring a new person, launching a new team, producing a new product, buying a new company – whatever it is, there will be risk involved. These leaders recognise that risk is worth taking; it leads to innovation and, in turn, to growth through advantage and market leadership. Growth, competitive advantage and market leadership lead to wealth beyond measure.

The difference, though, between a winning company and an average (or worse) company is that in the former, leaders invest heavily in the things that work, but *quickly* cut the things that don't.

In my interview with Jacqueline Gold, she told me about a business unit that didn't work out for Ann Summers:

> I don't regret trying it, because you have to try new ideas, but my biggest regret was not recognising sooner that it wasn't going to work. Instead of losing a million, I may have only lost half a million. The trouble is that when you're passionate about something, you do keep pursuing it and saying, 'It's going to come right in the end' and if you've got a team of people on board and they're all passionate about it, then, yes, it's a hard decision to cut the cord sooner rather than later. But cutting the cord sooner is something I'd definitely do today without hesitation.

I'm not suggesting that you take action before a new unit has had enough time to get through its initial teething problems – after all, you don't want to cut a department or new initiative just before a major upswing; it's just that sometimes folk end up waiting for an eternity for that upturn. Sometimes you have to draw a line in the sand and call the shot.

It's not always easy to know when it's the right time to call the shot. For example, for its first two years, Twitter didn't really get much traction at all. This is why great leadership is often more of an art than a science, why this chapter is called 'Tough Calls' and why intuition always has a part to play in every decision.

Firing people due to a gross lack of integrity

As a leader you should display zero tolerance for any signs of the above, so fire 'em quick and let everybody in your organisation know why you've let those people go (subject to local employment laws, obviously).

Firing low performers or those who do not live up to organisational values

As we discussed in chapter 25, you have to let people who aren't performing go – it's part of the job for the leader of an individual team or an entire organisation. Plus, if you're serious about values you have to be willing to swing the axe to defend them. However, as we've gone into it in detail earlier in the book, we won't go into it here – again, please just check and follow local employment laws!

Having the conviction to follow through with tough decisions

Tough decisions are tough decisions, so when you are required to make cuts, here are six tips that will help:

1. *Remember three words:*

    Respect – always respect the people that you're dealing with and treat them in a fair manner.
    Empathy – have genuine empathy for those people.
    Communication – always communicate in a clear and open way.

2. *Keep your emotions in check.* According to Daniel Goleman, 'The people that are most effective don't tune out in order to protect themselves and turn off to other people; they stay open [to emotion], but they're able to pass through that and to manage their own inner state – to let it roll off.' The key is to care and empathise, but also to let go of the emotion; this is a great technique to carry over when making tough calls.

3. *Feel the fear, take a deep breath and do it anyway.* This is another great technique, discussed in chapter 6. Everybody has fear and nerves, but, as Sir Terry Leahy says, as a leader, you need to 'take a deep breath and do it anyway'.

4. *Focus on the right thing.* Earlier in the book we discussed the importance of 'focus' and the concept of 'you get what you focus on' (chapter 19). When you're executing tough decisions, keep bringing your focus back to what's right for the company long term.

5. *Have a deadline.* As these decisions are tough, it's very easy to allow procrastination to slip in, so make sure you have drawn a line in the sand — a deadline for action. Some leaders have what I call 'horizon deadlines', i.e. they're always on the horizon!

6. *If you are going to do something, do it swiftly.* Swift correction is far better than long, drawn-out correction. As Brian Tracy says, 'If you are going to eat a live frog, it's far better to eat it quickly rather than slowly.' Not the prettiest metaphor, but it paints a pretty clear picture!

Leaders do need to make tough calls, so live and breathe the courage to always do the right thing for your organisation, even if that means over-coming personal feelings or anxiety. In fact, build a brand on doing so.

The idea in brief:

- *Leaders need to both build and cut, as and when necessary*
- *Always put the organisation first. Leaders who don't make the tough calls and act swiftly (i.e. cutting when something needs to be cut) have a huge impact on the bottom-line results.*
- *The best companies constantly invest in the 'new' — they cut what doesn't work quickly, and invest heavily in what does*
- *When making tough calls, always remember three words: Respect, Empathy and Communication; keep your emotions in check, feel the fear — and do it anyway, stay focused on the big picture and don't procrastinate*

32

Commit to innovation excellence

'Companies have to find a way to allow creativity to emerge. I always tell leaders of companies: you innovate or you stagnate. Sure, sometimes innovations fail, but stagnation is a sure failure ... Any firm that is not investing in innovative and creative work is going to miss the boat.'

Philip Kotler

From the teashops in Tokyo to the quesadilla restaurants in Mexico City, business leaders everywhere are talking about innovation; it's *always* a top priority for world-class leaders.

What's all the fuss about? They're fussing because they know it's the single most important factor that will determine their *future* success. It determines whether they'll be winning the race far out in front, or choking on the fumes of the competitors ahead of them.

Top leaders also know that they're fortunate enough to be living in a time of unparalleled opportunities, but wise enough to know that the world is changing fast, and new threats appear far more frequently than in placid times gone by. As such, they know that innovation, change and embracing the *new* can be a sustainable competitive advantage if they can instil the culture of agility and change in their organisations.

In fact the world's greatest leaders have innovation in their blood, and the world's greatest organisations have those innovators on the payroll.

So, if you like change, congratulations, you're living in the right century; if you don't, then don't worry – with technology growing exponentially, it won't be long until you have a time machine that can take you back to the early 1900s or something. Until then, however, there's no point in fighting the wave; ride it and make sure you and your followers enjoy the journey.

Some critical definitions for innovative leaders

What the heck is innovation, and how does it differ from creativity?

In my interview with Edward de Bono he shared the definition and the differences perfectly:

> Innovation means putting into operation something that is new for your organisation. That idea may be used elsewhere; it may be copied; it may be borrowed, stolen, bought – and that's good; that's excellent. It's not quite the same as creativity where you're generating an idea specifically for your circumstances. Innovation itself does not imply original creativity – it means putting something new in for your organisation.

To be an innovative leader you don't have to come up with original ideas yourself – that's creativity. To innovate, you can see what's working for your competition, or borrow ideas from other industry sectors. For example, it's always good to see what the gaming sector is doing (they're always pushing new things), or due to its extreme competitive nature, a lot of organisations have copied what the porn industry has done – not in terms of content but in terms of business models.

Wherever you get an idea from that might improve the way you do things in your organisation – go with it. In the words of Simon Calver, 'I am not precious where an idea comes from – some of the best ideas are stolen ideas'. Leaders are curious and are always on the hunt for new ideas that they can bring in to their team or their organisation to improve things. So always be on the lookout.

What the heck is disruptive innovation?

If you call somebody a disruptive innovator it sounds like they're doing something wrong! However, for any tech people or entrepreneurs out there, it's the biggest compliment. They might even go a shade of pink, become coy, and say, 'Oh thank you!'

Essentially, disruptive innovation is an idea that is so powerful that, once implemented, it could change the landscape of an entire industry. It's usually a new business idea that's founded on a new technology-enabling platform – like the Cloud, or a new business model that throws pricing on its head. Some examples would be: digital film vs standard film; video streaming vs DVD; online eTailers vs bricks and mortar; online subscription with monthly payments vs pay-up-front (such as Salesforce or Google Docs).

What the heck is kaizen?

Kaizen is a Japanese term that means continuous improvement (the translation of kai is 'change' and zen is 'good' so, 'change for the good'). This is essentially when companies work every day to improve their offerings, day in and day out. The ideas usually come from employees. Ideas and changes that come from continuous improvement are usually smaller changes, rather than radical changes brought about through disruptive innovation.

Which is better – kaizen or disruption? In the digital economy there's less 'buzz' about kaizen/continuous improvement and there's a lot more buzz about disruption (that's because the digital age is disruptive by nature). However, it's crucial to remember that both are vital in leading an excellent organisation.

And finally, what the heck is ideation?

Ideation is often confused with innovation, but the two are very different. Ideation is the process of *generating* new, original ideas; innovation
is the umbrella term for coming up with and *doing* 'new things'. The
word 'doing' differentiates between ideation and innovation. It's not until
you act and put the idea into practice that it actually becomes innovation – up until that point, it's lip service. Again, as Edward de Bono told
me: 'Innovation is a bit like climate change – it's a bandwagon; all the
politicians say, "We're very concerned with climate change" and all the
managers say, "We're very concerned with innovation" – but because we
come up with ideas but fail to implement them, very often it's just lip
service. Nothing actually happens.'

By committing to action, leaders allow innovation to take place.

Innovation isn't just about shiny new products ... it happens at departmental level too

Although most of the discussion to follow is about product or services
innovation, innovation isn't *just* about new products, new tech stuff, new
services or new business plans, it just means putting into practice new
stuff that helps your company. Many organisations never create a good
innovation culture. Why? Because the vast majority of the people, like
Agnes in payables, don't think it's their job. They think it's something
that the crazy folk over in research and development or marketing do.
But Agnes and the rest of 'em are wrong – innovation is *everybody's* job.

As Tom Peters (author of *In Search of Excellence*) told me: 'Innovation
as a word is as important in accounting, logistics or HR as it is in new
product development.'

You see, finding out a way to save one hour a day of work in the
maintenance room or a way to increase productivity in the accounting
department is innovation just like any other form. As such, the leaders
of those departments need to flick the 'How can I improve things?'
switch in the heads of their teams. Things can always be done better in
every department.

When talking to students at Stanford University about her time at
Google, the magical Marissa Mayer (now CEO of Yahoo!) said of its

innovation culture was: 'We expect everybody to have ideas.' Your job as leader, right now, is to make sure everybody in your organisation knows that innovation is their job – you might find they salivate at the opportunity of being able to change things for the better.

Phew, that's departmental innovation ticked off, now let's move on to more traditional territory: products and services. Why is this such an important topic? Because, as Brian Tracy told me, '90 per cent of business success is having the right product in the first place.' Amen to that.

Remember that innovation is NOT the customer's job

'If I had asked my customers what they wanted, they would have said faster horses.'

Henry Ford

Many leaders think that if they listen to their customers enough then one day Sally Smith, a customer from Newport, will present a mind-blowingly brilliant, game-changing idea that's going to disrupt the entire industry and provide them with a cash cow for the next one hundred years. This rarely happens in reality.

Customers are *usually* very good at telling you what they like and what they don't like about your current offering, but rarely will they give you a brand-new product idea. In other words, they're great at kaizen, not at disruptive innovation. Edward de Bono said: 'Customers on the whole are good at telling you what they like and don't like, but you shouldn't rely on them to come up with the big innovations and big breakthrough ideas.'

Jeff Bezos supports this idea, saying: 'It's really important to invent. [At Amazon] what we talk about is "inventing on behalf of customers". It's not a customer's job to invent for themselves. Sure, you need to listen to customers, but they won't tell you everything, so you need to invent on their behalf.'

As a leader, you need to be flying the flag for innovation – it's your job. The breakthroughs come from you, and your whip-smart team. To do that job properly, you need to make sure that everybody in your organisation is always 'switched on'. As Brian Tracy put it: 'You have to be like a radar screening the horizon – reading, listening, talking, asking questions, and then every so often it's like a lightning strike in the cartoons; one idea can save you five or 10 years of hard work.'

Sir Terry Leahy echoed this idea, when he told me:

> I think there's a great advantage in an organisation to have your radar switched on and looking at the world around you, and that's tough in organisations because the pressure is always on – you've got your nose to the grindstone, deadlines and what the boss wants, but actually just being curious about the world – how it's changing, and what the implications are for your organisation – is incredibly valuable.

All the greatest entrepreneurs and business leaders on the planet seem to say one thing: 'We innovate on behalf of our customers.' For example, Steve Jobs said: 'It's not about convincing people that they want something they don't. We figure out what we want. And I think we're pretty good at having the right discipline to think through whether a lot of other people are going to want it too. That's what we get paid to do.'

Innovate the 'Google Way'

It's well known in the tech world that Google has allowed all of their engineers to spend 20 per cent of their time to focus on ideas that they think are – to use a 'tech' word – cool. Marissa Mayer explained it sent a clear message to their employees that said: 'this is a company that really trusts them and wants them to be creative – and wants them to explore whatever it is that they want to explore, and it's that license to do whatever they want that ultimately fuels a huge amount of creativity and a huge amount of innovation'. So as a leader if one of your team comes up with a great idea, you might want to let them spend some time to pursue it – it's worked for Google, so well in fact that some people are calling it the 'Google Way'. Why not give it a try in your organisation? It could lead to the next big thing.

Leaders build a culture of challenging assumptions – internally and externally

Challenging assumptions can reap great rewards and should be practised by leaders, both externally in their wider industry and internally within the company they run. So let's look first at how two great leaders challenged external assumptions with great success:

Challenging assumptions externally

It wasn't so long ago that the business model for supermarkets was 'bigger is better', but Sir Terry Leahy challenged this industry wisdom and thought, Hmmm, what about small? Here's what he told me in our interview:

> I use the example of Tesco Express. The industry logic said that big stores were what worked in the economics of the industry, but actually, when we spoke to ordinary people, they said 'We're getting busier and busier in our lives; we have less time to go to big stores.' So, against the industry wisdom, we developed miniaturised stores that we could place adjacent to people in high streets and office parks, university campuses and villages, which proved to be hugely successful.
>
> Now Tesco Express's turnover is in the billions of pounds and there are thousands of them all over the world – and they're the most popular format. Now that innovation, which was highly profitable, came from listening to what customers were saying about their lives!

By challenging the supermarket industry assumption that 'bigger is better', Sir Terry Leahy found that both big and local have their time and place in the market and he succeeded in providing an alternative, highly profitable, revenue stream for his company.

Starbucks is another company that challenged assumptions as to what people are willing to pay for their coffee. I just about remember a time before Starbucks came along, when I was drinking steamy, watery coffee from little white polystyrene cups with plastic lids at a cost of about 30p. If you'd asked me back then whether I'd pay 10 times more for my morning coffee, then I'd have said, 'No way, I love my polystyrene flavoured coffee', yet now I pay a small fortune for my 'venti caramel macchiato with whipped cream and extra caramel' without giving it a second thought.

So are there any external assumptions that might be holding your business back? If so, you might want to test to see if they're actually true, including what people will pay for your product/experience – the only way to find our whether an assumption is true is to test the market.

Challenging how you make money (yes, innovation of the sacred 'business model')

There's something very hot out there in the world of business: it's not supermodels but business models. They're back in vogue. Why? Because business dynamics and the business plans that support them are changing, and they're changing faster than ever before. Technology is changing what is possible in the world and those companies that are able to respond fast and well to future opportunities will be the ones that survive and prosper. Consequently, leaders around the world are not just having to innovate on product, but also at the very core of their organisations: the way they make money.

Looking at the way they generate money freaks a lot of leaders of big, established companies out, yet it delights a lot of new companies and entrepreneurs who salivate at the idea of disrupting established industries. This threat of the teen-or-twenty-something tech-guru has made many big companies extremely paranoid that smaller, more agile competitors with jeans-wearing, disruptive tech folk will discover inefficiencies they can exploit and eat up their breakfast – and paranoid is quite a good state to be in, in this day and age as complacency kills.

All good CEOs are paranoid – even those running the most successful companies in the world. When asked what keeps him up at night, Bill Gates said: 'I'm worried about some guy in a garage inventing a new technology that Microsoft has never thought about.'

But why is it more difficult for large companies to innovate at the business-plan level, when that's what the new companies do all the time? It's because the CEOs don't want to play around with the elements of their businesses that make them money. They become scared that if a business model has been working for them since 1985, who are they to change it? Instead of innovating, they decide to leave the problem for their successor.

As Microsoft's CMO, Philippa Snare, put it: 'Some companies are lucky in that they don't have any legacies and therefore they don't have those huge revenues coming in from their cash cows or their big old products they've had for years. They don't have that and therefore they're not stifled by that.'

As a leader, you should make sure you set aside time to investigate new business models – to read widely, be curious about what's working in other industries, keep an eye on fast-moving competitors, anything – just be on the hunt for game-changing ideas that you can apply to your own company.

To give you a specific example of why this is important, consider the way pricing models have changed over the last few years. A few years back 'freemium' was a buzzword being thrown around the business circuit.

Although freemium is a model that's been around for decades, it really took hold because of the fact that in the digital economy it became easy and cheap to implement. (This is a fascinating area and for further reading, I recommend Chris Anderson's excellent book *Free: How today's smartest businesses profit by giving something for nothing.*)

The idea is that businesses provide users with a basic product or service for free. If the user likes the free version, they might then upgrade to a more advanced premium service/product (this is pretty much the way the app market operates). Think, for example, about how Skype uses its free service to compete with BT and AT&T and then sells paid-for products/services/upgrades to the customers who have been using their service for free.

Providing customers with a free service also encourages them to share or recommend the service to others, which leads to free marketing for your product. Mass 'virality' isn't going to happen from behind a paywall, and customers are always much more inclined to share content with their friends, tennis partners, colleagues, lovers, or anybody else if it's free.

The reason this example is so relevant here is that the leaders who heard about the model, stole the idea and made it their own, often fared far better than those that didn't.

So always be on the lookout for new pricing or business models. Even if it does mean playing and tinkering with the holy grail of your business – it's what the leaders of tomorrow are doing.

Challenging assumptions internally

Companies can become very set in their ways and sometimes their'ways' are prehistoric, flat out wrong, stupid or costly. To be a great leader you need to get into the habit of challenging perceived corporate wisdom and ingrained assumptions about the best way to do things. It's important to keep in mind that, just because you tried something 20 years ago and it didn't work, doesn't mean it won't work today.

Andy Cosslett told me: 'Sometimes what didn't work for your organisation in the past will work now. There's so much that goes on in business that is conventional wisdom, corporate orthodoxy. Why do we do that? Because we've always done that. And you have to have facts, not opinions, that demonstrate every assumption.'

For example, if you keep telling people that your company doesn't need to spend any more marketing money on direct mail and that you can go 100 per cent online, but everyone tells you it's not possible, then take a lesson out of Henry Ford's book. As Sahar Hashemi, cofounder of Coffee Republic, told me: 'Henry Ford was trying to make a conveyor belt go faster and the guys on the conveyor belt said, 'Sorry, Mr Ford, we've been on this conveyer belt for 30 to 40 years and believe us, this conveyor belt cannot go any faster.' Henry Ford's reaction was, 'Okay then, go and find me a 19-year-old who has got no idea this can't go any faster, because that 19-year-old can make it happen'. There is a Chinese proverb pertaining to this, which is, 'The person who says it cannot be done should not interrupt the person who is doing it.'

So are there any internal assumptions in your organisation that are plain wrong, or at least that you can bring a challenger mentality to? If there are, commit to discovering how you could do things differently.

To bring it around in a giant circle, don't forget your assumptions could be wrong too, which brings us to the wonderful, lucrative and exciting world of testing assumptions and moving quickly to exploit the successes.

Foster courage, risk-taking and permission to fail

We all know that the more things you try, the more successes you have and the more failures you'll have. The secret to success therefore lies in a willingness to invest in many new ideas and then swiftly investing more in the things that work for your company, and culling what doesn't.

So let's look at the failure side of the equation for a second. Some leaders go around saying, 'Sure, Jimmy, that sounds like a fab idea, give it a go – what have we got to lose?' and then when the project fails, poor Jimmy finds out what he's got to lose: his job. When some leaders even just hear the words 'mess-up', 'screw-up', 'fail', 'failure' they immediately bring out the firing gun, but then proceed to scratch their heads wondering why they don't have a healthy culture of innovation and risk-taking in their organisations. Even Thomas Watson, the legendary former CEO of IBM, once said, 'If I had to do it all over again, I would have encouraged employees to make more mistakes'.

Similarly, Greg Dyke told me: 'I remember one day standing up at the BBC and saying, "Look, I give you my word that if you try something and it goes wrong, and you've done it in the best interests of the organisation, we'll support you – because I want you to try some things and do some things, as opposed to waiting for permission for everything."' (We need more Dyke-style leaders hanging around HQ.)

And Sir Terry Leahy, speaking about the magic he worked at Tesco, said: 'Not shouting down an idea, and then not punishing failure, are the key ingredients to getting an organisation to try new things.'

But going further than that, if you want to embed a culture of risk-taking in your organisation, then rewarding people for doing it is a great way to achieve this. So every month, or every quarter, have innovation awards, where you recognise the best new ideas in every department. Or, if you don't want to do it group wide, then at least do it for individual teams. It really makes people realise that it's important – and it is.

As a leader if you allow for a lot of tests, quickly cut the ones that don't work (without reprimand) and invest in those that do work – your rockstar status will be guaranteed, after all that's what all great leaders (and companies) do.

Test, test, test and test some more . . .

The bottom line is that nobody knows if an idea is really going to work. To find out for sure, you need to put it out into the market and test it. For example, not one mobile operator ever thought text messaging was going to take off. It was only when they tested it in the market that they saw people's phenomenal desire to send short messages to each other.

Indeed, entrepreneur Doug Richard (who was one of the original dragons on the BBC programme *Dragons' Den*) told me that if Biz Stone, Jack Dorsey or Evan Williams had walked into the Dragons' Den with the idea for Twitter (before it had gone live), all of the dragons would have turned down the opportunity to invest. The proof is always in the adoption, not in the conviction or emotion of the idea-holder.

The best way to test is through prototypes. As entrepreneur Sir Stelios Haji-Ioannou told me:

> There are no shortcuts – you have to try it. But just make sure that when you test something, test it with the amount of money that you can afford to lose. I've done it a number of times – more times than most people – and I still can't tell in advance that the risk I'm taking is worth it, but I know that I'm taking a risk; I can quantify it, and I know where to look for the outcome. If you're not testing anything, you're unlikely to make any superior returns.

The potential for big wins far outweighs the potential for losses. As Mark Zuckerberg said, 'In a world that's changing really quickly, the only strategy that is guaranteed to fail is not taking risks.'

'Better Done Than Perfect'

In most industries (perhaps not pharmaceuticals!), there's no harm in whacking together a beta (i.e. in testing phase) and throwing it out there to gauge market attraction. Users are familiar with innovative companies that test ideas on a small scale to get feedback before rolling it out more widely. These prototypes don't need to be perfect, so don't worry about it; just get things out there and perfect them with feedback.

Michael Birch said that at Bebo: 'Our nature was to always spend a few weeks building something, put it live, and see how it looked. It's obviously different if you've spent three years building something and $10 million making it – and then find out that it was a crap idea in the first place!'

Testing using prototypes also allows room for the evolution of an idea. When talking about the phenomenal success of internet companies Google, eBay and Facebook, Ed Wray said: 'Google didn't start out making any money from search. It was a search business, but it hadn't worked out how it was going to make any money. eBay changed its business model, Facebook changed its business model. None of those guys said, "This is how I'm going to do it" and stayed there. They were continually evolving their businesses [by testing and trying new things].'

Take the venture capital approach to testing

If you go into any vibrant and successful organisation, they'll be testing things and trying things – and inevitably with this comes projects that don't work. So as a leader, you must make this an accepted and inevitable part of the process.

For example, venture capitalists know that if they back several companies, only a few will be successful, but the ones that do succeed will (far) offset their losses.

Here's what Sir Stuart Rose says about this: '[Success in business] is about spotting the trend and going for it. But there might be 10 things you spot. What you should do is chase all 10 of them – not bet the ranch on any one of them, knowing that only two or three might go somewhere, and if one of them does go somewhere, that one will pay for the others that didn't go anywhere.'

Adopting this approach is a good way to promote a culture of healthy risk-taking in your organisation, a culture of testing new ideas and then not immediately firing the team if it doesn't work.

Furthermore, all great leaders know that the people they employ want to be involved in testing and trying new things – it's interesting and it's cool to be on the experimental bleeding edge. So build a culture of trialling new things in your business, if something works you can scale it up, if it doesn't, move on – and let all your staff enjoy the journey of experimentation and adventure that comes with the testing process.

Use the power of 'what if?'

As we've established, you and the people in your organisation can come up with new ideas for your business from a variety of places: from what's working at your competitor to what's working in a different country to what's working in a different industry that might cross-pollinate to yours. But there's another important way to do this, which mustn't be neglected: good old original thinking!

You don't need to make all the things that you do original ideas – that's a lot of pressure. And there's nothing wrong with taking what works elsewhere and deploying it in your organisation. But the best leaders know there *is* great power in original thought. As Greg Dyke said, 'The people with ideas are worth their weight in gold.'

A powerful leadership technique for generating original ideas is scenario planning, which starts by simply asking 'what if?':

- What if we closed the Horsham factory?
- What if we doubled our sales force – what would happen to our bottom line?
- What if we added another product for people to up-sell and buy?
- What if we tried a subscription service?
- What if we increased our price point by 10 per cent?
- What if we offered a version of our product for free?
- What if we merged with another company?

Here's an example of 'what if?' in practice: I was once consulting for a smaller web-design company who had about 15 staff, but only *one* out of the 15 was responsible for sales and winning new business. So I asked the MD, 'What if you hired another one or two sales people?' After all, he was paying the fixed overhead costs anyway and so the cost increase would be a small percentage.

We did some scenario planning and showed that the additional cost to the business of just one extra sales person would be approximately

£35,000, but the revenue (based on moderate assumptions) would be £375,000 which, after the cost in servicing the revenue, would generate an additional £220,000 in profit for the year. That more than doubled their profit for the next 12 months and the business went from strength to strength on this one idea alone. So always ask yourself 'what if?' and encourage your employees to do the same – one innovative idea executed well can transform your business.

As a leader have an ideas net

As a leader you're going to come across ideas all the time – from your own meetings, from competitors, or from investors. Some will be good ideas, others less useful or even utter twaddle, but it's always important to capture them *all* at the time so you can digest and review them at a later date. For example, Larry Page always sleeps with a pad and pencil next to him. He told the University of Michigan that he once woke up in the night and asked himself, 'What if we could download the whole web and just keep the links?' Then he co-founded a company you may have heard of: Google.

To make sure you don't forget or overlook these potential nuggets of gold, create an ideas 'net' so that whenever you come across an idea, it's captured. You could use a notebook, a file, or an electronic document, just get into the habit of writing down ideas as they come to you. In the future you can weed out the good from the bad, but at least you will be confident that everything has been caught.

Ban the word *'cannibalisation'* – and replace it with *'future proofing'*

Many times loser leaders or muppet managers will shout, 'We can't implement those new ideas. I don't care how much the customers think they want it; it's cannibalistic to our current product offering.' But the truth is that if you don't, somebody else will. Being afraid of cannibalisation is short-term thinking and a dangerous trap for leaders (for more on this, see chapter 38).

Embrace diversity and expose yourself to new perspectives

To have the best innovation, you need a highly diverse organisation. If everybody is the same, then everybody will think the same. As Olaf Swantee, Chief Executive of EE, said to me, 'You get power in your company if you have diversity from the top down.'

As well as hiring for diversity, make sure that you, the leader, expose yourself to different perspectives frequently. One easy way to do this is to go out for lunch with different people! As Tom Peters said:

> For senior people in big corporations, exposing yourself to variety is literally number one. You have to expose yourself to new stuff, wild stuff, crazy stuff. The deviation from the norm as to the number of different people you go to lunch with is horrifyingly small for most of us. [If you go out to lunch with the same people all the time], the wonderful news is that you like your workmates; the bad news is you go to lunch with the person that you really like, and that you've been to lunch with 27 times in the last month – a lovely month but you're not going to learn anything new!

Create a federal structure with small, high-impact teams

Small, focused, highly charged and emotive project teams are a powerful way of testing and trying new ideas. These mimic the creativity that is formed in the start-up world and are a really powerful way for big companies to ensure that they've got innovative thinking going on in their organisation. In fact, Larry Page, the cofounder and CEO of Google, once said: 'We've tried very hard at Google to maintain an entrepreneurial culture and the way we do this is by having small teams work on things; you must have a small team that's really excited about it, that do everything like you would in a small start-up.' Plus, your employees love it. After all, why would Billy leave to go somewhere else when he can work on what's cool and what's new in your organisation – and keep the staff canteen!

And finally, think in terms of solving unmet customer needs

Business, at the end of the day, is about solving unmet customer needs. It's scratching an itch or solving a pain. The bigger the need the bigger the opportunity. By always focusing on how you can solve unmet customer needs, you'll never stray too far from the lucrative world of innovation.

The idea in brief:

- *Innovation – doing new things – is on the minds of all great leaders today*
- *Make it everybody's job to innovate and come up with new ideas*
- *Customers can tell you their needs, but don't rely on them for big innovations*
- *Challenge assumptions – both internal and external*
- *Become positively dissatisfied – it's a great way to come up with new ideas*
- *If you were starting out today, ask what you would do*
- *Have the courage to fail and allow for risk*
- *Get loads of stuff out there – test a lot to find the winners*
- *Ban the word 'cannibalisation'*
- *Small, high-impact teams are best*
- *Be switched on to new ideas – it's a mind-set*

33

Align your business with future trends

'A leader's job is to look into the future and see the organisation; not as it is, but as it should be.'

Jack Welch

Wayne Gretzky, who was known as the 'greatest hockey player ever' (for Brits reading this, that's the game on ice, not grass), once said: 'A great player plays where the puck is going to be.' This is true in business and leadership too – a great leader aligns themselves with where the next future trend is going to be.

I can hear you saying, 'What? I've got a P&L to manage, Melinda's just quit and our CRM system isn't working properly – now you want me to be a futurist too? Are you kidding me?' Well, let me explain the case.

Sir Ronald Cohen, who founded Apax Partners (now one of the most respected venture capital firms in the world) and who is widely known as the 'father of British venture capital', wrote a book called *The Second Bounce of the Ball.* In it he points out that companies that meet current customer needs are doing their job today (the first bounce of the ball) but companies that prosper in the future are those that anticipate the next major trend (the second bounce of the ball) and align themselves and their organisations to maximise the benefits accordingly. He points out that: 'If you want to build a thriving business, you have to see beyond today's certainties to tomorrow's uncertainties. You have to look at what is going to happen next in your field and put yourself in a position to take advantage of it.'

For a new company, this means making sure you align your organisation with a major trend. For a large, established company, this is all about, as Sir Stuart Rose puts it: 'reinvention'. Unlike the previous chapter on innovation, this isn't about doing new things, it's about aligning your entire organisation with the 'future new' …

(Please note, this chapter isn't saying that you should all take your focus off the first bounce of the ball – you should definitely focus on what's making you money. But it's also about investing in possible new future revenue streams. After all, the ball is always moving. It's when you do this that you might suddenly find that one of those so-called 'future revenue streams', becomes your primary one.)

All great business leaders have an opinion on the future trends in their industry

If aligning your company with future trends is what visionary leadership is made of, to be a visionary leader, and to align your business with the future, you have to have an opinion on the future.

When, during a public interview, I asked Sir Stuart Rose without a second's notice to give me his opinion on future trends in retail, he was able to give an answer immediately, eloquently, logically and with great enthusiasm for the road ahead. That's one of the reasons he's so great – this is what visionaries are made of. (Pretty much all 200 heads in the audience were nodding in agreement with his prophecy too.)

Let's check you out for a second

If I was interviewing you in front of 200 people and asked, 'So, what do you think are some of the key trends coming up in your industry, and what do you think the picture will be like in five years' time?', would you answer confidently or bolt for the fire escape or feign fainting?

Sure, you're busy with other things, but having an opinion as to the developments in your industry is essential for visionary leaders – if you don't have a clue about second bounces then there's no way that you'll be able to align yourself and your team to take advantage of the next one.

Placing bets on future trends

So why bother with trends?

In April 1994, Jeff Bezos was working at his computer (a big fat computer back then) when he came across a study showing that the internet was growing at a rate of 2,300 per cent per year. He was totally stunned. In fact he became fascinated by the growth of this space.

He soon realised that more and more people were getting online, and that pretty soon 'this thing was going to be *everywhere*'. Desperate to beat other mainstream bookstores (and ensure he was the first to the second bounce), he spoke to his parents, Jackie and Mike Bezos, and convinced them that this trend was going to be big and it was going to be the future. He did a good job: after he explained what the internet was, they gave him $300,000 – almost all of their money – to start Amazon.

Why was Jeff so successful? It was because he'd picked a trend – a colossal trend. As such, his business grew like a rocket – and his mum and dad made one of the best investments of the century.

Similarly, why was Michael Birch able to sell Bebo to AOL for £850 million, even though it was losing ground to the market leader (Facebook)? As Michael told me: 'Facebook won social networking; it just happened to be such a big space that you could be number two or three and still exit for a lot of money.' Along with the likes of Mark Zuckerberg, he'd aligned himself with a very powerful second bounce of the ball.

Another example is Sir Terry Leahy, who told me about the origins of his big bet on online retail:

> I went with my colleague, Tim Mason, to an installation called 'The Store of the Future' done by Andersen Consulting, who are now Accenture. The final exhibition was a kitchen, and despite the fact that this was 1995, there was a computer in the kitchen.

You'll have to think back, but that was very odd, because if you had a computer you certainly didn't have it in the kitchen! So we all asked the curator, 'Why is there a computer in the kitchen?' and he said, 'Ah, one day people will be able to order their shopping, their food shopping, from home' – to which we all fell about laughing and thought that was absolutely ridiculous, and we spent about an hour telling him why that would never work. We said, 'How would you communicate the order? How would you pick it?' And so on and so on. Then as we left, Tim and I said, 'But customers would like it, wouldn't they, if you could do that? I mean, I know it's ridiculous, but it would be really popular.' Within six months we'd launched Tesco.com.

Tesco.com went on to become the biggest online food business in the world.

It's all about evolution, baby

If you're the leader of a company that's been around for several hundred years, then congratulations – you'll know about the importance of rising tides and reinvention. Reinvention is critical, particularly in this day and age, where everything is constantly changing. Think for a second: do you think Facebook will be offering the same thing in 10 years' time? Google? Twitter? No. Why? Because companies need to change; they need to adapt to market needs, demands and opportunities.

When I asked John Studzinski about Goldman Sachs, he said:

Why is Goldman Sachs so successful? Because if you look at Goldman Sachs, since it was founded it's been the most astute organisation at marginally, incrementally reinventing itself and always staying a step ahead of the market – in a very entrepreneurial eye-opening way, managing capital, managing risk, but also doing it in a marginally fearless fashion. It has reinvented itself and that is why, from a Darwinian point of view, they're still the strongest.

So make sure that you are still picking the next trends and reinventing your company accordingly. Sir Stuart Rose told me: 'You've got to find that seam, and when you find it you've got to keep mining it, but remember, the mine is not inexhaustible, so then you've got to find another mine; that's what good management does, they reinvent.'

I hope that I've built the case for futurology and reinvention, because ...

I don't want to sound like a drama queen, but, if you don't reinvent and bet on new trends, it will be lights out

Take the example of Kodak. Do you remember those gorgeous little iconic yellow boxes with films in them, and everybody running around shouting, 'Cheese'?

Up until a few years ago, Kodak was full steam ahead with its print offering – holding a 90 per cent market share of photographic film sales in the US – but it was full steam ahead off a cliff, a giant, unforgiving cliff called the 'Digital Revolution'. Despite the decline in sales of photographic film during the 1990s, up until 2006 Kodak remained primarily focused on its print business and not on the digital business. I repeat, 2006! Although the business continued to execute well on its core offering, its slowness to embrace digital photography meant that the company began to struggle so much that it filed for bankruptcy protection in 2012. (Ironically it was Kodak that invented digital photography in its Japanese labs, yet even after inventing it, the leadership team did not see the rise of it as a medium, until it was too late.)

According to an article by *Forbes* contributor Chunka Mui, 'This strategic failure [not to reinvent] was the direct cause of Kodak's decades-long decline as digital photography destroyed its film-based business model.'

On the other hand, companies like FUJIFILM, who *had* invested in the rising trend of digital photography, laughed all the way to the bank – if you search for Google images of the FUJIFILM executives , everybody is smiling for the camera over there!

So, what's the next trend in your industry – have you placed some bets on it, or buried your head in the sand?

Don't be in denial about trends or market changes that might hurt you – face them head on and turn them to your advantage

As well as not having the time to consider future trends, many leaders put their heads in the sand when they see a potential bounce that could take a huge amount of time and effort or could be disruptive. After all, many market leaders are quite happy with the profits being made today. They like today's landscape because they're winning – and they don't want to start playing Mahjong if they are winning at the game of chess.

Sir Terry Leahy of Tesco pointed out that, as a CEO, you have to face the truth head on, whatever that might be: 'Face the truth of what's coming: the rise of China, the ageing demographic, climate change – big forces that are happening. But then, however bad it looks, believe that you can survive it if you're able to change and adapt to it.'

Some CEOs who don't invest in innovation are woefully guilty of not wanting to rock the boat. On this Sir Terry said: 'In the worst case, the CEO will say, "You know what? I'm here for three years, my share price is X, my bonus is Y and I'll just keep it calm, get out the way and leave it for the next guy". I think that really lets the organisation down.'

How can you keep your finger on the pulse of what's coming next?

Make time to read, absorb and think

The first step is to recognise that it's your job as the leader to predict future bounces of the ball. If it's your job, the only way it will get done is if you dedicate time to it. Ronan Dunne, the CEO of O2, told me:

> As a practice, I sit at the beginning of every quarter with the person who runs my office and we set out my non-BAU [business as usual] priorities. Essentially, what I try and do is to think about the things

that my colleagues aren't currently thinking about because they're rightly thinking about the priority that I gave them yesterday. It's a case of trying to be one quarter, one year, ahead and thinking, What are the evolving trends?

Remember also the enabling power of emerging technologies. Take time, for example, to reflect on what impact a new technology like 'The Cloud' might have on your industry and the opportunities it could bring which might result in a game-changing idea.

Invest in prototypes and scale up what works

As a leader, it's essential for you to make sure your organisation is constantly testing new ideas and scaling up those that work. For more on this, see Chapter 32.

Create a dedicated team

Although everybody in the organisation should be focused on trend-spotting – and you need to lead by example – while visiting Stanford University, Michael Dell (founder of Dell) said:

> [As well as getting everyone focused on it] we also have a group at Dell whose only job is to focus on things that are 18 months or further in the future; so they're not focused on the products coming out this year, or even next year – they're focused beyond that, on all the materials and things that could dramatically change the world. And then we meet with them every six weeks and we talk about two or three key things that might be really important.

As a leader your job is to be future orientated so invest some time in thinking and aligning yourself with the next bounce of the ball, the next rising tide, the next trend (or whatever you might call it) – failure to do so might result in the failure of your organisation. On the other hand, an ability to do so is likely to result in unprecedented niches and guaranteed success. But remember: the ball never stops bouncing, which is why, for great leaders, futurology is the name of the game.

The idea in brief:

- *A great hockey player skates where the puck is going to be; it's true in business too – what's the next opportunity to start aligning your business with?*
- *All great companies (new or big) always have a future-thinking team that can spot trends on the horizon*
- *Be agile enough to adapt to new trends, even if you don't like them! Don't be in denial – face the truth; it takes courage*
- *Develop a future-orientated mind-set*
- *Don't lose focus on your winners today (the first bounce of the ball) but spend enough time to make sure you're investing in your winners of tomorrow (the second bounce of the ball)*

34

Execution – winning by outproducing your competitors

'Ideas are easy. It's the execution that's hard.'

Jeff Bezos

About five years ago I was flying back to London after a trip to Singapore, and I remember getting very strange, and in fact, slightly worried looks from fellow passengers. I then realised why: I was reading Larry Bossidy's book *Execution*.

On the front cover there was hardly any text apart from the word 'Execution' on a red background. At 30,000 feet over the South China Sea, reading what others must have thought was some sort of do-it-yourself guide, I must have seemed quite scary. Anyway, it's one of the best management books out there today and I highly recommend it – although, if you do decide to read it, you might want to choose your reading place more wisely.

In the book, Bossidy points out that it doesn't matter how great your strategy, your vision or your people are, if you don't execute well (in other words *do it*) then you will fail. So many potentially great companies have great visions, but poor execution – and therefore never fly.

For example, when I asked Ed Wray why Betfair was able to beat Flutter.com (a competitor with significantly more funding), he told me: 'We executed better. People used to say it's first mover advantage. I think it's first *good* mover advantage.'

Execution is the organisational equivalent of action-orientated leadership, discussed in Part One (nothing happens unless you act). Just as visualisation is worthless without action for individuals, it is equally true that vision is worthless for organisations without execution. After all, as Warren Bennis (who is one of the pioneers in leadership academia) once said, 'Leadership is the capacity to translate vision into reality.'

The planning gap

Many leaders fall into what Bossidy describes as the 'planning gap'. This is essentially where a leader presents a set of goals for the future without ever working out the steps they need to take to get there.

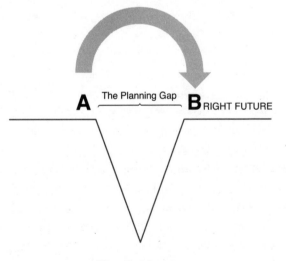

The planning gap

In my interview with Mike Harris, founder and CEO of First Direct Bank, he told me, 'Execution is best broken down into steps at a time.' Companies and their leaders that have broken down goals into small chunks and thought of how they're going to actually achieve them will be the companies and individuals that actually do so. The leaders who stare at you with a frozen expression and don't have a clue, are the ones with a planning gap that will prevent their organisations from achieving their goals.

So how can you avoid the planning gap and develop an action bias in your organisation that will enable the execution of your goals? Apart from always asking, 'What's the next step?' and then taking it, here are a few others:

Fly up to 35,000 feet and then come back down to the runway

As a leader, there will be times when you have to zoom out and go up to 35,000 feet to set the vision and the direction of your organisation. But to execute that vision, you also need to be able to zoom in and come back down to the runway to make sure that the strategy is getting implemented and is done well on the ground.

If you don't have these two perspectives then, again, you can fall short as the leader of an organisation – both matter. A perfect example of this is when I called the main switchboard at EE to find the office number for its CEO, Olaf Swantee, who I was due to interview the following week. The lady who answered the call asked why I wanted the number and I informed her that it was because I was interviewing him in a week's time and needed to check with his office about something. At this point she got all excited and asked what I was interviewing him about and when I told her it was about leadership, she said, 'Olaf will be perfect for that – he's a great leader. Not only is he a visionary, but also just last week he was listening in on my calls to check how I was doing. It was nerve-wracking for sure, but it shows how much he cares about us and our role with customers.'

This is a perfect illustration of the various perspectives of a great leader. Olaf was able to set the strategy (he decided to bring 4G into this country before anybody else), but the next day he had headphones on and was listening to calls!

Ask a heroic number of questions

As a leader, one of the most powerful techniques to use when you're on the runway is to ask a heroic amount of questions. For example, if one of your team says to you, 'We will increase our sales by 30 per cent this year', say, 'Alan, that's excellent news. I'm really looking forward to your achieving that growth. Now, how are you going to make it happen?' If Alan looks upwards for divine help with his answer, make sure he writes a plan for the execution of his goal.

Use your powers to remove obstacles

One of the best questions a leader can ask is: how can I help people to do their jobs better? Some of the most successful CEOs out there use their power in order to simply remove obstacles that make it more difficult for people to do their jobs. I was recently speaking to a friend working for a newly appointed CEO and one of the most important things that the new CEO did was to go around and ask the employees, How can I help? What's slowing you down? If you become Chief Obstacle Mover, your organisation will love you for it.

Employ great managers

> 'You need leaders who are inspirational, leaders who question, who challenge, who can see market opportunities and business opportunities that others may not see, but they need to be backed up, and supported by, people that can execute and convert the strategies into operational practices and activities [managers] – so yes, the two absolutely complement each other.'
>
> **Professor Richard Scase**

Although this book is called *The Book of Leadership* not *The Book of Management*, I see management as a very important skill for leaders. All leadership positions have a management component, just as all management positions have a leadership component. That said, on the whole, leaders and managers play very different roles in organisations. For leaders, management is not the primary modus operandi for doing their jobs. As the late Stephen Covey once said, 'Management is efficiency in climbing the ladder of success, leadership determines whether the ladder is leaning against the right wall.'

When it comes to execution, managers are vitally important. Take the example of a ship: if a ship's captain has pointed the ship in the right direction, but doesn't have the people to operate the engines, the ship won't even leave the port.

If an organisation has an abundance of great leaders but hardly any managers or the leader doesn't value the management component of their role, it will have one heck of an execution problem; every organisation needs somebody to set the vision, but also to manage the execution of that vision. As Allan Leighton, former CEO of Asda, told me, 'The great managers are the ones who keep the thing going the whole time.' So, if you want your organisation to execute on its strategies in the best way possible, you need to make sure you have the right team of managers in place that live and breathe for follow through, detail and getting people to get stuff done.

Roll out successes through great processes

'Vision – sure. Strategy – yes. But when you go to war you need to
have both toilet paper and bullets at the right place, at the right time.'

Tom Peters

If you're a start-up company with fewer than five employees, then business-process management or business-process reengineering probably isn't blocked out in your diary this week. This is because, at this size, internal communication is quite easy. The process for making anything happen is not much more sophisticated than, 'Check in with Nick, he'll know.' However, once your company starts to grow from five people all the way up to 300,000, like Tesco, it's essential to put processes and systems in place to execute your vision. Considering how processes can be improved might seem boring to some leaders, but taking the time to do so has been the maker of many billionaires.

When I interviewed Andy Cosslett, he told me about the processes used by the InterContinental Hotels Group to execute effectively:

We're opening a hotel every day, which is a very big demand on management resources, so you have to have good processes in place to be able to deal with it. So we have a very sophisticated 'New Hotels Operating Process', which has many stages on the way through, from signing the original deal for a new hotel in Paddington to opening it three years later. Every stage is monitored and managed and it's a well-oiled machine.

But how do you create a process? Here, I defer to Sir Terry Leahy:

You have to write down a process [associated with each best practice], which is just a series of steps or actions that have to happen. You have to be mindful that people are involved, so you have to define the roles that people must perform and, if you want to replicate it and make it reliable, you have to write an IT system for it. There are simple steps: data, decision, discipline, people, process, system. It's as boring as hell, but that's the meat and drink of successful organisational performance.

The best leaders are those who don't just spurt vision and strategy, but are those who spurt vision and strategy as well as ensuring everybody is focused on the how, the when and the nitty gritty of the execution of vision and goals. Be a leader who is known for getting things done.

The idea in brief:

- *A great way to beat the competition is to get more of the right stuff done (execution)*
- *Execution is doing things; it's productivity – the how to hit the goals, mission and vision*
- *As a leader, go to 35,000 feet then land back down on the runway*
- *Develop an action bias – just do it!*
- *Managers are crucial for execution – with no managers, nothing gets done in organisations and they'll never win*
- *Processes allow great execution*

35

Values and culture – moving beyond lip service

'Culture is what's happening when nobody is watching.
At O2, our values in the business are bold, open,
trusted and clear. At a moment of crisis, people align to
those values and behave in that way.'

Ronan Dunne

There are many people in organisations today who consider the issues of organisation values and culture to be soft, namby-pamby, clap trap nonsense. Although these folk might take some convincing, the truth is quite the opposite.

When I interviewed Sir Terry Leahy, a no-nonsense, tough guy from Liverpool, he said: 'I found – not just in Tesco, but in all my business life – that the softer side of management: values, vision and culture, is more important in sustaining business success than the hard side like marketing strategy, information technology or accounting. The reason for that is it speaks to the heart of the people.'

So, with these words of wisdom in mind, it's definitely worth:

1) Defining the values of your organisation as a whole
2) Making them visible
3) Using those values to underpin and create the culture of your organisation

Another thing to put up on the walls? Are you kidding me?

No, I'm not, but with good reason. Your organisation's values should be made as visible as possible so that all your employees are living and breathing your standards, your uniqueness and your organisational DNA, day in, day out. If you check out the world's most successful businesses, they have values displayed in their offices, in their communications and on their website. When researching this chapter I looked at the websites of hundreds of successful companies, including Dell, Microsoft, Facebook, InterContinental Hotels Group, O2 and Google, and every single one, without exception, had its values proudly on display.

Clear, considered and meaningful values give everybody in your organisation something to be proud of and allow you to define how your company is different. In practical terms, setting values as a clear bench-mark for success enables you to reward behaviour, build positive habits and hire people that have congruency with your values.

A case study: Zappos

I don't know if you've heard of the online shoe store, Zappos, but along with its magical founder Tony Hsieh, it has created one of the coolest organisational cultures in the world.

As one of the coolest and smartest companies on the planet, Zappos was (and still is) acutely aware that as small, founder-led com-panies grow, they can become cathedrals of dullness. They know that fast-growth companies and their workforces can become process driven, inward facing and systematised. Understanding the danger, Zappos has created a culture that is anything but this by going on the offensive and unleashing their company values early on. Those values were, and still are, big, bold and everywhere – like all companies that live and breathe their values, they are front and centre whenever you interact with the company (online, in store, at their head offices, etc.).

Having hung out at Zappos for a bit now, here is my impression of their values:

1) They believe in creating a magical customer experience

2) They have a love for change and new things

3) They believe in having fun and being authentic in everything they do

4) They have thirst for adventure (it seems they really believe that business isn't dull but a creative pursuit)

5) They believe in giving all their employees the opportunity to learn and develop

6) They believe in transparent communication (a 'say what you mean, mean what you say' approach)

7) They have a focus on creating a family spirit in their teams

8) They have a love for being smart with time and resources (über-productivity)

9) They are committed and passionate about achieving their goals

10) They are determined not to let their massive success (Zappos was sold to Amazon in 2009 for $1.2 billion) go to their heads

How to come up with the right values

Many people think that developing values involves a mystical process that requires the help of outside consultants who will charge you your next five years of earnings to help work them out. This simply isn't true. What you need to do, in reality, is to speak to people on the front line, get their input and then shape some values that everyone in your organisation can buy into. At the end of the day, developing values is often no more complicated than asking your employees, 'So, what do we really value around here?'

If you're not sure where to start, why not take some advice from Andy Cosslett, CEO of Fitness First? Here's what he told me about the way he developed the values for the InterContinental Hotels Group:

We went out to 900 employees, from Shanghai to Swindon, and asked for their language and their input. We asked them which words we were using that they didn't understand or didn't like, and then we gathered all that information together. It's amazing how many common themes and responses we got. We ended up with [a list of values called] The Winning Ways that don't just define our attributes and who we are, but have quite precise language underneath them about how we can act and behave on the front line to make a difference – and they've exploded. They're amazing. People have even written songs about them – oh my, they've been embraced. Why have they worked? It's because they're written in the language of the employees (they were written by them, after all), with input from the people that really matter, the people on the front line.

It's important, as Andy said, to involve the people in your organisation in developing its values. If you get a whole bunch of top execs together, then it will be so infused with management techno-babble that it will make sense to the board of directors but will be totally and utterly mean-ingless to the people on the ground.

Using values to create an awesome culture

It's not enough just to come up with a list of values; you also need to embed those values into the core of your organisation, by creating a cul-ture with those values as its basis, so that your employees can automatically incorporate those values into everything they do.

Here are some key ways to do this:

Hire (and fire) based on your values

Richard Reed, cofounder of Innocent Drinks, said to me:

You don't create a culture; it's the people you recruit who do this. The single biggest business decision you make is who you get to join your business. At Innocent we were clear about what we wanted in terms of values and brand, so we've been very strong at recruiting based on the values of the business. It's such an important philosophy to have your values, what you care about – and bring in people that care about those things too.

Likewise if you really want to instil the culture, you have to be willing to pull the trigger (not literally) on anybody that fails to live the values in your organisation, and show them the door.

Make sure your workspace reflects your values

If, for example, one of your values is to 'make work fun' or something similar, but you have a dull, dull, dull, work environment where people walk around like zombies, then there's a lack of congruency with reality. You can't just put your values on a piece of paper – you have to live and breathe them, and be willing to go crazy and paint the walls a sunshine-orange colour if it creates a more fun environment for your employees.

Please make sure *you* reflect your values

You will know from chapter 20 how important it is to be what you want others to be and when it comes to culture creation it's crucial that you are visibly embracing the values of your company through your own behaviour. Simon Calver said to me, 'Once you've set those values, you've got to live and breathe them. If you do that, and it will take a bit of time, then the organisation will begin to do it too.'

Associate specific behaviour with each value so your employees understand how they can apply them to everyday life

Listing examples of behaviour under each value will help translate theory into practice as well as removing any doubt about what the heck you're on about. By way of example: Coca-Cola has identified 'work smart' as one of the company's core values, and has associated it with the following behaviours:

- Act with urgency
- Remain responsive to change
- Have the courage to change course when needed
- Remain constructively discontent
- Work efficiently

Reward based on values

It's important to reward the employees who are contributing to the creation of the organisation's culture through their integration of its values into their individual work. Simon Calver told me: 'Every month we have an all-hands meeting, where we communicate where we are and how we're doing – and I give awards to people in the business based on those values, which constantly reinforces the five values that we have.'

But it doesn't always have to be a material reward, sometimes just showing your appreciation and recognising when an employee is upholding the organisation's values with a genuine thank you, or pat on the back, can be worth even more.

The test: are you living up to your values in the eyes of *all* your beloved stakeholders?

To ensure that the values and culture of your organisation are coming across to every stakeholder in your business, both internal (your staff) and external (your suppliers and customers), you need to be obsessed with the experiences these stakeholders are having when they come into contact with your company. Here are some stakeholders you can ask for feedback on whether the values and culture of your company are reaching them:

- A candidate for a job vacancy who isn't hired
- Somebody waiting at reception
- A supplier you've just started to work with
- A customer with a complaint
- A customer with a new idea
- A customer with a query
- A new hire
- An employee who's celebrating their birthday
- An employee who's leaving the organisation
- A supplier the company has worked with for a long time
- A visitor to your website
- An investor in your company
- A director in your company
- A bank manager that the company works with

These are all areas (and there will be many more) in which you need to make sure your values are alive and kicking. Check they're actually coming across, because when they are, that's when your values really are coming to life; this is what leads to a great culture that will differentiate you from your competition and enable you to rule the day.

The idea in brief:

- *Values define who you are and your culture*
- *Values make for great organisations (and great profits) – think Zappos*
- *Hire people that have your values in the first place!*
- *Make sure all of your customer touch points reflect your values*
- *Does your physical workspace reflect the company values? If it doesn't, then it should*
- *Reward employees based on values*
- *Make sure your stakeholders' experiences with you reflect your values and culture*

36

Know your organisation from the drains up

'Everybody that joins Dyson on the first day builds a vacuum cleaner, because then they know they're in the vacuum-cleaning business, and if you're in the vacuum-cleaning business, you'd better understand how one works.'

Allan Leighton

It might sound illogical to suggest anything different, but great leaders know all aspects of the organisations they lead. By this I mean *really* know it and *all* aspects of it. In fact, the *great* leaders become quite obsessed with all aspects of their organisation, their product and the systems that support it, and *totally* obsessed with their customer: why they buy from the company, their experience, their insights and what they might buy in the future.

This might sound obvious, but you'd be surprised at how many CEOs or business leaders lead an organisation without knowing it from the drains up. As I wrote in the introduction to Part One: 'If the blind lead the blind, both shall fall into the ditch.'

Sure, you don't have to be the expert at everything – after all, it's also the leader's job to hire in the experts. As Tom Peters said, 'If you are the boss, you are not paid to be the best sales person, the best accountant or whatever; you're paid to develop the best sales person, the best accountant' – but if that's the case, you'd better have a first-hand knowledge of whatever it is those experts are talking about.

So the question is *how*? How can you make sure that you know the business from the drains up? Here are three key techniques that all the great CEOs I've interviewed deployed to do just that.

Empirical lessons – sweat it out on the front line

Whenever any of the CEOs I interviewed joined an organisation, one of the very first things they did (I mean, literally, the first or second day in office) was to follow the journey of a product or service from conception to consumption. So if you're in a 'we make something' business, then make the product yourself. If you're in the service business, serve your customers. If you're in the hospitality business, be the host; it's through those experiences on the front line, rather than through hearsay at the company headquarters, that you'll learn what it is that your company *really* does.

To give you an idea of how this works in practice, Allan Leighton, who has achieved success in every organisation that he's touched, gave me three specific examples to illustrate this point:

1) *Dyson:* When Allan joined the board at Dyson, his first job as a director was to go and build a vacuum cleaner; after all, there's no better way for the bigwigs to find out the nuances, processes and intricacies of the business that they're leading than first-hand knowledge of the product.

2) *Royal Mail:* Allan borrowed Dyson's idea when he became chairman of the Royal Mail. Not only did he insist on posting a letter and literally following its journey until delivery, but when Allan appointed Adam Crozier as the Chief Executive of the Royal Mail he got him to go down and deliver mail at 4.00 in the morning! Talking to me about this, he said: 'Everybody who joined the board has been out delivering the mail at 4.00 a.m.

with the postmen. In fact, what we get them to do is to follow a letter. So they're actually out for 24 hours, because then you understand how the thing works.'

3) *Asda:* Similarly, Allan said that when he was CEO of Asda he 'used to make everybody go and work on the checkouts. If you were in finance, your first day wasn't in finance – it was in the store!'

(If you take nothing else away from this section, at least you know what you'll be doing in your first week if you go and work for Allan!)

Know your differentiators and USPs clearly

I don't need to tell you that we're living in a competitive world. So it is worth a mention at this point that a big part of knowing your organisation from the drains up is a clear understanding of what makes your organisation different from your competitors. You see, in a world where everybody wants to snatch everybody else's business, you must know the reason why a customer would want to buy your product/service instead of what's being offered by the company around the corner. As Jacqueline Gold told me:

> Your USP is one of your keys to success – you don't want to be copying anybody else. You have to be unique; you have to have something that sets you apart from your competition, whether it's a great service, fantastic value for money or a fantastic product, you have to identify what makes you different.

Could you easily and swiftly tell me right now, why a customer would choose your company over a competitor? If you can't, get out there right now and find out.

Get data, get information and walk around

Allan Leighton put it best when he said: 'I'm not one for royal visits; I just turn up. It's not because I want to catch everybody doing it wrong, but I want to see what things are really like. Anyone can make anything look good if they know you're coming. Often the best way to find out what's going on is to just turn up.' So make sure you're always walking around and speaking to people and getting feedback and insight from all departments.

Another method great leaders use to find out what's really going on in their organisations is to insist on seeing unfulfilled or inbound complaints from customers. Not only does this give the leader the chance to deal directly with their organisation's customers, but it also provides them with critical customer insights and again, sets an example to the entire organisation about what's important.

According to Allan Leighton, leaders also need a 'radar' – a network of people and inbound opinion, information that tells you what's *really* going on. Creating a radar will help you to go a level deeper than the stuff people want you to hear. Allan himself doesn't just build a network for people to talk to or rock up to sit on his employee's desks for a chat (which he does all the time), he also allows people to email him directly regarding information and opinion – yes he gets a tonne of emails, but it's better to be in the loop and have open communication than not have the information at all. A lot of CEOs do this: I know that, for example, Sir Martin Sorrell (CEO of the WPP Group) is legendary at answering his own email – yes, he delegates it out like a speed-demon, but he's scanning it to find out what's going on. So allow people to email you directly, come and see you – whichever way you choose, just be approachable.

Simon Calver echoed this when he told me, 'Being the CEO can be a pretty lonely job. You're the guy at the top and you're the guy that might have to tell people things they don't want to hear. My advice would be to build a network within the organisation that you can reach down into to find out what's really going on. The best people to speak to about what is happening in a job are the people that are doing the work – and they will say to you, "You know what, Simon? This just isn't working" or "This is mad" or "This isn't happening" and you may not get that message back through otherwise. Spend time in all departments.'

And don't forget the power of using the good, old-fashioned telephone to reach out to staff. I know one CEO of a major pharmaceutical company who just picks a name at random from the company telephone directory and phones that person to find out about what's going on with them – any challenges they're facing, any interesting news etc. I'm sure it freaks the employee out to have the CEO on the line while they quickly finish their mouthful of homemade cheese and pickle sandwich, but it's a great way for the CEO to hear directly from the people in the business.

Be fluent in finance, or at least know the numbers

When I asked Jon Moulton (one of the world's greatest turnaround champions) what his one piece of advice on business was, he said: 'Numbers – anybody that doesn't follow the numbers in the business they're in always fails. I don't think you can do it without having a high degree of financial astuteness; self-taught or not – you have to have a real feel for the financial workings.'

Whatever business you're in – even if it's in the charity sector (or especially if it's the charity sector) – make sure that you know the financials. Try to hang out with the finance team as much as possible; you could even work in finance for a day a week for a month or so, but if they won't take you, then at least take some of those folk out to lunch once in a while. Finance guys and gals often love talking strategy and their opinion of the business can be shrewd, strategic and objective (and they love a free lunch!)

The idea in brief:

- *Great leaders know all aspects of their organisation and the customer proposition*
- *As a leader it's very powerful to go back to basics and do the thing that your organisation does; if that's sending the post, send the post!*
- *Hang out at the coal face of customer and front-line staff interaction*
- *Get data coming in to you from your team organisation – via email, through a network, taking people out to lunch or just from walking around*

37

Leadership in a crisis – testing leaders under pressure

'I think you can only tell a leader when the going gets tough.'

Sir Stelios Haji-Ioannou

Wouldn't it be blissful if we could just lead during the good times? But when the good times aren't rolling and you're just getting smashed against a wall with one crisis after another, then what?

Let's look at a quote on this topic from my interview with the founder of easyJet, Sir Stelios Haji-Ioannou. He said: 'I think you can only tell a leader when the going gets tough, when there's difficult times – whether a financial crisis, a problem created by weather or a technical issue ... so that's the time to judge a leader.' This idea isn't new: Publilius Syrus, whose writing flourished around the first century BC, said, 'Anyone can hold the helm when the sea is calm.'

Indeed, many would argue that when a crisis hits, it's the true test of, not just the leader, but also the organisation. So, with this in mind, this chapter will discuss two time ranges: long-term crises (for example, the economic crisis which began in 2008) and short-term crises (such as an unexpected weather front moving in, a technical breakdown or publicity crisis).

Long-term crisis

The financial crisis of 2008–2014 was a long and protracted one, and I hope and pray that it's a long, long time until the next one. However, when it comes to leadership, there are many lessons that can be taken from the leaders of the organisations that fared well during this period.

Be a dealer in hope

During the economic crisis many leaders totally lost it, and therefore their companies suffered big time. Conversely, many leaders got it spot on. During my interview with Daniel Goleman he shared some wise words about leading in a downturn:

> Leaders get results through others. And one of the leader's tasks, at a primal level, is to help their people be in the best emotional state and brain state, so they can work at their best. That means two things: manage fear and inspire hope to keep people focused on where they're going – not on how bad it is now, but on how it can be when we get through this and go onward. This activates the left prefrontal cortex, which is the centre for positive emotion and also for continuing to work toward goals no matter what the obstacles are today. So there might be a lot of things that aren't working out for an individual or for a company, but if we can keep everybody's minds focused on that goal, it activates a centre that gives us a visceral sense of how good it's going to feel when we get there, and that feeling is the primal and motivating driving force that keeps people going forward no matter how tough it may be.

Andy Cosslett nailed it when he said: 'You have to be very focused on today and making sure you're doing what you need to do in terms of managing your costs: thinking about the cash, thinking about your customers. But people also need hope for the future and they need to know there's a better day.' (For more on this, I'd suggest revisiting chapter 19.) Indeed, as Napoleon once said, 'A leader is a dealer in hope.' Sometimes the leader's primary job is to remind people of this point, yet during the 2008–2014 economic meltdown, some CEOs and leaders of businesses that went under forgot the 'hope' and 'better day' component and therefore lost the plot.

Cut the right costs

Tough times will make it necessary for you as a leader to make some tough calls, particularly when it comes to costs, but to steer your team successfully through difficulties, you need to be clear on the difference between tough calls (which might be painful to make at the time, but will be positive in the long run) and dumb calls (which will damage your business). John Wayne put it bluntly when he said, 'Life is tough, but it's tougher when you're stupid.'

There are three areas with high potential for dumb calls, in which you should be very wary of cutting costs:

1) *The customer experience.* We discussed in chapter 30 how important customers are to your business and you should never forget that in tough times; if you lose customers, eventually you'll lose your company. Andy Cosslett said: 'Continue to invest in the customer experience, because there's a great temptation in a poor economic environment to reduce the amount of spend, but if you're doing that you won't be delivering the right customer experience now or in six months' time. So make sure you continue to invest in the customer.'

2) *Innovation and ideation* (discussed at length in chapters 32, 33, and 34).

3) *Revenue centres that are generating internal return on investment.* For example, if your marketing spend has an ROI of 400 per cent, then that means if you spend £10,000 there, you get £30,000 in profit. Why oh why would you cut that cost? You'd only do that if you thought your £10,000 spend could generate you a higher ROI somewhere else, but still, that's a risk. This is a similar scenario. If you're paying a sales person £30,000 a year

and they're bringing in £100,000 in revenue, you'd better be
very sure where you're going to get that £70,000 from. The best
CEOs do scenario planning, and they really think about the right
people to lay off and the consequences to the business.

Yes, you need to cut to bring your cost base in line with the new economic reality, but the best leaders are careful about which costs they cut.
They realise they might actually be directly cutting their profits; far better
to cut nice-to-have costs – after all, something's got to go: perhaps bowl-
ing and beer nights need to be postponed until the boom time. As
Jacqueline Gold said to me: 'It's about priorities; it's about which costs
will drive sales vs the "nice-to-haves."'

The key to making cuts is transparency and openness. Tell it like it is –
your staff aren't stupid (hopefully) and will understand that if the business hasn't got the money, it can't spend the money (at least if they don't
want the administrators and bankruptcy lawyers involved), but they will
appreciate honesty about the situation.

Be bold and continue to innovate – but bootstrap

In my interview with Sahar Hashemi, she said, '[During bad times] there's
a tendency for companies to huddle up and not take any risk. It's a time
for being bold, and taking risks, but you should bootstrap your ideas.'

By bootstrap, Sahar was referring to rolling up your sleeves and doing
things on a shoestring budget: really thinking of the best and cheapest
way of coming up with ideas and putting them to market. It's these
bootstrapping ideas that will put you in a good position when the economy picks up again.

Focus on the life-saving 80/20 principle

The downturn has meant that we all have to be über-productive and
focus on our winners, our strengths and the things that will bring massive value (for more detail on this, see chapter 9). Reminding ourselves
once in a while what are our absolute core strengths and the value we
bring to the world, is always a good thing to do, but especially so during
difficult times.

Short-term crisis

So everybody's idea of a crisis is different. For some it's that there's been a delay in delivering their baby-blue Louis Vuitton handbag, for others it's when their cricket team is all out for three runs or it's that the hairdresser didn't seem to listen when they said *'not too short please'*. But looking at any crisis, probably ones a bit bigger than the aforementioned, here's what great leaders of organisations do.

Keep calm and carry on leading

In my interview with Daniel Goleman he spoke about how important it is for leaders to stay calm in a crisis, and brought reference to the moment in the 2008 US election (John McCain vs Barack Obama) when the financial crisis hit. It's a fascinating insight:

> The reason that Obama won [the 2008 election] was because of his mode of handling the financial crisis. He embodied the ability to stay calm under pressure; he showed us that he could be cool in crisis. In a crisis, everyone looks to the leader to get a sense of how we should be reacting, and if the leader is panicking, then why are we going to stay calm? But if the leader is calm, cool, collected, focused – and Obama was – then we feel confidence; we feel there's someone steering the ship who knows how to get us out of this trouble.
>
> The critical point came in the US election: McCain and Obama were neck and neck in the polls and then the financial crisis hit and all of a sudden McCain lost it! One day McCain said, 'I'm going to stop campaigning. I'm going to go to Washington and solve this problem.' He did; he flew to Washington, and nothing happened. Obama, on the other hand, said, 'You know if you're president, you should be able to do two things at once: campaign and handle the crisis.' So he kept going on both tracks and he was actually calm.
>
> People who stay calm in a crisis can use their cognitive abilities better, because of the way the brain is designed. In a crisis, when we're angry, or we're distressed or anxious, that actually handicaps the thinking brain, the cognitive centres, that help us pay attention –

to stay focused, to take in information, to understand it, to respond well – and Obama showed us that he had that capacity [to stay focused]. And I think that's why Americans then shifted – and he won, basically, in a landslide after that.

For more on this, check out chapter 12, which looks at improving your emotional intelligence and chapter 13, which suggests ways to manage stress. The techniques outlined there should help you to stay zen during rough times.

Fix the problem, react swiftly, take responsibility and don't start throwing the blame around

Whatever the crisis at hand, you have to be seen to be tackling the problem and acting swiftly to solve it – everything else is noise. As such, you need to have a contingency plan for a crisis.

Some leaders are so bad at dealing with a big crisis that the organisation would be better off if its leader was sunbathing on a beach somewhere. They get into such a frantic panic that they lose their executive function (i.e. ability to think) but retain their ability to bark orders with rapid fire (a dangerous combination).

Other leaders stay calm, cool and do the right thing. When there was a significant problem with the O2 coverage in some areas of Britain in 2013, Ronan Dunne recalled: 'The customer wanted to know three things: 1) what's happened, 2) why did it happen, and 3) what the BLANK BLANK are you going to do about it?'

In situations like these you have to be seen to have urgency. As Ronan said: 'That night I didn't go to bed – I stayed up and I communicated with my network team [the folk fixing the problem] and my shareholders in Madrid.'

Ronan's approach to the crisis showed his staff and his customers that he was doing everything he could to resolve it. This is why, if a leader is spotted drinking cocktails on board a yacht somewhere when all hell is breaking lose back at home, people go ballistic.

In a crisis, some weak leaders immediately start looking for people to blame. This is remarkably dysfunctional and those leaders should be given their marching orders at the first opportunity. As Henry Ford once said, 'Don't find fault, find a remedy.' When facing a crisis, it's also useful to remember this quote from the Disney film *A Bug's Life*, 'First rule of leadership: everything is your fault.' It sucks but it's true.

Communicate good news, bad news, or no news, with authenticity

Your consumers aren't stupid – they understand that sometimes SH*T happens. After all, companies like O2 are pioneers, so their consumers forgive them if there's a blip. But you do have to overcommunicate, even if it's just to say, 'There's no update, but we are working on it.' According to Ronan Dunne, it's a case of 'be prepared, and then be decisive and then communicate, communicate, communicate'.

During the network coverage crisis, O2 never lost their cool or their authenticity. Some of the customers were angry and had things perhaps a bit out of perspective, yet O2, true to their brand, remained positive, caring and quirky. In fact, many people gave credit to O2's handling of the crisis, saying that it was like a *'masterclass in social media'*. In my interview with Ronan Dunne, he said, 'I think that one of the real qualities of a leader is authenticity: that means being the same person inside the office, outside the office, in a crisis, not in a crisis – it's just being real.' As Allan Leighton said, the best strategy is to 'tell them how it is'. Your job as leader is also to keep calm and diffuse the situation so don't forget the power of humour. Even while President Reagan was being rushed to the operating room after being shot in 1981, he looked up at his wife Nancy and said, 'Honey, I forgot to duck.'

Oh, and finally, 'thinking' can be quite useful too

Very often in a crisis leaders just react without pausing to think things through (well, the loser leaders do anyway). The best leaders spend time thinking – even if it's a case of thinking on their feet.

In an interview with CNBC, Donald Trump said: 'You learn during bad times about yourself: you learn if you can handle pressure, you learn if you can think quickly and on your feet – and if you can't, you're going to go out of business and it's the end of the game – it's "take me home, mummy."'

To think on your feet, you need to stay calm – so, whether you're experiencing a short-term crisis or a long-term crisis, good luck with it and just don't forget to breathe.

The idea in brief:

- *Leaders make cuts, but they also deal out hope in buckets*
- *Stay calm – if you freak out, the entire team will do the same and that doesn't bode well*
- *Cut the right costs: be wary of cost involving customer experience, innovation or revenue generation (where you're getting an ROI)*
- *Innovate, but innovate on a shoestring or, for the posh folk: encourage lean innovation*
- *Communicate good news, bad news and also no news – and do so with authenticity*
- *Don't forget to use your God-given thinking ability to actually think and not just react*
- *Do what you need to do in the moment, but remind everybody that you'll all pull through and that there are better days on their way …*

38

Keeping a challenger mentality – avoiding complacency and staying hungry

'It's all right to be Goliath but always act like David.'

Philip Knight

Do you recall the biblical story of the giant Philistine warrior Goliath being beaten in combat by the young shepherd David? In business today, it's much more fun being David – the challenger, the underdog – and trying to work out how to beat somebody 10 times the size of you. But what if *you* are Goliath – the market leader everybody is trying to beat? You can't use the underdog position to muster up fighting spirit from your troops. After all, you're the big player now and everybody inside and outside your company is aware of that.

If you're a leader in the number one company in your market, congratulate yourself – it's a great achievement. But don't let your team put on their slippers and get complacent. Never get complacent, for it is when you stop doing what you did that enabled you to get to number one in the first place (being aggressive and testing, plotting, executing and outthinking) that you might suddenly find you're getting overtaken left, right and centre and lose momentum. This is as true for your individual leadership success as it is for your organisation's success – hence the need for chapter 11 on being addicted to learning.

Time and time again, it's been shown that when an organisation becomes top dog (or market leader), they stop doing the things that enabled them to get there in the first place (including taking risks). Odd yes, but a common occurrence. Why does this happen? Well, the market leader has a lot more to lose than the other mavericks out there, and this can make companies cautious. They begin to prefer the status quo to innovation; they become defensive rather than offensive, and worst of all, complacent rather than hungry. To illustrate this point, Sir Terry Leahy told me that when he first took over Tesco his major competitors 'liked the environment that made them number one, so they were more reluctant to change that environment' (hence giving him a significant opportunity to come from nowhere and overtake at breakneck speeds). Business is an offensive, not defensive game. Just like you can't defend your way to the top, you can't just defend when you get there either.

So there *is* a danger when you're number one. However, I have interviewed many CEOs and entrepreneurs who made their companies number one in the market and kept them there. We'll now share some of their secrets about keeping everybody hungry. For example, when Tesco overtook their competitors, Sir Terry grew the company to several times the size of their closest competitor (not just fractionally better) – so it absolutely can be done, and that success can be sustained, by keeping the challenger mentality alive.

One of the best examples of retaining the challenger mentality that I've come across in my interviews with leaders is from Simon Calver, who was running LOVEFiLM in the UK before Netflix came along and disrupted the market by providing online streaming:

> If you're going to do something that's going to prepare you for the future and change your business model, that's not about cannibalisation, that's about being smart and really driving the business forward.

So get rid of the word 'cannibalisation' and make sure you're focused on the customer proposition and how that is changing. [For LOVEFiLM this meant] constantly fighting about the best way for a customer to watch a film when they want to watch it, how they want to watch it – and challenging yourself more than anything else.

The reason that I like to build this challenger mentality is so that internally you don't become complacent. And you are looking at yourself and you are saying, 'What can we do next?' 'How can we do that?' I've been in lots of situations in business where you achieve the goal that you set out – it could be leadership in DVD rental, for example – and then you go, 'Okay, what next?' and the whole organisation makes a massive sigh. It's important to celebrate success, but what's really important as well is to set the next hurdle for the business, because they need a goal and a challenge to go for. For [LOVEFiLM] it's about film-watching, and about how we can make that transition from physical to digital and lead the way in digital – and how we get people to our site for film information. All of those are responsibilities in their own right that we need to give people accountability for – so that we never become complacent; we never sit back and rest on our laurels.

When Netflix launched in the UK market almost overnight, LOVEFiLM wasn't squashed (far from it) because of its investment in and hunger for the next big thing – streaming (see chapter 33 for more on this). Yet had LOVEFiLM been complacently counting its DVD money and not worrying about the future, it would have been toast. What happened instead was that LOVEFiLM was bought by Amazon for a fortune and now Amazon and LOVEFiLM are taking on Netflix. (I might be a geek, but I can't help but love watching this battle unfolding.)

So here are a few neat tactics to keep the hunger alive and complacency at bay:

Self-imposed pressure – paranoia

As mentioned earlier, when Tesco became number one in the supermarket industry, it didn't stay just slightly ahead of its main rivals – in market capitalisation terms it grew about six times bigger than its next competitor, with a market cap of around £35 billion. There was absolutely no complacency at Tesco with Sir Terry Leahy at the helm.

When I asked him about it, he said: '[Staying ahead is] very difficult – being paranoid helps and constantly putting yourself under pressure, because if you put yourself under pressure there's less chance of someone else putting you under pressure and actually just being a pain in the backside.' Similarly, Ronan Dunne cited paranoia as a driver of O2's success: 'Let's be honest: we're paranoid about the fact that somebody will come and steal our lunch.' Paranoia forces you to think and constantly be striving to produce a better service for your customers. It can be a driving force, and it sure beats complacency (think Kodak) so embrace it.

Focus on the next hurdle

Running a successful organisation is like riding a bicycle: you have to keep pedalling to go forward; otherwise you'll stop and fall over. So as soon as one hurdle is reached, it's time to focus on the next big thing, as Simon Calver advocates. In my interview with him he told me, 'It's important to celebrate success but what's really important as well is to set the next hurdle for the business – because [your employees] need a goal and a challenge to go for.' Entrepreneur Mike Harris echoed this idea when he said, 'You can create energy [in a sleeping giant] by setting a future goal that seems impossible but very desirable.' In an article for *Business Insider,* Max Nisen wrote about LinkedIn's strategy for maintaining this focus on the next hurdle:

> Every time Duke University's highly successful college basketball team completes a play, its legendary coach Mike Krzyzewski yells out, 'Next play', regardless of how well things went. They don't over-celebrate successes. And they don't dwell on failures, either.
>
> That strategy inspired LinkedIn's approach to its highly successful IPO … employees wore shirts with the company's 'LNKD' ticker symbol on one side, and 'Next Play' on the other.

So the first thing to do as the market leader is to continue to raise standards and not to see your competitors as the benchmark – you're number one, so it's time to set your own benchmarks and goals. You have to set a challenging goal for your organisation that's going to demand innovation, and creative thinking – always get the team focused on the 'next play'.

Let's look at Apple. Shortly after its launch, the iPod counted for as much as 40 per cent of Apple's sales. But did Steve Jobs bask in the glory and take a chill pill and relax under a coconut tree for a year? Certainly not, he was straight on to the next version, the next improvement, the next product that would kill even the iPod. It's this relentless hunger for the next improvement, the next new thing, that enables market leaders to stay market leaders.

In a similar vein, when I asked Robert Senior about how he'd got Saatchi & Saatchi to the top of the advertising industry, he said:

> I don't ever think that there's a top. Nelson Mandela on his 90th birthday had a birthday party involving all the leaders of the time, and he did a little speech. After the speech, he then asked if there was any questions, to which George W. Bush put his hand up and said 'What next Nelson?' and it got a laugh. Then Nelson looked at him deadpan in the eye, and said, 'George, what's next for me is what's next for everybody in this room, to climb a higher mountain.' There is no top, it doesn't exist.

Matthew Key, also spoke about this in my interview with him:

> I think a lot of it comes down to the people in the business. Employ people who have the attitude and the mentality to always be striving for something better. Never be comfortable with where you are – always look to the next game. Whatever industry you're in, somebody else is going to come along and beat what you're doing today. The trick is that, when they beat what you're doing today, you have already moved on another step.

Absolutely right – the only thing that I'd add to that is to make sure that, as you're striving for better things and climbing higher mountains, you take a moment once in a while to make sure you're thoroughly enjoying the journey – which takes me all the way back to the first chapter of the book: 'Leadership starts (and ends) with a love of what you do'. Good luck.

The idea in brief:

- *You have to keep fighting; slowing down is not an option – organisations are like bicycles, they have to keep going forward otherwise they fall over*
- *If you're the market leader then you have to win in new areas and define your own benchmarks*
- *Always stay hungry by setting new goals and setting new challenges*
- *Stay paranoid!*
- *Don't rest on past successes – always be striving for something better (but in the meantime enjoy the journey)*

Congratulations on getting to the end of Part Three. Now that's you, your team AND your organisation sorted, let's move on to a quick conclusion so we can get out and do our thing ...

Conclusion

Thank you, dear reader, for reading this book. Before you close it for a final time there are three things I'd like to emphasise:

Firstly, I'd like to ask you a question: What do *you* think is the best way for you to become a world-class leader?

I would argue that while reading, watching videos, and further study are noble things (and are essential components of learning), nothing beats getting out there and leading others. The best way to learn any game – leadership, chess or any other – is not *just* by studying the game, but having the courage to go out there and play it. By doing so, you'll test any theory you might have picked up in your study, and you'll find out if they work for you in the real world – only then do they become those rich empirical lessons that bring true wisdom and mastery in your field. As Sir Antony Jay rightly said, 'The only real training for leadership is leadership.' At the end of the day, if you want to learn how to swim, you have to get into the pool.

Secondly, I'd like to ask you another question: What do you want to be remembered for at your funeral?

Think about it: if a family member stands up and gives a speech about you, what would you want them to say? Would you really want them to struggle for material and say, 'Tim or Kim reached the Vice

President of Marketing at the age of 53, and, well, that's about it actually ... let's sing hymn number ...'? Or would you want them to talk about other really important roles in your life? If you would, then, as we discussed previously in this book, if there's anything important to you – you have to schedule time for it, and protect it. It takes self-discipline to create amazing moments in life, but, as Joel Osteen said, 'The pain of discipline is minuscule compared with the pain of regret.' So make sure you prioritise the truly important things in life (including your health) today.

And finally (well for now, at least), I'd just like to point out that:

The world needs more inspiration and passion

The world needs more role models setting high standards and living noble values

The world needs more people with compelling visions

The world needs people that are willing to serve others – and to help others in their own journeys

The world needs more people to be courageous and to fight for what they believe in

The world needs more hope for a better day

The world needs more people who live every day with integrity

In essence, the world needs more great leaders ...

As such, I wish you well on your journey to leadership excellence. I just hope that there have been a few pages in this book that have sung out to you and helped you somehow on your way. Just remember: the more shots you take, the luckier you'll get.

Here's to you having a life filled with a love for what you do – a life filled with dreams that have been achieved and a life of inspiring others and helping them through the awesome power of leadership.

Reach the author

What do you think makes a great leader? What do you think about this book? I'd love to hear *your* thoughts on leadership or on the preceding three-hundred or so pages, so feel free to reach out to me via the 'Get in touch' section on my website, www.anthonygell.com

Index